THE
POETIC
SCRIPTURES
OF SIX WRITERS

THE POETIC SCRIPTURES OF SIX WRITERS

GOD'S WORD IN RHYTHM & RHYME

MICHAEL D. WESTER

LIGHTHOUSE PUBLICATION
SPREADING THE WORD OF GOD, ONE BOOK AT A TIME.

Copyright © 2020 by Michael D. Wester.

All rights reserved. No part of this publication may be reproduced, distributed, or transmitted in any form or by any means, including photocopying, recording, or other electronic or mechanical methods, without the prior written permission of the author, except in the case of brief quotations embodied in critical reviews and certain other noncommercial uses permitted by copyright law.

Printed in the United States of America
ISBN 978-1-64133-634-5 (sc)
ISBN 978-1-64133-635-2 (hc)
ISBN 978-1-64133-636-9 (e)

Library of Congress Control Number: 2019917230

Artwork and Cover Design by **Cameron Klingenberg**

Inspirational / Worship and Devotion / Non-Fiction
20.02.17

Lighthouse Publication
1553 E. Caro Road
Caro, MI 48723

www.lighthousepublication.com

CONTENTS

Introduction vii

The Poetic Gospel of Matthew 1

The Poetic Gospel of Mark 179

The Poetic Letter to the Hebrews 289

The Poetic Letter of James 343

The Poetic Letter of Peter

    1 Peter 361

    2 Peter 381

The Poetic Letter of Jude 395

Endnotes 401

INTRODUCTION

"You will eventually go into heart failure. It is imperative that we do something soon to give you the best chance of success." My wife began to tear as the doctor gave me his prognosis after running me through a battery of tests. I had a rare condition that had gone unnoticed for several years. My heart had continually become irregular, with the lower chamber beating 50 unsteady beats per minute and the upper chamber beating 385 beats per minute. The many years of this constant abuse swelled the upper chambers to three times the normal size. The doctor stated that it would take several surgeries, and even after that, he gave it a 60% chance of success.

As I write these words, my heart is beating steady at 56 beats per minute. The doctor from Mayo Clinic repaired my heart in one long six-hour surgery. My wife occasionally puts her hand on my heart, smiling as she feels a strong, steady beat.

As I have witnessed many read scripture in rhythm and rhyme, I have seen smiles come to their faces and even tears come to their eyes.

This is the fourth and final book of putting the entire New Testament into rhythm and rhyme. The same format is followed as the previous book, with notation showing any poetic license. Two symbols note poetic license: an asterisk (*) and a diamond (♦).

The asterisk (*) indicates that I have added to the text in some way. For example, the genealogy of Jesus found in the first chapter of Matthew abounds with this notation because of the difficulty of rhyming names. So, I have added things, like a fact about the person named or the meaning of one's name, to produce rhyme.

Another example is in Matthew 4:1 which reads:

Then Jesus, led by the Spirit,
Went into the desert place
To be tempted by the Devil
Who would test Him face to face.*

That last line is not in the text of Matthew, but it summarizes what the next verses explain.

The diamond (♦) indicates that I have elaborated on a word or a phrase. For example, Matthew 5:3 reads:

Blessed are those who in their spirit
Are poor ♦and in desperate need
Because the kingdom of heaven
Belongs to them, *indeed.

Notice that the diamond immediately precedes the phrase *and in desperate need*. This further defines what Matthew means by poor. By the way, any time you see the word *blessed*, make sure you pronounce it as *blest*.

This work has been reviewed by a team of twenty-three students of the Bible, mostly pastors. Their task was to make sure the biblical text has been accurately reflected in this unique translation. I thank each one of the following for their invaluable reviews: John Botkin, Randy Brandon, James Conner, Dave Cooper, John D'Arcy, Dave Hoffman, Sam Hamilton, Marc Herron, Bill Livingston, Jim Marcus, Tom Metz, Kyle Roat, David Roberts, Steve Roe, James Solomon, Ted Stephens, Jon Terry, Jeff Vogel, Doug Wallaker, Art Werry, Pat Wester, Terry Wilson, and Bruce Winter.

May all who read this work be blessed by the rhythm and rhyme and be motivated by the meaning it conveys.

THE POETIC GOSPEL OF MATTHEW

1:1 The genealogical scroll
Of Jesus Christ *as Man,
Also called the son of David
And the son of Abraham.

1:2 Abraham became the father
Of Isaac, *the promised son;[1]
And Isaac became the father
Of Jacob, *the deceptive one.[2]

Now Jacob became the father
Of Judah and his brothers;
1:3 Judah fathered Perez and Zerah,
And Tamar was their mother.

Perez fathered Hezron who fathered
Ram, *whose mention is brief;[3]
1:4 And Ram fathered Amminadab
Who fathered Nahshon, *the chief.[4]

	And Nahshon became the father
1:5	Of Salmon who fathered Boaz
	By a foreigner named Rahab.⁵
	"The harlot" she was known as.*

       Boaz fathered Obed by Ruth
       Who came from a land abroad;⁶
       Obed fathered Jesse who fathered
1:6   David declared king *by God.

       Now David fathered Solomon
       By a woman who belonged
       To the Hittite⁷ named Uriah
       Whom he had severely wronged.*

1:7   Solomon became the father
       Of Rehoboam *who reigned*⁸
       The southern kingdom of Judah*
       Where David's line was maintained.*

       Rehoboam was the father
       Of Abijah *who just warred;⁹
       He was the father to Asa
       Who was faithful to the Lord.¹⁰

1:8   Asa fathered Jehoshaphat
       Who followed his father's deeds;¹¹
       Jehoshaphat fathered Joram
       ("Jehoram" the Hebrew reads).¹²

       From Joram's line, Uzziah came¹³
       Whose skin God did irritate;¹⁴
1:9   And Uzziah fathered Jotham
       Who built the Upper Gate.¹⁵

And Jotham then fathered Ahaz
Who practiced forbidden things;[16]
Ahaz fathered Hezekiah,
The greatest of Judah's kings.[17]

1:10 Hezekiah fathered Manasseh
Who at twelve began his reign;[18]
And Manasseh fathered Amon
Who dishonored the Lord's name.[19]

Now Amon fathered Josiah,
Who had the book of the Law*
Discovered in the temple read*
And was overcome with awe.[20]

1:11 From his line came Jechoniah[21]
Who had many in his clan.[22]
This occurred when deportation
To Babylon *was the plan.

1:12 Now after the deportation,
When the temple was just rubble,[23]
Jechoniah fathered Shealtiel
Who fathered Zerubbabel.[24]

(The rebuilding of the temple
Was the task given to him);[25]
1:13 Zerubbabel fathered Abiud
Who fathered Eliakim.

Eliakim fathered Azor
Whose life is not discussed;*
1:14 Azor was father to Zadok
Whose name means *righteous* or *just*.*

>
> Zadok was father to Achim,
> Meaning *the Lord will confirm*;*
> And Achim fathered Eliud
> (*God's my praise* translates that term).
>
> **1:15** Eliud fathered Eleazar
> Whose name means *God is my aid*;*
> Eleazar fathered Matthan
> Whose name means *a gift was made*.*
>
> And then Matthan fathered Jacob,
> Meaning *to forcefully seize*;*
> **1:16** Jacob was father to Joseph
> Whose name means *he will increase*.*
>
> He was the husband of Mary
> By whom was fathered *a son,²⁶
> He who is now called the Christ,
> Jesus, *the Promised One.
>
> **1:17** Therefore, all the generations
> Have three enumerations.*
> First,* from Abraham to David,
> Were fourteen generations.
>
> Second,* from the time of David
> 'Til the time of deportation
> To the kingdom of Babylon,
> Were fourteen generations.
>
> Lastly,* from the deportation
> To Babylon's *plantations
> Until the time that Christ was born,
> Were fourteen generations.

| 1:18 | Now the birth of Jesus, the Christ,
In this manner, did occur:
Mary was engaged to Joseph
While yet a maiden and pure. |

Yet she was found to be with child
By the Holy Spirit's *power.
1:19 However, her husband Joseph
Made plans to disavow her.♦

For he was just, but to shame her
In public, he did not will.
So, divorcing her secretly,
He intended to fulfill.

1:20 But while thinking about these things,
To him in a dream, behold,
An angel of the Lord appeared,
And these words to him he told:

"Joseph, son of David, don't fear
Taking Mary as your wife,
For by the Holy Spirit's *power
In her was fathered this life.

1:21 "And she will give birth to a son.
Call His name Jesus. You must.
For from their sins, He'll save His own,
His people *who in Him trust."

1:22	Now this entire thing has happened That this word which was spoken By the Lord through the prophet Would be fulfilled, ♦not broken:
1:23	"The virgin will become with child And will give birth to a son; Immanuel, which means 'God with us', They'll call the name of that One."
1:24	When Joseph awoke from his sleep, He did as the angel[27] said. He took Mary to be his wife But ♦without the marriage bed.
1:25	He did not sexually know her 'Til she gave birth to a son, And Joseph called His name Jesus. His commanded tasks were done.*

2:1	Sometime after Jesus was born In Judea's Bethlehem, In the days of Herod the king, There appeared *some Gentile men. Magi came to Jerusalem From a region in the east. The question that they were asking, Stirred the greatest and the least.[28]

2:2	"Now, where is the King of the Jews
Whose birth has finally come?
For we saw His star in the east.
We've come to worship that One."
2:3	When King Herod heard about this,
He was intensely stirred.
2:4	All the people's chief priests and scribes,
He gathered *to search God's word.
	He kept asking for the birthplace
Of the Christ *as prophesied.
2:5	"In Bethlehem of Judea,"
To him they at last replied.
	"For through the prophet, this is what
For us has been written down
About the birthplace of the Christ,*
The region and the town.*
2:6	"'You, Bethlehem, land of Judah,
Are by no means least of all
Among the rulers of Judah
Although you are very small.*
	"'For out from you, *O Bethlehem,
A great ruler will arise
To shepherd my people Israel
Although you are of small size.'"*
2:7	Then Herod summoned secretly
The magi to ascertain
The time the star had first appeared,
And this knowledge he did gain.

2:8	To Bethlehem, he sent them and said,
	"Go search for the Child with care.
	When you find Him, report to me
	That I may worship Him there."
2:9	After they listened to the king,
	They started toward Bethlehem.
	Then suddenly the star appeared,
	Proceeding ahead of them.
	This star which they'd seen in the east
	Was leading them on their way.
	It guided them until it stood
	Above where the Child lay.
2:10	When they saw the star before them,
	They were overcome with joy.
2:11	Entering the house, they saw Mary[29]
	Along with her baby boy.
	And falling down, they worshipped Him
	And opened up their treasures.
	Gifts of frankincense, gold, and myrrh
	They gave Him *in vast measures.
2:12	They did not return to Herod,
	Having been warned in a dream.
	They went back to their country
	By another way unseen.
2:13	After they departed, behold,
	While Joseph was still in bed,*
	An angel of the Lord appeared
	In a dream to him and said:

"Take the Child, and His mother too.
Quickly get up! Arise!
Run to Egypt and remain there
'Til I tell you otherwise.

"For Herod is about to search
For the Child with this in mind:
To bring the Child's life to an end.
Leave quickly so he won't find."*

2:14 He took the Child and His mother
At night, with haste applied,
And departed into Egypt,
2:15 Staying there 'til Herod died.

So, what was spoken by the Lord
Through the prophet (a minor one)³⁰
Came to be fulfilled, for it says,
"Out of Egypt I called My Son."

2:16 Herod became greatly enraged,
Realizing that he was tricked
By the magi *not returning,
And sent out ♦an evil verdict.

Children two years old and under
In Bethlehem and its borders
(The age derived from the magi)
Were killed as per his orders.

2:17 So, what was spoken *by the Lord
Through the prophet Jeremiah
Was fulfilled *in this failed attempt
Of killing the Messiah.*

2:18　　For this is what the Scripture♦ says,
　　　　"A cry in Ramah was heard,
　　　　One of weeping and much mourning.
　　　　Deep emotions have been stirred.♦

　　　　"For Rachel weeps for her children
　　　　And does not wish to be fed
　　　　By the comfort of anyone
　　　　Because her children are dead."

2:19　　While Joseph was still in Egypt
　　　　And after Herod was dead,
　　　　An angel of the Lord appeared
　　　　To him in a dream and said:

2:20　　"Rise! Take the Child and His mother.
　　　　Go to Israel's land inside.
　　　　As for those seeking the Child's life,
　　　　They all have finally died."

2:21　　He took the Child and His mother,
　　　　After getting up from bed,
　　　　And entered the land of Israel
　　　　Just as the Lord's angel said.*

2:22　　However, when he heard this news,
　　　　Archelaus, Herod's heir[31]
　　　　Was ruling over Judea,
　　　　He was scared to enter there.

　　　　After he was warned in a dream,
　　　　To Galilee's parts he went.
2:23　　He came to the city, Nazareth,
　　　　And lived ♦in that settlement.

This resulted in being fulfilled
What the prophets *had foreseen,
For this thought[32] was spoken through them,
"He'll be called a Nazarene."

3:1 Now in the Judean desert,
     In those days there did appear
3:2 John the Baptist preaching, "Repent!
     For heaven's kingdom is near."

3:3 For through Isaiah the prophet
     This person was spoken about:
     "'Prepare the Lord's[33] way! Straighten His paths!'
     In the desert, a voice cries out."

3:4 John wore a robe of camel's hair.
     A leather belt wrapped his waist.
     Mainly locusts and wild honey
     Were the food that he would taste.

3:5 Then people from Jerusalem
     To him were coming out
     With those all over Judea
     And from Jordan all about.

3:6 And as they confessed openly
     Their sins *which they recognized,
     In the Jordan River by him
     They all were being baptized.

3:7	Now many of the Pharisees
	And Sadducees *one day
	Were coming to John's baptism.
	When he saw them he did say:
	"Who warned you, you brood of vipers,
	To flee from the coming wrath?
3:8	Therefore, produce fruit that's worthy
	Of a repentant path.
3:9	"Don't think to say among yourselves
	'Abraham is our father.'
	That won't exempt you from His wrath.*
	To think this, do not bother.♦
	"For I tell you, God is able
	To raise up for Abraham
	Children out of these very stones.
	Are you ready for His exam?*
3:10	"Already the axe has been placed,
	Ready to strike each tree's root.
	So, those are chopped and thrown in fire
	Which do not produce good fruit.
3:11	"For the purpose of repentance,
	In water you, I baptize,
	But there's One stronger than I am
	Who after me will arise.
	"Even His sandals I'm unfit
	To carry *as His for hire.
	He Himself will baptize you
	In the Holy Spirit and fire.

The Poetic Gospel of Matthew

3:12 "With sorting fork in hand He'll clean
The threshing floor and supply
Wheat for His barn, burning the chaff
In a fire that will not die."

3:13 Then from Galilee before John
At the Jordan there did appear
Jesus to be baptized by him,
To this, John would not adhere.*

3:14 John was stopping Him by saying,
"I'm the one that needs to be
Baptized in the Jordan by You,
Yet You are coming to me?"

3:15 Jesus answering, said to him,
"Let go now, for it's fitting
For us to fulfill all righteousness."
So Him, John was permitting.

3:16 Now after Jesus was baptized,
He went up without delay
From the water, and then behold,
The sky opened right away.

He then saw the Spirit of God
Descending just like a dove,
Coming on Him *so as to rest,[34]
3:17 And behold, ◆words from above!

A voice from heaven spoke these words,
The Scriptures being cited:[35]
"This is My Son I dearly love,
In whom I am delighted."

4:1 Then Jesus led by the Spirit
Went into the desert place
To be tempted by the Devil
Who would test Him face to face.*

4:2 Fasting for forty days and nights,
From eating, He did refrain.♦
After this, He became hungry.
Then to Him, the tempter came.

4:3 "So, since[36] You are the Son of God,"
The tempter to Jesus said,
"Issue a command to these stones
So that they become Your bread."

4:4 "It's been written," He answered back,
"'Man must not live on just bread.
No!* He must live on every word
That comes from God's mouth instead.'"

4:5 Then into the holy city
The Devil took Him away,
And on the temple's highest point
He stood Jesus, just to say:

4:6 "Because You are the Son of God,
Throw Yourself down from up there,
For it's been written, 'He'll command
His angels to serve your care.

"'They will carry you in their hands
Lest you fall upon the ground
And strike your foot against a stone.'
So, go ahead. Jump down!"♦

4:7   Then Jesus answered back to him,
"Again, *on the other hand,
'You must not test the Lord your God'
Is written *as a command."

4:8   Again, the Devil took Jesus
To a mountain very high
And displayed all the world's kingdoms
And their glory for Him to eye.

4:9   Then the Devil proposed to Him,
"To you, I will give them all
If You only will worship me
As before my feet You fall."

4:10   Jesus told Him, "Depart, Satan!
This is written *to observe:
'You must worship the Lord your God,
And only Him you must serve.'"

4:11   Then the Devil abandoned Him,
And behold, the angels came.
To Him, they were ministering
So His strength He would regain.*

The Poetic Scriptures of Six Writers

4:12	Now, He withdrew to Galilee
	When He heard of John's arrest.
4:13	After coming to Nazareth,
	To leave there, He was pressed.[37]
	He then lived in Capernaum,
	Which is right next to the sea,
	Located in the region of
	Zebulun and Naphtali.
4:14	This resulted in fulfilling
	Isaiah's prophetic word
	As spoken through him *by the Lord,
	Which says this *to be heard:
4:15	"Zebulun's land and Naphtali's
	By the roadway of the sea,
	Just beyond the Jordan River
	Where Gentiles live – Galilee!
4:16	"The people sitting in darkness
	Saw a great light *in the air.
	In a place where death's shadow is,
	It shined on those sitting there."
4:17	From that time on, Jesus began
	To proclaim this loud and clear,
	"Keep repenting for this reason:
	Heaven's kingdom has drawn near."

4:18	Now, while walking along the coast
Of the Sea of Galilee,
Jesus saw two brothers throwing
A net into the sea.
	For both of them were fishermen.
Now Simon was the brother
Who was better known as Peter,
And Andrew was the other.
4:19	He said to them, "Come follow Me.
I'll make you fishers of men."
4:20	And instantly, leaving their nets,
They followed Jesus right then.
4:21	And traveling on from that place,
He saw in a boat two men
With their father named Zebedee,
And He summoned both of them.
	The brothers known as James and John
Were mending their nets that day.
4:22	Leaving the boat and their father,
They followed without delay.
4:23	Now, throughout all of Galilee
He traveled and was teaching
Wherever there were synagogues.
Of the kingdom, He was preaching.
	This preaching of the kingdom
Was the gospel, ◆the good news.
Disease and illness in the people,
He healed and did not refuse.[38]

4:24	And into all of Syria The report of Him did run. They brought Him all those suffering, And He healed them, ◆every one.
	The demon-possessed and oppressed, Those diseased and racked with pain, The lunatics and paralytics, He healed, ◆thus spreading His fame.
4:25	From Jerusalem, Judea, Decapolis, Galilee, And beyond the Jordan River, Great crowds followed eagerly.
5:1	When Jesus saw the massive crowds, The mountainside He climbed high. He sat down; His disciples came; And the crowds gathered nearby.[39]
5:2	Opening up His mouth to speak To the disciples gathered 'round, He was teaching these words to them Which the crowds would deem profound:[40]
5:3	"Blessed[41] are those who in their spirit Are poor ◆and in desperate need Because the kingdom of heaven Belongs to them, *indeed.

5:4	"Blessed are those who are in mourning,
	For they'll find comfort *of worth.
5:5	Blessed are the ones who are gentle,
	For they'll inherit the earth.
5:6	"Blessed are those who for righteousness
	Just hunger and thirst inside
	Because completely they will be
	Filled up and satisfied.
5:7	"Blessed are the ones who show mercy,
	For mercy, they will obtain.
5:8	Blessed are the ones whose hearts are pure,
	For to see God, they will gain.
5:9	"Blessed are those who endeavor
	To bring peace to those at odds,
	For they will most certainly be
	Branded as sons of God.
5:10	"Blessed are the ones persecuted
	For the sake of righteousness
	Because the kingdom of heaven,
	They within themselves possess.
5:11	"Blessed are you when they insult you,
	And when they pursue you about,
	And when against you, because of Me,
	All kinds of evil they spout.
5:12	"Rejoice and exult! For your reward
	Up in heaven is immense,
	For against the previous prophets
	Persecution was intense.

5:13	"You all are the salt of the earth, But if the salt were to lose All of its salty properties, How will it be salt to use?
	"It's good for nothing anymore. It can only be assigned As something to be thrown outside To be trampled by mankind.
5:14	"You all are the light of the world. It's not possible to hide A city on a mountaintop From the view of those outside.*
5:15	"Nor do they light a lamp to put Under a basket to hide. They set it on the household stand, And it shines for all inside.
5:16	"Let your light shine before mankind In a way so they can view Your good works and then glorify Your heavenly Father too.
5:17	"Don't think that I came to destroy The Law or the Prophets *of old, No!* I have not come to destroy But to fulfill *what God has told.
5:18	"For to you all I speak this truth, Until heaven and earth flee, Every dot or stroke in the Law Will stay[42] 'til all comes to be.

5:19 "Therefore, whoever breaks one law,
Although it's the least command,
And teaches folks to do the same,
Least in God's kingdom⁴³ he'll stand.

"But if one lives the entire Law⁴⁴
And practices each command,♦
Teaching folks to do the same,
Great in God's kingdom⁴⁵ he'll stand.

5:20 "I say, into heaven's kingdom
You won't be able to squeeze,
Unless your righteousness exceeds
That of scribes and Pharisees.

5:21 "You've heard what the ancients were told,
'Murder, you must not commit'
And 'Whoever kills will be judged
By a court that won't acquit.'

5:22 "But I tell you, that all who are
Continually throwing a fit
Against their brother will be judged
By a court that won't acquit.

"And whoever decides to say
To his brother, 'Stupid fool!'
Will be judged by the highest court,
And guilty will be its rule.

"And whoever decides to say
To his brother,* 'You blockhead!'
Will be guilty enough to go
To Gehenna's fiery bed.[46]

5:23 "While putting your gift on the altar,
If you[47] at that place recall
That your brother holds against you
Some matter, *then do not stall.

5:24 "Leave your gift there at the altar.
Go to your brother straightway.
First be reconciled. Then come back
And offer your gift, *I say.

5:25 "Work hard and quick in making friends
While on your way to court
With the one who is suing you,
Or to this he might resort:

"He might give you up to the judge,
And the judge to his deputy,
And then into jail you'll be thrown.
So, when will freedom you see?*

5:26 "Truly, I am informing you,
From there you'll in no way go
Until the time you have paid up
The very last cent you owe.

5:27 "You've heard what has long been said,
'Adultery do not commit',
5:28 But I tell you *that your own heart,
You have to examine it.*

"All who keep eying a woman
To lust for her sexually
Has already in their own heart
Committed adultery.

5:29 "If you keep stumbling *into sin
Through what your right eye might view,
Then immediately take it out
And throw it away from you.

"For it's better that for one part
Destruction you require
So your whole body not be thrown
Into Gehenna's fire.

5:30 "If you keep stumbling *into sin
Through what your left hand might do,
Then immediately cut it off
And throw it away from you.

"For it's better that for one part
Destruction you require
So your whole body not depart
Into Gehenna's fire.

5:31 "And it was said, 'Whatever man
Sends his wife away by force,[48]
He's commanded to give to her
A document of divorce.'

5:32 "But I tell you that all who send
Their wife away with demand
(Except due to fornication)
Will wrongly make her stand.[49]

"She will be made out as the one
Who has committed ◆the wrong,
Branding her as an adulteress
Though innocent all along.*

"And whoever marries that wife
Who's been sent away by force,
That one commits adultery⁵⁰
Though she has a bill of divorce.*

5:33 "Again, what was taught the ancients
You've heard *and are hearing still,
'You must not make a vow that's false,
But to the Lord your vows fulfill.'

5:34 "But I Myself am telling you,
No vows at all must you swear.
Do not make a vow by heaven,
For the throne of God is there.

5:35 "Or don't make a vow by the earth,
For it's His footstool, *I state,
Or don't vow t'ward Jerusalem,
The city of the King who's great.

5:36 "Or don't make a vow by your head.
It's an empty vow to swear*
Because you can't make white or black
A single strand of your hair.

5:37 "But let your word of 'Yes' mean yes
And your word of 'No' mean no.
All the things that do more than this,
From the evil one they flow.

5:38	"You've heard, 'Eye for eye, tooth for tooth.'
	It's been long taught ◆in our midst,
5:39	But I Myself am telling you,
	The wrongdoer, don't resist.

"Whoever is slapping your cheek,
Let's assume it is the right,
Turn to him the other one too.
This person you must not fight.◆

5:40	"The one who wants you to be judged
	For the purpose to receive
	The inner garment that you own,
	The outer one also leave.
5:41	"Whoever uses his power
	To force you to bear his load
	For the length of one whole mile,
	Bear it for two miles *of road.
5:42	"Give to him who keeps asking you,
	And to him who wants, *I say,
	To borrow from you some money,
	From him don't be turned away.
5:43	"You have heard what has long been said,
	'Selflessly love your neighbor.
	However, hate your enemy
	For showing you disfavor.'*
5:44	"But I tell you, as a lifestyle,
	Show selfless love to your foes,
	And keep praying for all of them
	Who pursue you to oppose.

5:45	"Do these things so that you might prove To be sons of ◆God above, God the Father who's in heaven, For ◆He shows this kind of love. "He makes His sun to rise ◆and shine On both the bad and the good; And on the just and the unjust, He sends rain for their livelihood.*
5:46	"For if you unselfishly love Just those who love you this way, What reward do you really have? Tax collectors do this, don't they?
5:47	"And if you greet just your brothers, What higher life might this be? Do not even Gentile people Practice this philosophy?
5:48	"Therefore, ◆in light of all I've said, Mature ways you must secure As shown by your heavenly Father Who is already mature.

6:1	"Be attentive not to practice Your righteousness before men For the purpose that it be seen And so receive praise* by them.

> "But if indeed attentiveness
> To this you do not bother,
> You've no reward in the presence
> Of your heavenly Father.

6:2
> "So, when you're making donations,
> Don't do as hypocrites do.
> They blow their trumpet in the streets
> And in the synagogues too.
>
> "They do this for just one purpose,
> To be glorified by men.
> Truly I tell you, they receive
> Their only reward right then.

6:3
> "But when you're making donations,
> Your left must never permit
> Your right to learn what it's giving,
> Or else you're a hypocrite!*

6:4
> "Do this so that in your giving
> Secrecy you will not lack.
> Your Father who sees secrecy
> Will certainly pay you back.

6:5
> "And whenever you are praying,
> As the hypocrites do not be,
> For they have a deep affection
> To voice prayers publicly.
>
> "In synagogues, on street corners,
> They stand to be seen by men.
> Truly I tell you, they receive
> Their only reward right then.

6:6	"But when you are about to pray,
	To your inner room first go,
	And then, after shutting your door,
	Let prayer to your Father flow.
	"That's to say, pray to your Father
	Who's hidden from public view.
	Your Father who sees secrecy
	Will certainly reward you.
6:7	"And don't pray like the Gentiles do,
	Saying words many times each,
	For they think that they will be heard
	In their voluminous speech.
6:8	"Therefore, do not become like them,
	For your Father truly knows
	What you need before you ask Him.
6:9	So, pray thus[51] *as I propose:
	"'Our Father, who is in heaven,
	Sanctified be Your name,
	Set apart, unique, and holy♦
	In all that we proclaim.*
6:10	"'And let Your kingdom soon arrive.
	Let Your will have its own way
	Upon the earth as in heaven.
6:11	Give us our bread for this day.
6:12	"'And forgive us of all our debts
	Just as we ourselves have done
	To all those indebted to us,
	Forgiving them, ♦every one.

6:13	"'And do not lead us down a road That enters temptation's snare, But deliver us, ◆rescue us From the evil one *out there.'⁵²
6:14	"For if you forgive human beings The trespasses which they do, ⁵³ Your Father who is in heaven Will certainly forgive you.
6:15	"But if you don't forgive people Of the sins that they commit,* Then as for your own trespasses, Your Father will not remit.
6:16	"And whenever you are fasting, Don't look sad and full of gloom As the hypocrites when they fast, For their faces they don't groom. "They do this so that their fasting Might be noticed by all men. Truly I tell you, they receive Their only reward right then.
6:17 **6:18**	"But oil your head and wash your face During the time of your fast So that to men it might not be Something that you broadcast. "But only make it obvious To your Father who's unseen. Your Father who sees secrecy Will reward you. *So, look clean.

The Poetic Scriptures of Six Writers

6:19 "Stop storing for yourselves on earth
       Treasures *of any type,
       Where moth and rust just eat away,
       And where thieves break in and swipe.

6:20 "But practice storing for yourselves
       Treasures in heaven. *That's ideal.
       There moth or rust don't eat away,
       And thieves don't break in or steal.

6:21 "For wherever your treasure is,
       That is the very same place
       Where your own heart will truly be.
       Store treasures in heaven's space.*

6:22 "The lamp of the human body
       Is the eye *which gives it sight.
       Therefore, if your eye is healthy,
       Your whole body will be bright.

6:23 "But your whole body will be dark
       If your eye is bad, ♦full of sin.
       So, if the light inside you is dark,
       How great is the darkness within!

6:24 "Nobody can serve two masters,
       For conflict will come thereof.*
       He will end up hating the one,
       And the other, he will love.

> "Or else, he will hold on to one,
> And the other, he will scorn,
> For you cannot possibly serve
> Both God and riches, *I warn.

6:25 "Because of this, I'm telling you,
Worry from your mind delete.◆
Stop worrying about your life
As to what to drink or eat.

"Stop worrying about your body
As to what clothing to possess.
Is not life more than nourishment
And the body more than dress?

6:26 "Birds in the sky don't sow or reap
Or gather so as to store,
Yet your heavenly Father feeds them.
Are not you worth so much more?

6:27 "And who is there among you all
Who has the power ◆and might
To add by the act of worry
One cubit to his height?

6:28 "Learn from the lilies of the field.
Learn how they grow *without stress.
They do not work or spin their clothes.
Why worry about your dress?

6:29 "But I am declaring to you
Regarding Solomon's clothes,
In all his glory he wasn't clothed
Like a single one of those.

6:30	"If God so clothes the field plants now,
	Though later they're thrown in fire,
	Then, O people of little faith,
	Much more will be your attire.
6:31	"Therefore, do not worry and say,
	'What food might we prepare?'
	Or 'With what might we quench our thirst?'
	Or 'What clothing might we wear?'
6:32	"For seeking ♦food, drink, and clothing,
	Gentiles keep doing, *indeed.
	For your heavenly Father knows
	That these you constantly need.
6:33	"But keep seeking God's kingdom first
	And the righteousness He gives,
	And all these things He'll add to you.
	This is how one truly lives.*
6:34	"Therefore, do not ever worry
	About tomorrow, *I say.
	Tomorrow will care for itself.
	There's enough evil this day.

7:1	"Stop the habit of playing judge
	That judgment you won't incur,
7:2	For by the judgment with which you judge,
	You will be judged for sure.

       "And by the very same standard
       With which you measure others,
       You will be *most assuredly
       Measured the same way, *brothers.

7:3   "And why do you keep noticing
       In your brother's eye the dot,
       Yet stop noticing in your eye
       The gigantic beam you've got.

7:4   "How will you say to your brother,
       'That dot from your eye let me take'
       And yet, behold, still in your eye
       Is that mammoth beam *you forsake?

7:5   "You hypocrite! First from your eye
       Throw out the beam, then thereby,
       You'll see clearly enough to take
       The dot from your brother's eye.

7:6   "Don't give to dogs what is holy.
       Your pearls before pigs don't cast,
       Or they'll trample them underfoot
       And tear you apart, turning fast.

7:7   "Keep asking and you will receive.
       Keep seeking and you will find.
       Keep knocking and it will open.
       Persistence won't be declined.[54]

7:8   "For all who keep asking, receive.
       All who keep seeking, find.
       All who keep knocking, open it will.
       Persistence won't be declined.*

7:9 "Or what man exists among you,
Who will give his son a stone
If that son asks him for a loaf?
Such a father is unknown.⁵⁵

7:10 "Or what man exists among you,
Who will give his son a snake
If that son asks him for a fish?
No father would give what's fake.⁵⁶

7:11 "Therefore, if you know to practice
(Though evil you truly are)
Giving good gifts to your children,
Much truer is this by far:

"Your Father (the One in heaven)
Who is good and without sin*
Will most certainly give good things
To those who keep asking Him.

7:12 "Therefore, as the heart of the Law
And the Prophets does proclaim,⁵⁷
How you wish people to treat you,
Practice treating them the same.

7:13 "Enter through the gate that's narrow,
For to destruction is where
The wide gate and the broad path lead.
Many are entering there.

7:14	"But leading to eternal life
	Is the narrow way, *I state,
	Yet the pathway is oppressive,
	And few are finding this gate.
7:15	"Keep looking out for false prophets
	Who come to you in sheep's clothes
	But inwardly are vicious wolves.
7:16	You'll know by the fruit one shows.
	"People don't gather grapes from thorns.[58]
	From thistles, figs aren't gotten.
7:17	So, each healthy tree's fruit is good.
	Each bad tree's fruit is rotten.
7:18	"A healthy tree is unable
	To make bad fruit, *as you know.
	Likewise, a bad tree cannot make
	Good fruit *from itself to grow.
7:19	"Every tree not bearing good fruit
	Is chopped and in the fire thrown.
7:20	Therefore, by the fruit that they bear,
	All false prophets will be known.
7:21	"Not all who say 'Lord, Lord!' to Me
	Will enter heaven's empire,
	Only the one who practices
	My heavenly Father's desire.
7:22	"Many will tell Me on that day,
	'Lord, did we not in Your name
	Prophesy, or cast out demons,
	Or many wonders make plain?'

7:23	"And then I will confess to them,
	'I never truly knew you.
	Depart from Me, evil workers,
	For it's lawlessness you do.'◆
7:24	"So, all who hear these words of Mine
	And practice them will be compared
	To a wise man who built his house
	On the rock foundation prepared.
7:25	"The rain fell; rivers overflowed;
	Against that house winds did knock,
	And yet the house did not fall down
	Since it had been built on rock.
7:26	"And all who hear these words of Mine
	But don't heed them will be compared
	To a fool who built his own house
	On the sand foundation prepared.
7:27	"The rain fell; rivers overflowed;
	Winds blew on that habitation.
	As the winds struck, the house fell down,
	And great was its devastation."
7:28	After Jesus finished these words,
	Amazement the crowds expressed,
7:29	For He taught with authority,
	But not as their scribes possessed.

8:1	When He came down from the mountain,
	Large crowds followed Him around.
8:2	Behold, a leper came to Him,
	Bowing to Him on the ground.
	"Lord, if you wish, You can cleanse me."
	The leper to Jesus pled.
8:3	Stretching out His hand, He touched him.
	"I wish it. Be cleansed." He said.
	Immediately, his leprosy
	Was cleansed. ◆His skin was made pure,
8:4	But Jesus then instructed him,
	"Of this tell no one. Make sure.
	"Go and show yourself to the priest
	And offer the gift *for your cure
	Which Moses ordered *in the Law.
	It's proof to them *that you're pure."
8:5	When He entered Capernaum,
	Before Him with urgency,
	A commander of one hundred[59]
	Came to Jesus with this plea:
8:6	"Lord, my servant who's but a child
	Has been confined to my home.
	He is suffering terribly
	A paralyzing syndrome."

8:7   He said to him, "I am coming.
The child, I Myself will heal."
8:8   The commander of one hundred
Responded with this appeal:

"I'm not worthy enough for You
To come under my roof, sir,
But only say a single word,
And his healing will occur.

8:9   "For I myself am a person
Who's under authority,
Entrusted with one hundred men
Who are soldiers under me.

"I tell this one, 'Go!' and he goes;
To others, 'Come!' They obey.
To my slave I command, 'Do this!'
And he does just as I say."

8:10   When Jesus heard this, He marveled.
To those following Him around,
He said, "Truly, in Israel
Such faith I've not even found.

8:11   "I tell you that from east and west
Many will come and recline
With Abraham, Isaac, and Jacob
In heaven's kingdom to dine.

8:12   "But into the outer darkness
The kingdom's sons will be cast.
In that place the gnashing of teeth
And the weeping will be *vast."

The Poetic Gospel of Matthew

8:13   He told the centurion, "Go!
        For as your faith has appealed,
        Let it be accomplished for you."
        And right then the child was healed.

8:14   When Jesus entered Peter's house,
        He saw in a bed confined
        The mother-in-law of Peter
        With a fever *of some kind.

8:15   He went over and* touched her hand,
        Since her, He desired to heal.*
        The fever left her. She got up
        And then served to Him a meal.

8:16   After that evening had arrived,
        To Jesus the people brought
        Many who were demon-possessed
        And who with illness were fraught.*

        And by a simple spoken word,
        Jesus cast the spirits out
        And healed all those with illnesses
8:17   So as to bring this about:

        Words of Isaiah the prophet
        Through whom was spoken before,
        "He Himself took our weaknesses,
        And our diseases, He bore."

The Poetic Scriptures of Six Writers

8:18 But seeing a crowd around Him,
 Jesus ordered that there be
 For Himself and His disciples*
 Arrangements to cross the sea.

8:19 A certain scribe approached Jesus.
 From his mouth these words did flow,
 "I will follow you anywhere,
 Whatever place You might go."

8:20 Jesus told him, "Foxes have dens,
 The birds of the sky have nests,
 But the Son of Man has nowhere
 To lay His head when He rests."

8:21 Another of the disciples
 Said to Him, "Lord, ✦if You may,
 Allow me first to leave from here
 To bury my dad *someday."

8:22 But Jesus answered back to him,
 "Keep following Me, *I say.
 Leave those who are spiritually dead[60]
 To bury their dead *someday."

8:23 Now, His disciples followed Him
 As into the boat He stepped.
8:24 Behold, a great storm shook the sea.
 Over the boat the waves swept.

	But He was sleeping, so they came
8:25	Right to where He was lying.
	They woke Him up, saying, "O Lord,
	Rescue us! We are dying!"

8:26 He said, "Why fear, you of small faith?"
Their request He rose *to fulfill.
He rebuked the winds and the sea
Which became perfectly still.

8:27 The men marveled as they conversed.
"Just what kind of man is He
That nature itself♦ obeys Him,
Even the winds and the sea?"

8:28 He crossed and entered a region.
The Gadarenes[61] is its name.
Two demon-possessed men met Him.
From among the tombs, they came.

They were so fierce that nobody
Was strong enough to pass through
Using the road beside the tombs.
None dared to challenge these two.*

8:29 They shouted out, "O Son of God,
You come to us for what reason?
Have You come here to torment us
Before the appointed season?"

8:30 Now, there was a large herd of pigs
Being fed a distance away.
8:31 So, the demons were urging Him,
For this is what they did say:

	"If You plan on casting us out,
	Send us all into that herd.
8:32	So, He said to them, "Go away!"
	And they came out *by His word.

They entered the pigs, and behold,
The whole herd with them inside
Rushed down the slope into the sea,
And in the waters they died.

8:33 The ones feeding them ran away
Into the town to attest,
Telling all, even what happened
To the ones demon-possessed.

8:34 The whole town came to meet Jesus
With their own set of orders.*
When they saw Him, they all urged Him
To exit from their borders.

9:1 After getting into a boat,
He went back across the sea,
And then He entered His own town.
Capernaum, that would be.[62]

9:2 And behold, people were bringing
A man who was paralyzed
Who had been placed on a stretcher.
Their faith, Jesus recognized.

	To the paralyzed man, He said,
	"Be of good courage, O child.
	Your sins are now forgiven you."
9:3	And behold, some scribes *were riled.
	For they had said within themselves,
	"Blasphemy, this One imparts."
9:4	And perceiving their thoughts He said,
	"Why think evil in your hearts?
9:5	"To say to this paralytic,
	Which is the easier talk:
	'Your sins are now forgiven you'
	Or is it, 'Get up and walk'?
9:6	"But in order that you might know
	That the Son of Man retains
	Authority upon the earth
	To forgive sins *as He claims –"
	Then to him who was paralyzed,
	Jesus said, "To your feet stand.
	Pick up your stretcher and go home."
9:7	And he obeyed His command.[63]
9:8	When the crowds saw him walking home,
	To fear and awe[64] they resigned.
	They praised God for giving to men
	Authority of such kind.

9:9	As Jesus proceeded onward,
	In a tax booth He could see
	A man called Matthew sitting there.
	He said to him, "Follow Me."
	Matthew got up and followed Him
9:10	And a great feast for Him threw.[65]
	Jesus and His disciples ate.
	Taxmen and sinners ate too.
9:11	When the Pharisees observed this,
	His disciples they did entreat,
	"Tell us, why with tax collectors
	And sinners, does your teacher eat?"
9:12	When Jesus heard them, He then said,
	"The healthy don't have a need
	For a doctor *to tend to them,
	But the ailing do *indeed.
9:13	"'I want mercy, not sacrifice.'
	Go learn what by this is meant.
	I've not come to call the righteous
	But the sinners *to repent."
9:14	Then John's disciples came to Him
	And asked Him, "Why *this contrast?
	Pharisees and we give up meals.
	Your disciples never fast."

9:15	Jesus said, "Wedding guests can't mourn While the bridegroom is still there, But days will come when he's taken. Then they will fast *in despair.
9:16	"Nobody throws an unshrunk patch On a garment that is old, For as it shrinks the garment tears, And a worse tear will unfold.
9:17	"Nor does anyone pour new wine Into wineskins that are old, For if they do, the wineskins burst, And the wine, it cannot hold.◆ "The wine spills out, and the wineskins Are ruined as expected. Pour new wine into fresh wineskins, And both are then protected."
9:18	As He was telling them these things, One Jewish ruler, behold, Came and was bowing before Him, And these words to Him he told: "My daughter, she has just now died. Please grant this request I give.* Come and lay Your hand upon her, And I know that* she will live."
9:19	Jesus got up and followed him. His disciples followed too.
9:20	And behold, there came a woman Behind Him ◆just out of view.

	She had been bleeding for twelve years.
	So she touched His garment's border,
9:21	Thinking, "If I just touch His clothes,
	I'll be healed *of this disorder."

9:22 Turning to see her, Jesus said,
"Be courageous ♦and assured.
Your faith has healed you, O daughter."
Right then the woman was cured.

9:23 Into the Jewish ruler's house,
Jesus entered and there viewed
The flautists playing and the crowd
In a most disturbing mood.

9:24 He was saying, "Get out of here,
For she did not really die,
But the girl is only sleeping."
Ridicule was their reply.

9:25 Now once the crowd was forced outside,
He went in and grabbed her hand,
And the girl got up on her feet.
9:26 This news spread throughout that land.

9:27 As Jesus proceeded from there,
Two blind men followed behind.
They were shouting, "Son of David,
Have mercy on us. *We're blind."

The Poetic Gospel of Matthew

9:28   After Jesus entered the house,
       He was approached by these two.[66]
       Jesus asked them, "Do you believe
       That this I'm able to do?"

       They replied to Him, "Yes, O Lord."
9:29   He touched both their eyes right then.
       He said, "According to your faith,
       Let this happen to you, ◆men."

9:30   Their eyes were opened, but He warned,
       "Tell nobody. Understand?"
9:31   But when they left, they spread the news
       About Him throughout that land.

9:32   After they left, behold, a man
       Who could not with words express
       Was brought to Jesus to be healed,
       And he was demon-possessed.

9:33   And when the demon was cast out,
       Words from the mute man just spewed.
       The crowd marveled, "In Israel
       Never has such thing been viewed."

9:34   But the Pharisees were saying,
       "This person derives His clout*
       By the ruler of the demons
       In casting the demons out."

9:35   To all the cities and small towns
       Jesus was traveling around,
       Teaching in all their synagogues,
       Wherever they might be found.*

| | The gospel about the kingdom,
He was preaching everywhere,
Also, healing every disease
And every ailment out there. |

9:36 And when He saw the multitudes,
Compassion for them He applied,
For they were troubled and scattered
Like sheep with no shepherd *to guide.

9:37 Then He said to His disciples,
"There's much to harvest. *It's true.
But the number of laborers
At this time* are very few.

9:38 "Therefore, the Lord of the harvest,
You all must beg ♦and implore
That He might send more laborers
Into His harvest galore."

10:1 He summoned His twelve disciples
And gave them power to cast out
Unclean spirits, also to heal
Each disease and ailing bout.

10:2 The twelve apostles' names are these:
Peter and his brother Andrew;
Zebedee's sons called James and John;
10:3 Philip and Bartholomew.

	Thomas and the taxman Matthew;
	Alphaeus's son named James;
10:4	Simon the Zealot, Thaddaeus,
	And Judas, *making twelve names.

At first, Peter was called Simon[67]
Before the Lord changed His name.[68]
Judas was the Iscariot
Who betrayed the Lord *in shame.

10:5 These twelve apostles, Jesus sent,
Laying these instructions down:
"Don't go onto a Gentile road
Or to a Samaritan town.

10:6 "Instead, go to Israel's house,
The sheep who have lost their way.
10:7 The news, 'Heaven's kingdom is near!',
You must continue to say.

10:8 "Practice healing those who are sick.
Keep raising to life the dead.
Practice cleansing the leper's skin.
Demons cast out. *Go ahead.

"Because you have freely received,
Then freely give *all the more.
10:9 No gold, silver, or copper coins
In your purses must you store.

10:10 "Don't carry a bag for the trip.
A second garment exclude.
No extra sandals or a staff,
For the worker deserves his food.

10:11 "The city or town you enter,
Search within it to and fro.
Find someone worthy, and stay there
Until from the town you go.

10:12 "Entering, greet the house *with peace.
10:13 If worthiness it does not lack,
Let your blessing of peace abide.
Otherwise,⁶⁹ let it come back.

10:14 "Whoever does not welcome you
And listens not to your talk,
As you exit that house or town,
The dust from your feet just knock.

10:15 "'Twill truly be more bearable
On that final judgment day
For Sodom and Gomorrah's land
Than for that city, I say.

10:16 "I am sending you out as sheep
In the midst of wolves, you see.
In light of this, be wise as snakes
Yet harmless as doves would be.

10:17 "Be on the lookout for such men,
For you to the courts, they'll hand.
They'll whip you in their synagogues,
And before rulers you'll stand.♦

10:18 "Because of Me, you will be brought
Before rulers and kings ♦at trials
As a testimony to them,
As well as to the Gentiles.

The Poetic Gospel of Matthew

10:19   "When they give you up for trial,
             Do not be anxious at all
             As to how or what you might say,
             For words from your lips will fall.♦

             "In that hour will be given you
             The words to be testified,
10:20   For it will not be you who speak
             But your Father's Spirit inside.

10:21   "Brother will hand brother to death,
             A father his progeny.
             Children will stand against parents,
             Making death the penalty.

10:22   "You'll be hated by all people
             Solely because of My name,
             But he who endures 'til the end,
             That one will be saved from blame.

10:23   "Whenever they in one city
             Persecute you *due to Me,
             Run away to another one.
             If they come there, likewise flee.*

             "For I am telling you the truth,
             You will in no way be done
             Reaching Israel's towns before
             The Son of Man will have come.

10:24   "A disciple's not greater than
             The teacher by whom he's taught,
             And a slave's not superior
             To the master that he's got.

10:25	"It's enough for a disciple To be like his teacher, *that's who. And it's sufficient for a slave To be like his master too. "If the name of Beelzebul They apply to the household's head, How much more to those who belong To his house will this be said.
10:26	"Therefore, don't be afraid of them. For there's nothing which won't be shown That's already been covered up, Or hidden which won't be made known.
10:27	"What I tell you in the darkness, In the light you are to share. What you hear in the ear from Me, Upon the rooftops declare.
10:28	"Don't fear those who kill the body But can't make the soul expire. Fear Him who can kill both body And soul in Gehenna's fire.[70]
10:29	"Isn't a farthing for two sparrows Required for acquisition? Yet not one will fall to the ground Without your Father's *permission.
10:30 **10:31**	"But even the hairs on your head Have been counted. So don't fear! You yourselves matter so much more Than many sparrows. ◆You're dear!

10:32 "All who'll confess to be in Me
   Before mankind's very eye,
   I will confess that I'm in him
   Before My Father on high.[71]

10:33 "But whoever would deny Me
   Before mankind's very eye,
   Certainly* I will deny him
   Before My Father on high.

10:34 "Do not assume that I have come
   To put peace upon earth's land.
   I did not come to put peace here
   But a sword *in mankind's hand.

10:35 "For I came to divide a man
   Against his father, *I tell.
   I came to divide a daughter
   Against her mother as well.

   "And against her mother-in-law,
   I came to divide a bride.
10:36 I've come to make a person's foes
   Those who in his house abide.

10:37 "You who for your own dad or mom
   A deep fondness do possess
   That exceeds your fondness for Me,
   Aren't worthy of Me, *I stress.

   "You who for your son or daughter
   A deep fondness do possess
   That exceeds your fondness for Me,
   Aren't worthy of Me, *I stress.

10:38	"And the one who does not receive The cross which he is assigned And keeps following after Me, Is not worthy to be Mine.
10:39	"The one who has secured his life, That life he will lose for sure. He who loses his life for Me, That life that one will secure.
10:40	"Now the person who welcomes you, That one welcomes Me as well; And the person who welcomes Me, Welcomes My Sender, *I tell.
10:41	"The one who welcomes a prophet Who's a prophet of the Lord* For the sake of the prophet's name Will receive a prophet's reward. "The one who welcomes a person Who is righteous *in the Lord For the sake of his righteous name Will gain a just man's reward.
10:42	"He who in a disciple's name To give a cold drink does choose To just one of these little ones, His reward he'll never lose."

The Poetic Gospel of Matthew

11:1 When Jesus finished commanding
The twelve disciples *He sent,
He left from there to teach and preach
In the cities where they went.⁷²

11:2 Now John, after hearing in jail
About the works Christ had done,
Sent word through his own disciples,
11:3 Asking Him, "Are You the One?

"Are You Yourself the Coming One,
Or another must we await?"
11:4 Jesus said in reply to them,
"Go and ♦this message relate.

"State to John what you hear and see:
11:5 The blind are gaining their sight;
Lame people are walking around;
Lepers are cleansed *from their plight.

"The deaf hear; the dead have been raised;
The poor hear the gospel call;⁷³
11:6 And blessed is the one who in Me
Isn't made to stumble ♦or fall."

11:7 After these disciples of John
Left there from Jesus's midst,
He began to say to the crowds
Concerning John the Baptist:

"You went out into the desert
To observe what? *Tell Me, please!
A reed being swayed here and there
From the variable breeze?

11:8 "But what did you go out to see,
A man wearing fancy things?
Behold, those who wear fancy clothes
Are in the houses of kings.

11:9 "But what did you go out to see,
A prophet? I tell you, yes!
Yet he is more than a prophet.
11:10 Of him the Scriptures address:

"'See My messenger whom I send
Ahead of Your very face.
He will prepare the road for You.
Ahead of You him, I'll place.'

11:11 "There's no one who has arisen
(Of this truth I now inform)
Who's greater than John the Baptist
Among those from women born.

"But the least in heaven's kingdom
Is greater than he *anyhow.
11:12 Look at what's happened* from the days
Of John the Baptist until now.

"Heaven's kingdom is being stormed.
The violent are grabbing on,
11:13 For all the Prophets and the Law
Just prophesied until John.

11:14	"If you're willing to accept it,
	Elijah who's to appear[74]
	Is fulfilled in John the Baptist.
11:15	He who has ears, let him hear.
11:16	"To what out there will I compare
	The generation today?
	Small kids sitting in the markets,
	Calling to others to say:
11:17	"'We played the flute for you to dance,
	But dancing you did not do;
	We sang a dirge for you to mourn,
	But you did not *heed our cue.'
11:18	"For John the Baptist came this way:
	He consumed no wine or bread,
	Yet they say, 'He's demon-possessed!'
	And then what else have they said?*
11:19	"The Son of Man both eats and drinks.
	They say, 'Look at whom He befriends.
	This Man's a glutton and a drunk.
	He's with sinners and publicans.'
	"Yet wisdom's proved right by her works."
11:20	Then the towns He began to shame
	Where He did many miracles,
	For repentance was not their aim.
11:21	"O Chorazin and Bethsaida,
	How horrible it will be
	On the day of judgment for you
	For the miracles you see.

"For if the miracles you see
In Tyre and Sidon were wrought,
They'd be in sackcloth and ashes.
Repentance they long would have sought.

11:22 "But it will be more bearable
For Tyre and Sidon, I say,
Than for you, ◆that is your people,
In the time of judgment day.

11:23 "And as for you, Capernaum,
Will you be lifted up high
As far as the heaven above?
No! In Hades you will lie!

"For if the miracles you see
Were wrought in Sodom, I say,
It would ◆never have been destroyed
But still would remain today.

11:24 "But it will be more bearable
For the land of Sodom, I say,
Than for you, ◆that is your people,
In the time of judgment day."

11:25 At that time, Jesus responded,
"Father, it's You whom I praise,
Lord of the heaven and the earth,
Because *of Your higher ways.

"From the wise and intelligent,
All these things You have concealed,
Yet to babes, ◆to the innocent
All these things, You have revealed.

The Poetic Gospel of Matthew

11:26   "Yes, Father,*it's You whom I praise,
           For it is this very way
           Which is well-pleasing in Your sight.
           This praise, I openly pray.*

11:27   "All things were delivered to Me
           By My Father. There's no one
           Except for the Father above
           Who does really know the Son.

           "No one really knows the Father
           Except for the Son, ♦He knows,
           And anyone to whom the Son
           Determines to disclose.

11:28   "All of you who labor so hard
           And also have been hard-pressed,
           Come before Me *with your burdens,
           And I will cause you to rest.

11:29   "Take My yoke, and put it on you,
           And from Me begin to learn.
           For I'm meek and humble in heart,
           Showering you with concern.*

           "If you do this, this will occur:*
           Rest for your souls, you will find,
11:30   For My burden is very light
           And My yoke is very kind."

The Poetic Scriptures of Six Writers

12:1	In that season on the Sabbath,
	Through the fields Jesus proceeded.
	Hungry, His disciples began
	To pluck and eat what they needed.

12:2	But the Pharisees told Him, "Look!"
	When His disciples they saw,
	"Your disciples on the Sabbath
	Do what is against the Law."

12:3	But He told them, "Haven't you read
	What David one time had done
	When he and those who were with him
	Became hungry *on the run?

12:4	"He entered God's house. Ate the showbread,
	Which the Law does not condone,
	Neither for him nor those with him
	Since it's for the priests alone.

12:5	"Or haven't you read in the Law
	That priests in the temple profane
	The Sabbath on the Sabbath day,
	Yet these priests are without blame?

12:6	"But I tell you, there is One here
	That's greater than the temple.
12:7	'I want mercy, not sacrifice.'
	That's Scripture plain and simple.[75]

	"The guiltless you would not condemn
	If those words you would obey,
12:8	For the Son of Man is Lord
	Even of the Sabbath day."

12:9	Then after proceeding from there,
	To their synagogue He went.
12:10	Behold, there was a certain man
	Whose hand was shriveled ◆and bent.

They questioned Him because a charge
Against Him they all desired.
"Is it against the Law to heal
On the Sabbath?" they inquired.

12:11 He asked, "If on a Sabbath day
Your one sheep fell in a pit,
Is there any man among you
Who would not go rescue it?

12:12 "Of much more value is a man.
A sheep's worth, his does outweigh.
Therefore, it is lawful to do
What's good on the Sabbath day."

12:13 He told the man, "Stretch out your hand."
He did *as per His command,
And it was completely restored
As good as his other hand.

12:14 But after the Pharisees left,
A plot they began to build
Against Jesus for one purpose,
The purpose that He be killed.

12:15	But when Jesus learned of this plot,
	He withdrew from there *with speed,
	Yet the many crowds followed Him,
	And He healed all *who had need.
12:16	He charged them not to make Him known
12:17	For the purpose to fulfill
	What the prophet Isaiah said,
	These words which God did instill:[76]
12:18	"Look, My servant whom I've chosen,
	The One I dearly embrace,
	In whom My soul finds good pleasure,
	On Him, My Spirit I'll place.
	"He'll announce judgment to the world.[77]
12:19	He'll not quarrel or cry out,
	Neither will any person hear
	His voice in the streets about.
12:20	"He will not break a flimsy reed
	Or put out a fading flame
	'Til He brings judgment to triumph.
12:21	The world will hope in His name."

12:22	Then one who was demon-possessed
	Was brought to Him mute and blind.
	He healed him so he could speak and see.
	The man, Jesus did unbind.[78]

12:23	And all the crowds were marveling, Discussing who He might be. "This person cannot be ♦the Christ, The Son of David, can He?"
12:24	Now when the Pharisees heard this, They said, "He doesn't cast out Demons except by their ruler, Beelzebul! *There's no doubt!"
12:25	But knowing their thoughts, He told them, "Every kingdom ♦or nation That's divided against itself Comes to ruination. "In the same way, every city Or household *in any land That's divided against itself Will never be made to stand.
12:26	"And if Satan casts out Satan, Against himself he's divided. Therefore, how will his own kingdom Be made to stand united?
12:27	"And if I cast out demons by Beelzebul's authority, By what do your sons cast them out? Therefore, your judges they will be.
12:28	"But if I cast out the demons In the Spirit of God's power, Then surely the kingdom of God Has arrived on you *this hour.

12:29	"Or how can one enter the home
Of a man whose strength is great
And seize his goods unless he first
Puts him in a tied-up state?
12:30	"The one who does not stand with Me
Stands against Me *in all matters.
The one who gathers not with Me
Is a person who just scatters.
12:31	"Because of this, I say to you,
That sin of every kind
Even the sin of blasphemy
Will be forgiven mankind.

"However, ♦there's a certain sin
Where forgiveness won't be applied:♦
Blasphemy against the Spirit.
Forgiveness will be denied. |
| **12:32** | "And whoever speaks any word
That's against the Son of Man,
Even though it is blasphemy,♦
Forgiven, that one will stand.

"But if one speaks against the Spirit,[79]
Forgiveness, he will have none,
Not ever in this present age
And not in the age to come. |
| **12:33** | "Either produce a tree that's good
Which makes good fruit *as it should,
Or produce a tree that's worthless
Which makes fruit that is no good. |

	"For by its fruit, a tree is known.
12:34	So then, how can you be viewed
	As speaking good when you're evil?
	You are just a viper's brood!

"For out of the heart's abundance,
The mouth makes its oration.
Whether that abundance be good
Or a bad aggregation.[80]

12:35 "The good man takes out good items
From the good that's stored inside.
The evil man takes out bad things
From the bad that does reside.

12:36 "I tell you, every useless word
People will decide to say
Will be paid back to their account
In the time of judgment day.

12:37 "For by the words which you express,
Righteous you will be declared,
And by the words which you express,
You will be condemned, ♦not spared."

12:38 Some of the scribes and Pharisees
Then said to Him in reply,
"Teacher, we want a sign from You
That we can see ♦with the eye."

12:39	But answering back, He told them, "Only a generation That is evil and faithless seeks A sign for affirmation. "Yet no sign will be given it, Not one sign which it wants done.♦ Only the prophet Jonah's sign Will be given by the Son.[81]
12:40	"Jonah was inside the belly Of the monster of the sea For a period of days and nights, Which period numbered three. "So, just as it was for Jonah, The Son of Man also will stay For only three days and three nights In the heart of the earth, *I say.
12:41	"The men of Nineveh will stand With today's generation In the judgment and will pronounce Upon it condemnation. "Why? Because those men repented At Jonah's proclamation. Look! One greater than Jonah's here Among this generation.*
12:42	"The Queen of the South will rise up With today's generation In the judgment and will pronounce Upon it condemnation.

"For to hear Solomon's wisdom
From the earth's limits she came.
Look! There is One already here
Who exceeds Solomon's name.

12:43 "Whenever an unclean spirit
Exits from whom he possessed,
He goes through waterless places
Looking for a place of rest.

"Yet he finds none, and so he says,
12:44 'To my house I will return,
The one from where I exited.'
He does, and what does he learn?

"It's been swept and put in order,
But it is unoccupied.
12:45 So, he then goes and brings with him
Other spirits to reside.

"He finds seven evil spirits.
His wickedness theirs excel.
They then go into the body,
And that body they indwell.

"That person's last state is much worse
Than his first state *of damnation.
So also, it will be the same
For this evil generation."

12:46 Now, there had been standing outside,
While to the crowds He was speaking,
His own mother and His brothers.
To talk to Him, they were seeking.

12:47	To Him someone relayed, "Take note, Your mother, Your brothers too, They all have been standing outside Desiring to speak to You."[82]
12:48	But He replied to the person Who had relayed this demand, "Who are My mother and brothers?"
12:49	Then He extended His hand.
	He pointed◆ to His disciples, And then these words He told, "Who are My mother and brothers? These disciples are!* Behold!
12:50	"For whoever would do the will Of My heavenly Father, That person is ◆My family: My brother, sister, or mother."

13:1	On that same day after Jesus Had from the house vacated, He was sitting beside the sea.
13:2	Large crowds just congregated.
	He climbed into a boat to sit Before the large crowds, therefore. Now the whole crowd had *eagerly Been standing along the shore.

13:3	Then He spoke many things to them,
	But in parables He'd tell:
	"The sower went out to sow seed.
	Take note *where all the seeds fell.
13:4	"In his sowing, some of the seeds
	Fell just alongside the road,
	And when the birds came, they consumed
	All of these seeds that he sowed.
13:5	"But others fell on rocky earth
	Where not much soil was intact.
	Shoots sprang up immediately,
	For depth of soil that ground lacked.
13:6	"When the sun rose up ♦in the sky
	And shined upon every shoot,*
	They were scorched and withered because
	None of them had any root.
13:7	"But among thorns, other seeds fell,
	And as plants from these did sprout,*
	The thorns sprang up around them high,
	And they choked the plants right out.
13:8	"Other seeds fell on healthy ground
	And began producing fruit,
	Multiplying themselves much more,
	For these seeds the soil did suit.[83]
	"Some multiplied one hundred times,
	Some sixty times *in that year,
	And some multiplied thirty times.
13:9	He who has ears, let him hear."

The Poetic Scriptures of Six Writers

13:10   When the disciples came to Him,
        They asked Jesus this question:
        "Why do You speak in parables
        To the crowd *in this session?"

13:11   In reply, Jesus said to them,
        "It's been given you to know
        The mysteries of heaven's kingdom,
        But for them, this is not so.[84]

13:12   "For whoever has this knowledge,
        To him will be given more,
        And he will be completely filled
        With the knowledge I outpour.[85]

        "But whoever has no knowledge,
        Even what he has, I say,
        Regardless of what it might be,*
        Will from him be snatched away.

13:13   "I tell them parables because
        In their seeing they don't see
        And in their hearing they don't hear.
        They can't learn *God's mystery.

13:14   "And so, Isaiah's prophecy
        Is fulfilled in them. I quote:
        'You'll hear the word yet never will
        Understand *what I denote.

        "'And in your seeing, you will see
        But will not perceive at all
13:15   Because the heart of this people
        Has become extremely dull.

"'And they have barely heard a word,
Even with their ears *exposed,
And the two eyes that they possess,
They have shut them tight; ◆they're closed.

"'This way they don't see with their eyes,
Or hear with their ears anymore,
Or with their own hearts understand
And turn so them I'd restore.'

13:16 "Since your eyes see and your ears hear,
Your eyes and ears are both blessed.
13:17 Many prophets and righteous ones
Longed for this day, I attest.

"They desired to see what you see
Yet did not see what they sought,
And they longed to hear what you hear,
Yet to hear it, they did not.

13:18 "Therefore, you yourselves listen now
To the parable that was told
Of the sower who sowed the seeds,
The meaning which I will unfold.*

13:19 "Everyone who hears the message
About the kingdom *of God
Yet does not understand that word,
The evil one *will defraud.

"The word that was sown in his heart,
The Devil◆ comes and snatches.
The seed that fell beside the road,
This explanation matches.

13:20	"But what was sown on rocky ground Matches him who hears the word And receives it immediately, His joyfulness being stirred.
13:21	"But having no root, it lasts not; For when oppression or trouble Because of the word arises, He is tripped up on the double.
13:22	"He who hears the word, but it's choked By wealth's guile and the world's care, Matches what was sown among thorns. No fruit can it possibly bear.
13:23	"But what was sown upon good ground Is he who grasps the word told And bears fruit, increasing thirty, Sixty, or one hundredfold."

13:24	Here is another parable Which Jesus to them revealed: "Heaven's kingdom is like a man Who sowed good seed in his field.
13:25	"But while men slept, his enemy Sowed tares among all the wheat And then departed *unnoticed. No one knew of this deceit.[86]

13:26	"When the crop grew and produced fruit,
	Then all the tares were exposed.
13:27	The household owner had some slaves
	Who to him this question posed:

        "'Master, did you not in the field
        Sow all good seed, *not just some?
        Then why does it have tares as well?
        From where *did the bad seed come?'

13:28	"He said to them, 'A foe did this.'
	His slaves asked *for their next deed.
	'Do you want us to go from here
	And gather up every weed?'

13:29	"But he said, 'No! For otherwise,
	In gathering the tares you may
	Uproot the wheat along with them.
13:30	Let both grow 'til harvest day.

        "'At that time, I'll tell the reapers,
        *First gather the tares *in the field.*
        Tie them in bundles for burning.
        Pile in my barn the wheat yield.'"

13:31	Here is another parable
	That to them He did proclaim:
	"Heaven's kingdom is likened to
	The mustard plant's seed or grain.[87]

	"And a man took the mustard seed
	And sowed it onto his field.
13:32	Although it's smaller than all seeds,
	What a large plant it does yield.[88]

"It grows larger than all the plants
And becomes a tree *of rest.
The birds of the sky come to it,
And in its branches they nest."

13:33 Here is another parable
Of the kingdom of heaven*
Which Jesus presented to them,
Comparing it to leaven.*

"Heaven's kingdom is like leaven
Which a woman took and blended
In one bushel[89] of wheat flour
'Til through all it extended."

13:34 All of these lessons to the crowds,
In parables Jesus taught.
Without a single parable,
To speak to them He did not.

13:35 He taught this way in order to
Fulfill what had been proclaimed
Through the prophet *found in the Psalms,[90]
From *Asaph's Maskil* as named:[91]

"I'll open My mouth in parables,
Giving a proclamation
Of what has long been covered up
Since the time of creation."

13:36 Then right after leaving the crowds,
Back into the house Jesus went.
"The field's tares," His disciples asked,
"Tell us what that parable meant."

13:37	In reply, to them He explained So that they could understand,* "The person who sows the good seed Represents the Son of Man.
13:38	"Now the field represents the world. And the good seed *that was sown, These are the sons of the kingdom, Heaven's kingdom as it's known.♦
13:39	"The tares are the evil one's sons. The foe *who stooped to the level Of sowing these *tares in the field, That one represents the Devil.
	"Now the harvest, it represents This age's culmination. The harvesters are the angels. So here's the correlation:
13:40	"Even as the tares are gathered And are burned up in the fire, So also the same will occur When this age comes to expire.
13:41	"The Son of Man will then send out His angels who will collect From His kingdom all stumbling blocks And who lawlessness elect.
13:42	"Then they will throw them all into The furnace of fire *beneath, Where there will be constant weeping, Also gnashing of the teeth.

13:43   "Then in the Son's Father's kingdom,
The righteous ones will appear,
Shining as the sun *in the sky.
He who has ears let him hear.

13:44   "Heaven's kingdom is somewhat like
Treasure buried in some field
Which a man eventually found,
But he put it back, concealed.

"From his joyous exuberance
Over this treasure revealed,
He goes and sells all that he owns
And buys the entire field.

13:45   "Again, the kingdom of heaven
Is very similar to
A merchant seeking certain pearls
Which are very fine ♦and true.

13:46   "But after he had discovered
One pearl with a price so great,
He went and sold all that he owned
And bought ♦that which was first-rate.

13:47   "Again, the kingdom of heaven
Is like a net which was cast
Into the sea ♦to gather fish.
All kinds of life were amassed.

13:48	"When it was filled, onto the beach They dragged it and sat about Then put the good in containers, But the worthless, they threw out.
13:49	"At the end of this present age So it will be as described. All the wicked from the righteous, Angels will go and divide.
13:50	"And they'll throw the wicked into The furnace of fire *beneath, Where there will be constant weeping, Also gnashing of the teeth.
13:51	"Have you comprehended these things?" They told Him, "Affirmative."
13:52	He said to them, "Because of this, This parable I now give:* "Every scribe made a disciple Of heaven's kingdom is as A house lord who takes new and old Out from the treasure he has."
13:53	When He finished these parables, Jesus went away from there.
13:54	After coming to His hometown, His words He began to share.◆ As He taught in their synagogue, They became amazed *that hour And asked, "From where did that One get This wisdom and all that power?"

13:55	"Is this not the carpenter's son? Is not Mary His mother? And are not James, Joseph, Simon, And Judas each His brother?
13:56	"Aren't all His sisters before us? So, from where have extended All these things to this one person?"
13:57	In Him they were offended.
	"A prophet," Jesus said to them, "Is not without honor shown Except in the town where he's from, And also in his own home."
13:58	And so, Jesus then decided That He'd no longer enact Very many miracles there Because of the faith they lacked.

14:1	Of Jesus, Herod the tetrarch At that time, heard the report.
14:2	"This is John the Baptist!" he said To the servants of his *court.
	"He Himself has raised from the dead, And that is the reason why Such powers are working in Him For miracles *to supply."

14:3	For because of Herodias,
	Herod's brother Philip's wife,
	He arrested John, tied him up,
	Then jailed him *for verbal strife.
14:4	For John kept on confronting him
	About this wrong relation.*
	"It's unlawful that you have her.
	It's an abomination!"*
14:5	And although he wished to kill him,
	The crowd, Herod greatly feared
	Since as a prophet *of the Lord,
	John the Baptist they revered.
14:6	But when Herod's birthday arrived,
	Herodias's daughter danced
	In the presence of everyone.
	Herod was pleased ♦as she pranced.
14:7	So, he promised to give to her
	Whatever request she'd make.
	He made this promise under oath.
	The promise he could not break.*
14:8	Being prompted by her mother
	What request to make, she said,
	"Give to me here on this platter
	John the Baptizer's head."
14:9	Although the king was very grieved,
	He ordered that the request
	Be granted to fulfill his vows
	In front of each dinner guest.

14:10	In jail he had him beheaded.
14:11	Then was placed the head of John
	On a plate and given the girl
	Who then brought it to her mom.
14:12	After John's disciples arrived,
	The corpse they carried away,
	Buried it, and came to Jesus,
	Telling Him *without delay.

14:13	As soon as He heard their report,
	Jesus went somewhere remote
	So that He could be by Himself,
	And He left there on a boat.
	When the crowds heard *He was leaving,
	From their cities they came out.
	They followed Him, except on foot,
	Walking on the land about.
14:14	Jesus saw the enormous crowd
	As out of the boat He got.
	Upon them He had compassion,
	And He healed the sick they brought.
14:15	Now, the disciples came to Him,
	Once evening did dominate,
	And said, "This place is a desert,
	And it is already late.

          "From this desert* release the crowds,
          This enormous multitude,♦
          To go into the villages
          And buy for themselves some food."

14:16   But He told them, "They need not leave.
          You feed them all *as I wish."
14:17   But they told Him, "We've nothing here
          Except five loaves and two fish."

14:18   He replied, "Bring them here to Me."
14:19   Then ordered the multitude
          To recline on the grass in groups,[92]
          And then He picked up ♦the food.

          He took the five loaves and two fish
          And looked up into the sky.
          He blessed the food and broke the loaves,
          Distributing the supply.♦

          He gave bits to His disciples
          Who gave to the crowds *as grouped.
14:20   Everyone ate 'til they were full.
          The leftovers, up they scooped.

          They collected twelve basketsful.
14:21   Now those who ate fish and dough
          (Excluding women and children)
          Were five thousand men or so.

14:22   He forced the disciples to board
          The boat without a delay
          And cross the sea ahead of Him
          While He sent the crowds away.

14:23	After sending the crowds away,
	Up the mountainside He went
	To be alone so He could pray.
	There alone that night He spent.
14:24	Now, by this time the boat itself
	Was a distance from the land,
	Being tossed around by the waves,
	For the wind was fiercely grand.
14:25	Now in the fourth watch of the night,
	Which was sometime after three,♦
	Jesus came to the disciples,
	But by walking on the sea.
14:26	Seeing Him walking on the sea,
	They were disturbed and did shout,
	"It's a ghost, ♦an apparition!"
	And from their fear, they cried out.
14:27	Immediately, He said to them,
	"Be of good courage. It's I.
	There is nothing* to fear. So stop!"
14:28	Then Peter said in reply:
	"O Lord, if it is really You,
	On these waters *let me tread.
	Order me to come before You."
14:29	"Come before Me!" Jesus said.
	Peter then stepped out of the boat,
	And on the waters he walked.
	He came all the way to Jesus.
	All the while the waters rocked.*

The Poetic Gospel of Matthew

14:30 But when he saw the mighty wind,
The fear within him just soared.
At that time, he started to sink.
So, he cried out, "Save me, Lord!"

14:31 Right then Jesus reached out His hand,
And of Peter He grabbed hold,
He asked him, "You of little faith,
Why by this doubt be controlled?"

14:32 After they got into the boat,
The wind, it no longer blew.
14:33 The ones in the boat worshipped Him,
Saying, "You're God's Son. It's true."

14:34 They came into Gennesaret,
Once they crossed over to shore.
14:35 The men belonging to that place,
Recognized Him *from before.93

Into the surrounding places,
They sent word, and there outpoured
People who brought those with ailments,
14:36 And Jesus they all implored.

They begged Him if only the sick
Of this act would be assured,
To touch the fringe of His garment,
And all who touched Him were cured.

15:1	Then there came from Jerusalem
	Pharisees and scribes *distraught.
15:2	"Your disciples do not follow
	What the elders ◆long have taught.

"Why do they break the tradition
When it is time to eat bread?
They don't practice washing their hands!"
These leaders to Jesus said.

15:3	But Jesus answered back to them,
	"Constantly you all defy
	For the sake of your tradition
	The commandments of God. Why?

15:4	"'Honor both father and mother,'
	God said. *So, do not defy!
	He also said, 'He who reviles
	Father or mother must die.'

15:5	"Yet you say this: 'Whoever says
	To his father or mother
	What's of mine that might be your help
	*Is a gift *to God, no other*

15:6	"'Must not then honor his parent.'
	So, you *by this position
	Invalidate the word of God
	Because of your tradition.

15:7	"Isaiah prophesied well of you
	For the hypocrites you are,
15:8	'This people honor Me with their lips,
	But from Me their heart is far.
15:9	"'They worship Me to no avail
	Because they just teach ♦and say
	That the precepts which men have made
	Are the teachings *to obey.'"
15:10	Jesus called the crowd to Himself,
	And this teaching He began,
	"Keep on listening to what I say,
	And work hard to understand.
15:11	"Whatever enters the stomach,
	That's not what defiles the man.
	However, what comes from the mouth,
	That's what defiles, *understand."
15:12	Then the disciples came to Him
	And asked Him, "Were You aware
	That the Pharisees took offense
	At the word they heard You share?"
15:13	"Every plant that's not been planted"
	Jesus told them in reply
	"By My Father who's in heaven
	Will be uprooted *to die.
15:14	"Leave these leaders alone. They're blind.
	If those who can't see at all
	Keep leading those who too are blind,
	Both into a pit will fall."

15:15	But in reply, Peter asked Him, "This parable to us explain."
15:16	He said, "Without understanding, Do you yourselves still remain?"
15:17	"Haven't you learned that everything Which into the stomach goes Is held in the belly, and then, Into the sewer it flows?
15:18	"But all that exits from the mouth, Originates from the heart. These are things which defile the man,
15:19	For all sin* comes from this part.
	"Murders, adulteries, thefts, and lies, Blasphemies and evil plans,
15:20	To do these defiles the person, Not to eat with unwashed hands."

15:21	Jesus left there and into parts Of Tyre and Sidon withdrew.
15:22	Behold, coming from that region Was a woman *not a Jew.
	The woman was a Canaanite And was crying out, "O Lord, Give me mercy, Son of David. My daughter *must be restored.

	"My daughter is demon-possessed
	To a degree that's absurd."
15:23	But Jesus did not answer her,
	Not even a single word.

His disciples came telling Him
As they all begged ♦and implored,
"She keeps crying out behind us.
Send her away from here, *Lord!"

15:24 But in reply, He said these words:
"I've not been sent *to this place
Except to the sheep who are lost
And belong to Israel's race.[94]

15:25 But she knelt before Him and said,
"Lord, help me!" But He said, *"No!
15:26 It's bad to take the children's bread
And it, to little dogs throw."

15:27 But she replied, "Lord, I agree,
Yet little dogs are able
To eat crumbs which happen to fall
From their master's table."

15:28 Jesus then answered her and said,
"O woman, your faith has power.
Let it be for you as you wish."
Her daughter was healed that hour.

15:29 Jesus left there and went along
The Sea of Galilee's shore.
He climbed up the hill and sat there.
15:30 Then large crowds to Him did pour.

They brought along the lame, the blind,
The maimed, the mutes, and much more.
They tossed them down beside His feet.
All of them He did restore.

15:31   The crowd was amazed when they saw
Mutes speaking, the maimed unflawed,
Lame ones walking, blind ones seeing.
So, they praised Israel's God.

15:32   Jesus summoned His disciples.
"I feel for the crowd," He explained,
"For already it's been three days
That before Me, they have remained.

"They have nothing that they can eat,
Yet I don't wish *on this day
To release them from here hungry
Lest they faint along the way."

15:33   "In the desert where can we find,"
The disciples to Him said,
"Satisfaction for this vast crowd
With the required loaves of bread?"

15:34   "How many loaves do you possess?"
Jesus to these men replied.
They told Him, "We have seven loaves
And a few small fish supplied."

15:35   Then after commanding the crowd
To recline upon the ground,
15:36   He took the fish and seven loaves,
Giving thanks *for what was found.

Then He gave to His disciples,
Breaking off pieces of food,
And the disciples *then in turn
Gave it to the multitude.

15:37 Everyone ate, and all were filled.
Then they picked up the supply
And filled seven large baskets up.
How the food did multiply.*

15:38 Now the number of those who ate
(Not included in the amount
Were the women or the children),
Four thousand men was the count.

15:39 After sending the crowds away
According to His orders,*
He got into the boat and went
Into Magadan's borders.

16:1 The Pharisees and Sadducees
Approached in order to test.
A miraculous sign from heaven
To Jesus was their request.

16:2 But in reply, He said to them,
"When evening arrives you state,
'Because the sky is fiery red
The weather, it will be great.'

16:3	"Morning comes, 'Since the sky is red,
	It's threatening a storm today.'
	The sky's face, you know how to judge,
	But the signs of the times, no way!
16:4	"Who keeps seeking after a sign?*
	Only a generation
	That is wicked and unfaithful
	Seeks one for affirmation.
	"Yet no sign will be given it.
	Not one sign that it wants done.♦
	Only the prophet Jonah's sign
	Will be given by the Son."⁹⁵
	And so, Jesus left their presence
	And proceeded on ahead.
16:5	The disciples crossed *the sea with Him
	But neglected to take bread.
16:6	"See to it that you all watch out,"
	To all of them Jesus said.
	"The Pharisees and Sadducees –
	Beware of the yeast *they spread."
16:7	Now, they began among themselves
	Discussing *what Jesus said.
	"Is He speaking this way* because
	We did not take any bread?"
16:8	Aware of this, Jesus then said,
	"You who have a faith so small,
	Why keep talking among yourselves
	That you don't have bread at all?

16:9	"Are you not yet comprehending? Remember the five loaves of bread? How many baskets did you fill After the five thousand were fed?
16:10	"And don't you also remember Having the seven loaves of bread? How many large baskets were filled After the four thousand were fed?
16:11	"How are you not comprehending? I don't speak to you of bread. The Pharisees and Sadducees – Beware of the yeast *they spread."
16:12	Then they knew that He did not mean To beware of the yeast from bread But from the teaching of Pharisees And of Sadducees instead.

16:13	After Jesus entered the parts Of Caesarea Philippi, He was asking His disciples A consensus to supply.*
	"Who are people really saying The Son of Man to be?"
16:14	They said, "Some think John the Baptist, Others, Elijah they see.

	"And others say Jeremiah
	Or one of the prophets *of old."
16:15	He asked them, "Who am I to you?
	What is the view that you hold?"*
16:16	Simon Peter said in reply,
	These words Jesus would applaud:96
	"You're the Christ, ♦the Anointed One,
	The Son of the living God!"
16:17	Then Jesus answered back to him,
	"Simon Barjona, you're blessed,
	For no man just My Father97
	Revealed *what you have confessed.
16:18	"You are Peter, ♦the Rock, I say,
	And on this rock *without fail,
	I'll build My church, and against it
	Hades' gates will not prevail.
16:19	"I'll give you heaven's kingdom's keys,
	A stewardship that's profound,98
	And whatever you bind on earth
	In heaven will have been bound.
	"And whatever you free on earth
	In heaven will have been freed."
16:20	Then He warned them to tell no one
	That He was the Christ *indeed.
16:21	From then on, to His disciples
	He began to clearly show
	That it was essential for Him
	To Jerusalem to go.

>   That the elders, chief priests, and scribes,
>   Great suffering on Him must lay,
>   And that He must be put to death
>   But be raised on the third day.

16:22   Peter began to rebuke Him
            By telling Him privately,
            "Heaven's mercy is on You, Lord!
            To You, this will never be."

16:23   Turning around, He told Peter
            (Who as the Rock was now known), [99]
            "Get behind Me, adversary![100]
            To Me, you're a stumbling stone.

            "For you are not thinking at all
            On the things that are of God.
            You are only thinking about
            The things that people applaud."

16:24   Then He said to all, "Let us say
            My follower one wants to be.
            He must deny self, lift his cross,
            And continue following Me.

16:25   "For he who wants to save his life
            Will destroy it *in his quest.
            He who destroys his life for My sake
            Will find it *and will be blessed.

16:26   "For what will it profit a man
            If the whole world he acquire,
            But *at the end of that process
            It makes his own life expire?

"Or, *to put it another way,
Just what will a person give
As an exchange for his own life?
What is worth more than to live?*

16:27 "The Son of Man in the glory
Of His Father will one day come
With His angels when He'll repay
According to what each has done.

16:28 "I tell you that some standing here
Won't ever taste death, it's true,
Before the Son of Man's coming
In His own kingdom, they view."

17:1 Now after Jesus said these words
(After six full days had gone),
He took with Him Peter and James,
Also James's brother John.

He brought them up, only those three,
On a mountain very tall.
17:2 Then He became completely changed
In the presence of them all.

Jesus's face shined like the sun.
His clothes were white as the light.
17:3 Moses and Elijah talking
With Jesus became the sight.

17:4	Peter reacted and said, "Lord, For us to be here is great! Assuming this is what You wish, Three tents I will here create.
	"I will create one just for You, And one for Moses I'll make, And lastly one for Elijah. I'll do this for each one's sake."*
17:5	While he was speaking with Jesus, A gleaming cloud did appear. This cloud overshadowed them all. A voice from it they could hear.
	The voice exclaimed, "This is My Son. He's the One whom I adore. I am very well-pleased with Him. Listen to Him. ✦Don't ignore."
17:6 **17:7**	And when the disciples heard this, To excessive fear they clutched. Each of them fell upon their face. Jesus came, and them He touched.
17:8	"Get up and stop being afraid," He said *in a pressing tone. Then lifting up their eyes, they saw No one but Jesus alone.
17:9	As they went down the mount, He charged, "'Til the Son of Man has risen Out of the grip of death itself, Tell no one of this vision."

17:10 Then the disciples questioned Him,
"Why do the scribes anymore
Say that it is necessary
For Elijah to come before?"

17:11 Jesus answered back by saying,
"All the scribes say anymore[101]
Is that Elijah is coming,
And all things he will restore.

17:12 "I tell you, Elijah's coming
Has already been fulfilled,
And they did not recognize him,
But did to him as they willed.

"The Son of Man too will suffer
By their hands *as they insist."
17:13 Then the disciples knew He spoke
To them of John the Baptist.

17:14 As they came to where the crowd was,
A man came to Him on his knees.
17:15 He said to Him, "Lord, there's my son.
Have mercy upon him, please.

"For he is an epileptic,
And suffers a lengthy spell,
Often falling into the fire
And into the water as well.

17:16 "And I brought to your disciples
My son *with my petition,
But they weren't able to heal him
Of this awful condition."*

17:17 He replied, "O generation,
In a faithless and crooked state.
How long must I be here with you?
How long must I tolerate?

"Bring the child over here to Me."
17:18 He rebuked *the unseen power.
The demon came out from the boy
Who was healed that very hour.

17:19 Coming to Jesus privately,
The disciples this question asked,
"Why were we ourselves unable
The demon from him to cast?"

17:20 "It's because of your little faith,"
Jesus to them did explain.
"I tell you, all you need is faith
As a mustard plant's seed or grain.[102]

"If you have it, to this mountain
You'll say, 'Move from here to there.'
Nothing will be impossible.
It will move as you declare."[103]

17:22 When they gathered in Galilee,
Jesus plainly said to them,
"The Son of Man is going to be
Delivered over to men.

17:23 "And these men will put Him to death,
Yet the third day He'll be raised."
They became excessively grieved
Over these things Jesus phrased.*

The Poetic Scriptures of Six Writers

17:24　　When they entered Capernaum,
　　　　 There came those who collected
　　　　 The didrachma[104] for the temple.
　　　　 Just male Jews it affected.[105]

　　　　 They came before Peter and said,
　　　　 "Does not your own teacher pay
　　　　 The didrachma for the temple?"
17:25　　"Of course." Peter did say.

　　　　 After Peter entered the house,
　　　　 Jesus approached him to ask,
　　　　 "Simon, tell Me, what do you think
　　　　 About the following task?*

　　　　 "From whom do the kings of the earth
　　　　 Collect tax (various ones)?
　　　　 Is it from strangers *in their land,
　　　　 Or is it from their own sons?"

17:26　　After he said, "It's from strangers."
　　　　 Jesus to him did reply,
　　　　 "So the sons are indeed exempt.
　　　　 To them it does not apply.♦

17:27　　"But so that we might not offend,
　　　　 Go cast a hook in the lake.
　　　　 Then reel in the very first fish
　　　　 That you just happen to take.

"When you open the fish's mouth,
You will find a coin[106] inside.
Take it and, for both you and Me,
Have the taxes applied."[107]

18:1 In that same hour, the disciples
Came before Jesus to say,
"Who then is the greater person
In heaven's kingdom anyway?"

18:2 After He called a little child,
He stood the child in their midst.
18:3 "Truly I tell you," Jesus said,
"As this child, you must exist.

"Because if you do not repent
And as this child become,
You will never ever enter
The heavenly kingdom.

18:4 "Whoever will humble himself
As this little child, therefore,
In the realm of heaven's kingdom,
That person's greatness is more.

18:5 "Whoever decides to welcome,
All for the sake of My name,
One little child such as this one,
That one welcomes Me the same.

18:6 "But whoever trips up just one
Childlike believer in Me,
That one would be much better off
At the bottom of the sea.

"It would be best for a millstone
That a donkey makes go 'round
Be hung on his neck as he's plunged
To the sea's bottom ♦and drowned.

18:7 "Because of the world's stumbling blocks,
I must pronounce on it 'Woe.'
For it is inevitable
For the stumbling blocks to show.

"However, the very same woe,
I also have to confer
On the one through whom the stumbling
Is occasioned to occur.

18:8 "If either your hand or your foot
Causes you to stumble,
Cut it off, and throw it from you
So you don't take a tumble.*

"It's better that you enter life
As one who is maimed or lame
Than be thrown with two hands or feet
Into the eternal flame.

18:9 "And in the same way, if your eye
Induces you to stumble,
Gouge it out, and throw it from you
So you don't take a tumble.*

　　　　　　"It's better that you enter life
　　　　　　As one-eyed *being your name
　　　　　　Than to be thrown with both your eyes
　　　　　　Into Gehenna's flame.

18:10　　"Don't scorn one of these little ones,
　　　　　　For I say, in heaven's space
　　　　　　Their angels are always seeing
　　　　　　My heavenly Father's face.[108]

18:12　　"Let us assume that some man has
　　　　　　One hundred sheep *to view,
　　　　　　And one of them is led astray.
　　　　　　What do you think he will do?

　　　　　　"Will he not leave the ninety-nine
　　　　　　On the mountain right away
　　　　　　And go and seek continually
　　　　　　For the one sheep led astray?

18:13　　"And if he happens to find it,
　　　　　　He rejoices more, I say,
　　　　　　Over it than the ninety-nine
　　　　　　Who have not been led astray.

18:14　　"Likewise, your heavenly Father
　　　　　　Does not possess a desire
　　　　　　For any of these little ones
　　　　　　To eternally expire.

18:15　　"If your brother decides to sin,
　　　　　　Go reprove him one on one.
　　　　　　If he listens to your reproof,
　　　　　　Then your brother you have won.

18:16 "But if he listens not to you,
Take with you one or two there
That every word might be confirmed
By what two or three mouths swear.

18:17 "If he ignores them, tell the church.
If he ignores the church too,
Let him be as the publican
And the Gentile are to you.

18:18 "I am telling you all the truth,
And it is very profound,*
Whatever you bind on this earth,
In heaven will have been bound.

"Whatever you free on this earth,
In heaven will have been freed.
I am telling you all the truth.*
This is the truth, indeed.*

18:19 "If two of you agree on earth
About anything you pray,
Then by My heavenly Father
It will be done as they say.

18:20 "For where two or three are gathered
For the purpose of My name,
There I am in the midst of them.
This to you all, I proclaim."[109]

The Poetic Gospel of Matthew

18:21   Then Peter came to Him and asked,
"Lord, what's the maximum count
If my brother sins against me
An exorbitant amount?*

"How often must I forgive him?
Would seven times be the count?"
18:22   Jesus told him, "Not seven times.
Seventy times that amount.

18:23   "For this reason, heaven's kingdom
Is similar to a king
Who wished to settle with his slaves[110]
Their accounts on everything.

18:24   "When he began the settlement,
One debtor to him was brought
Who owed him ten thousand talents,
18:25   But to pay him, he could not.

"Then the lord ordered that the slave,
His wife, and children be sold
Along with whatever he owned
To repay the debt he owed.

18:26   "Therefore, the slave fell to the ground,
And him, he begged and implored,
'Be patient with me. I'll repay
Everything to you, *my lord.'

18:27	"The lord felt pity for the slave, And so mercy he bestowed.♦ He released him and forgave him For all the debt that he owed.
18:28	"But after the slave went away, He hunted until* he found One of his fellow slaves whose debt To him *greatly did abound.
	"The debt - one hundred days' wages.[111] He grabbed him *in his attack And was choking him as he yelled, 'What you owe me, pay me back!'
18:29	"Therefore, his fellow slave begged him As he fell down *to his knees, 'I will repay all that I owe. Just be patient with me, please.'
18:30	"But unwilling *to hear his plea Of paying back the debt load,* He went and threw him into jail 'Til he repaid what was owed.
18:31	"When his fellow slaves observed this, Deep sorrow in them was stirred. They went and explained to their lord All the things that had occurred.
18:32	"Then the lord summoned him and said, 'You're a wicked slave indeed! All this debt I've forgiven you Because with me you did plead.

18:33	"'Was it not a necessity For you to shower as well Mercy upon your fellow slave Who also before you fell?'[112]
18:34	"His lord became very angry. No more mercy to him, he showed.* He handed him to the jailor 'Til he repaid all that he owed.
18:35	"So too, My heavenly Father Will do to each one the same If you do not from your own hearts Forgive your brother his blame."

19:1	When he finished saying these words, Jesus left Galilee's grounds. He then went beyond the Jordan, Entering Judea's bounds.
19:2	Large crowds followed along behind, And He healed them in that place.
19:3	Yet to test Him, the Pharisees Came before Him face to face. "Is it lawful for a husband For any reason at all To send his wife away from him, Making divorce the call?"♦

19:4   Jesus answered them back and said,
       "To read of this, did you fail:
       The Creator from the beginning
       'Made them male and female'?

19:5   "It also says, 'Because of this,
       His father a man must leave,
       And his mother he must also,
       And to his wife he must cleave.

       "'The two then must become one flesh.'
19:6   Therefore, a man and his wife◆
       Are not two *separate entities
       But one flesh *while they have life.

       "So in light of what Scripture says,¹¹³
       Whatever God has united,
       Is not lawful for any man
       To have the same divided."

19:7   They said to Him, "Why did Moses
       Command in her hand to lay
       A written statement of divorce
       And then to send her away?"

19:8   He said to them, "It is because
       Of the hardness in your heart
       That Moses made allowances
       To force your wives to depart.

       "However, from the beginning
       It has not been meant this way.
19:9   So, listen very carefully*
       To what I'm about to say.

"Whoever sends his wife away
(Except for fornication)
Commits adultery when entering
Another marriage relation."

19:10 The disciples then said to Him,
"If this is truly the case
Between a husband and his wife,
Then marriage, it has no place."

19:11 But He told them, "Not everyone
Can hold to this word *you give.[114]
Just those to whom it's been granted
Is able this way to live.[115]

19:12 "For there are the kind of eunuchs
Born thus from their mother's womb.
Others were made eunuchs by men,
And this life, others assume.*

"They make themselves to be eunuchs
For the kingdom of heaven's sake.
Let him who can hold *to such life
Hold to it. *It is no mistake."

19:13 Then small children were brought to Him
So that them, Jesus *could hold
And lay His hands on them and pray,
But them, the disciples did scold.

19:14	But He said, "Leave the children be.
	Don't keep them from coming, please,
	Because heaven's kingdom belongs
	To all people such as these."
19:15	After laying His hands on them,
	From there He then proceeded.
19:16	Then behold, one came to Jesus
	And asked Him *what was needed.
	"Teacher, what good thing must I do
	In order that I might gain
	What is known as eternal life?
	How might this life I obtain?"◆
19:17	He said to him, "About what's good,
	Why of Me do you inquire?
	There is only One who is good,
	But what is your real desire?*
	"If you want to enter that life,
	With the commandments comply."
19:18	"Which ones are you talking about?"
	He said to Him in reply.
	Then Jesus said, "You must not kill;
	To steal you must never dare;
	Do not commit adultery;
	False testimony don't bear.
19:19	"Honor your father and mother;
	As yourself love your neighbor."
19:20	The youth told Him, "I've kept these things.
	What lacks in my behavior?"

19:21   Jesus replied, "If you desire
To reach the goal,[116] here's one more:
Go from here and sell all you own,
And give it all to the poor.

"Do this,* and you will have treasure
Stored in heaven, *I guarantee.
Then once you have completed this,
Come back here and follow Me."

19:22   But when the youth heard this word said,
He left from there very sad,
For he was extremely wealthy.[117]
Great riches he himself had.

19:23   Jesus said to His disciples,
"This truth I make very plain:
The rich will with difficulty
Go into heaven's domain.

19:24   "It's much simpler for a camel
To go through a needle's eye
Than for the wealthy to enter
The kingdom of the Most High."[118]

19:25   But when the disciples heard this,
They, to an extreme degree,
Became astonished responding,
"Then saved, who can ever be?"

19:26   Looking at them, Jesus then said,
"This, no man himself can gain.
However, with God all such things
Are possible to attain."

19:27   Then in reply, Peter asked Him,
        "Take note of us carefully.[119]
        We've left all things to follow You.
        So, for us what will there be?"

19:28   Jesus said, "You who've followed Me,
        The truth to you, I now tell:
        You'll sit upon twelve thrones and judge
        The twelve tribes of Israel.

        "This will occur in the time of
        'The renewal,' *as it's known,
        When the Son of Man finally sits
        Upon His glorious throne.

19:29   "And all who left for My name's sake
        Brothers or sisters or homes,
        Father or mother or children,
        Or farms or *all that one owns –

        "All will get one hundred times more
        And eternal life inherit,
19:30   But many first ones will be last
        And last ones first. *I swear it.[120]

20:1   "For heaven's kingdom is just like
        A lord of a house who'd gone
        To hire workers for his vineyard.
        The day was about to dawn.*

20:2   "When he agreed with the workers
        That one denarius he'd pay,
        He sent them into his vineyard
        To work the entire day.

20:3	"About the third hour of the day, He went out again and found Other ones in the marketplace Who were just standing around.
20:4	"To those he said, 'You go also Into the vineyard for pay. I'll give you whatever is just.' They worked *the rest of that day.
20:5	"Again the lord went out roughly The sixth hour of that same day, And again about the ninth hour, Saying he would give just pay.[121]
20:6	"The lord went out *one final time When the eleventh hour came And found others standing around. So, he asked them *to explain.
	"'Why have you all been standing here Doing nothing?' he inquired.
20:7	They all answered back to the lord, 'Because us, no one has hired.'
	"He said to them, 'You also go Into that vineyard *of mine.'
20:8	When evening came, the vineyard's lord Told his foreman, *'It is time.
	"'Call in all the workers I hired. To each have their pay disbursed, Starting with the last group I hired And proceeding to the first.'

20:9	"The eleventh-hour workers came.
	A denarius, each one got.
20:10	When the first group of workers came,
	To receive more was their thought.
	"Yet each got one denarius too.
20:11	They (after getting their pay)
	Were grumbling against the house lord,
	And this is what they did say:
20:12	"'These who were last worked just one hour.
	As our equals, them, you did treat
	Although we bore the whole day's weight
	And felt the day's burning heat.'
20:13	"He said, answering one of them,
	'Comrade, I do you no wrong.
	Did you not for one denarius
	Agree to work *all day long?
20:14	"'Take what is yours and go from here.
	This last group, I wished to pay
	Even as I paid all of you
	At the end of the work day.*
20:15	"'Is it not perfectly lawful
	For me to do what I desire
	With whatever things that are mine,
	Giving to those whom I hire?*
	"'Or because I am generous,
	Does your eye to evil fall?'
20:16	So, the last ones will then be first,
	And the first ones, last of all."

20:17	Jesus went up to Jerusalem,
	And while He was on the way,
	He took the Twelve aside alone,
	And to them all He did say:
20:18	"Look, we're going to Jerusalem,
	But soon after He arrives,*
	The Son of Man will be given
	To the chief priests and the scribes.
	"And they will sentence Him to death.
20:19	To Gentiles Him, they'll betray
	To be mocked, scourged, and crucified,
	Yet He will rise the third day."
20:20	Then Zebedee's two sons' mother
	Came before Him to inquire.
	She knelt, wanting something from Him.
20:21	He asked, "What do you desire?"
	She said to Him, "In Your kingdom,
	Say that two seats You'll assign:
	One on Your right, one on Your left
	For these two sons of mine."
20:22	Jesus said to them in reply,
	"You know not what you request.
	Are you able to drink the cup
	That I'm about to ingest?"

	They said to Him, "We are able."
20:23	He told them, "My cup you'll drink,
	But to sit on My right or left
	Is not Mine to give *as you think.

"It's for those whom have been prepared
By My Father. *He knows best."
20:24 The ten were outraged with these two
Upon hearing *their request.

20:25 But summoning them, Jesus said,
"The rulers of the nations
Lord it over those whom they rule.
You know *these observations.

"Also 'the great' over others
Exert their authority.
20:26 But as it pertains to you all,
This is not how it will be.

"All who wish to be great among you
Must as your servant behave.
20:27 All who wish to be first among you
Must become just like your slave.

20:28 "So, the Son of Man did not come
So as to be served by any,
But to serve and to give His life
As a ransom for many."

20:29	As they came out of Jericho,
	A great crowd followed behind,
20:30	And behold, sitting by the road
	There were two men who were blind.
	After these men heard that Jesus
	Was about to pass them by,
	"Give us mercy, Son of David!"
	The blind men began to cry.
20:31	But so that they would be quiet,
	The crowd's rebuke did pour.
	"Lord, Son of David, pity us!"
	They cried out all the more.
20:32	Jesus stood still, called them, and asked,
	"What do you wish that I do?"
20:33	They said to Him, "Lord, that our eyes
	Be opened *so we may view."
20:34	Jesus touched their eyes *with His hands,
	Having been filled with pity.
	Immediately, they gained their sight
	And followed Him *to the city.
21:1	When they approached Jerusalem
	And into Bethphage went,
	Stopping at the Mount of Olives,
	Two disciples, Jesus sent.

21:2	He told them, "That town beyond you,
	Enter, and at once you'll see
	A donkey tied up and her colt.
	Untie and bring them to Me.
21:3	"If someone asks you anything,
	Then these words you must extend:
	'The Lord, He has a need for them.'
	And them, he'll instantly send."
21:4	Now, this happened in order that
	Prophecy might be fulfilled
	Which was spoken through the prophet.
	Here's that word *which was instilled:
21:5	"Tell the daughter of Zion, 'Look!
	To you is coming your King,
	Mounted humbly on a donkey,
	A colt, a donkey's offspring.'"
21:6	The disciples went and did as
	Jesus on them did impose.
21:7	They brought the donkey and the colt,
	And on them, they placed their clothes.
	He sat upon the clothes they placed
	And then proceeded ahead.*
21:8	Most of the crowd took their own clothes.
	In the roadway them, they spread.
	However, there were some others
	Who in the roadway did lay
	Some branches from the trees *nearby
	Which they had just cut away.

21:9   Now, the crowds going before Him
             And the ones following behind,
             All were crying these words loudly
             Which partly in Psalms we find.[122]

             "He's blessed who comes in the Lord's name.
             Hosanna to David's Son!
             Hosanna in the utmost heights!"
             Chanted and sang everyone.♦

21:10   Once He entered Jerusalem,
             The whole city was distressed.
             Those within the city questioned,
             "Who is this person *who's blessed?"

21:11   And the crowds were replying back,
             "The promised* Prophet is He,
             Jesus who is from Nazareth,
             The city* in Galilee."

21:12   Jesus entered the temple courts
             And drove out all suppliers
             Who were selling in the temple,
             As well as all the buyers.

             The tables of moneychangers
             He flipped *with pushes and shoves.
             He also overturned the chairs
             Of those who were selling doves.

21:13	He told them, "It's written, 'My house Will be called a house of prayer.' But you yourselves are making it A den of thieves *everywhere."
21:14	The blind and the lame in the courts Came to Him, and them, He healed,
21:15	But both the chief priests and the scribes, Indignation they revealed.
	For they saw the deeds which He did (Though wonderful was each one) And the boys shouting in the courts, "Hosanna to David's Son!"
21:16	They said to Him, "Are You hearing What these boys are conveying?" Jesus replied, "Affirmative! You've never read this saying?
	"It's found in the Psalms of Scripture.[123] 'From the mouth of nursing babes And from the mouth of little boys, You have perfected Your praise.'"
21:17	He went outside the city gates, After leaving from their sight, To the village of Bethany, And He stayed there for the night.

21:18 Early the following morning,
While proceeding to return
To the city, ◆Jerusalem,
For food, He began to yearn.

21:19 Sighting one fig tree up the road,
He came to it, yet He found
Nothing upon it, only leaves.
And this curse,[124] He did resound:

"Fruit will come from you no longer,
Not one fruit in any day."
As soon as Jesus said these words,[125]
The fig tree withered away.

21:20 When the disciples witnessed this,
They marveled and did inquire,
"How did the fig tree's withering
Immediately transpire?"

21:21 Jesus said in reply to them,
"If faith you constantly hold,
And if you don't waiver in doubt,
To you the same will unfold.*

"Not only will you do this thing
To the tree but this mount too.
'Rise and be thrown into the sea.'
If you say it, 'twill ensue.

21:22   "I am speaking the truth to you.
         Even all things you'll receive,
         Whatever you ask in prayer
         If you constantly believe."

21:23   He came into the temple courts.
         There approached Him while He taught
         The chief priests and the people's elders
         Who a certain answer sought.*

         They asked, "By what authority
         Do You do the things You do?
         Who gave You this authority?
         We demand You tell us, who?"*

21:24   And in reply He said to them,
         "I'll ask you one word as well.
         If you answer Me, then My source
         Of authority I'll tell.

21:25   "John's baptism was from what source,
         From heaven or humanity?"
         So they reasoned among themselves
         As to what their answer should be.*

         "If we say that it's from heaven,
         Then to us He will reply,
         'For what reason did you, therefore,
         Not believe him ◆and comply?'

21:26   "But if we say that it's from men,
         Then we'll have the crowd to fear,
         For John as a prophet *of God
         Is something that all hold here."

21:27   They answered Jesus, "We don't know."
He said, "Then I won't tell you
Who gives Me the authority
To do the things that I do.

21:28   "What's your view? A man had two sons.[126]
He came to the first to say,
'Child, go and work in the vineyard,
And you must do it today.'

21:29   "But in reply, the first son said,
'I don't want to *do as you say.'
But he repented later on,
And he went *and worked that day.

21:30   "The man came to the second son
And commanded him the same.
In reply, he said, 'Lord, I will.'
Yet to go, he did refrain.

21:31   "So then, of the two, which one did
The thing the father had willed?"
"The first one did," they all replied.
So these words, Jesus instilled:

"I am telling you all the truth,
That tax collectors and whores
Will enter the kingdom of God
Before it is ever yours.

21:32   "For in the way of righteousness,
John came to you face to face.
You did not ever believe him.
His words, you did not embrace.♦

"But the whores and tax collectors,
They trusted ♦and received him.
When you saw this, you still did not
Repent so to believe him.

21:33 "Now, hear another parable.
There was a house lord, a man
Who planted a massive vineyard.
A wall around it he ran.

"Within it he dug a wine press.
A tower, he did erect.
He leased it all out to farmers.
Then on a journey, he left.

21:34 "Now, when the season for grapes neared,
He sent slaves *he selected
To the farmers so that his fruit
From them might be collected.

21:35 "The farmers took the house lord's slaves,
And one of them, they belted.
Another one, they put to death.
With stones a third, they pelted.

21:36 "Again, he sent out other slaves.
Compared to the first that came,
This group was a much larger group,
Yet to them they did the same.

21:37 "Later, he sent his son to them.
'They'll respect my son,' he thought.
21:38 But when the farmers saw the son,
Among themselves they did plot.

	"'This one's the heir. Come, let's kill him
	And take what to him was willed.'
21:39	After grabbing him, him, they threw
	Outside the vineyard and killed.

21:40 "So, when the vineyard's lord returns,
To the farmers, what will he do?"
21:41 They said to Him, "Those wicked men
He'll destroy with no mercy in view.

"And he will rent the vineyard out
To other farmers who'll pay
The crop of fruit that is due him
Each harvest *without delay."

21:42 Jesus replied back to them all,
"Have you never ever read
In the writings ◆of the Scripture
About what has long been said?*

"'A stone the builders rejected
Became the capstone that ties.
This has come about by the Lord.
It's marvelous in our eyes.'

21:43 "Due to this, the kingdom of God
From you will be snatched away
And then given to a people
Producing its fruit, I say.

21:44 "And those who fall upon this stone,
Into pieces will be dashed,
And those upon whom this stone falls,
By its great weight* will be smashed."

21:45	After they heard His parables, The chief priests and Pharisees Came to realize that about them That Jesus was speaking these.
21:46	Though they were seeking to grab Him, Fear of the crowds in them swelled Because Jesus as a prophet Was the view commonly held.

22:1	And Jesus spoke again to them In parables and replied,
22:2	"Heaven's kingdom is like a king Who a wedding feast supplied.
	"He prepared it for his own son.
22:3	Then sent out his slaves to call The ones whom had been invited To come to the banquet hall.
	"However, they were unwilling To come to the celebration.
22:4	He once again sent out his slaves, But another delegation.
	"He said, 'Tell the invited, *Look!* *My dinner I did prepare.* *My bulls and fattened calves are killed.* *Come! All is ready *to share.*'

The Poetic Gospel of Matthew

22:5 "But two of them just walked away
Without a concern displayed.
One returned to the field he owned,
Another one to his trade.

22:6 "The rest *of the ones invited,
After grabbing every slave,
Mistreated them all severely,
And then death to them, they gave.

22:7 "But the king sent out his soldiers
As with rage he did perspire.
He then destroyed those murderers
And set their city on fire.

22:8 "Then he told his remaining slaves,
'The wedding feast is prepared,
But those who had been invited
Were not worthy, *I've declared.

22:9 "'Therefore, go on all the roadways
And whoever you might find,
Invite them to the wedding feast.'
22:10 And those slaves went *as assigned.

"They went on the roads and gathered
All whom they found, *I stress all,
Whether they were evil or good,
And dinner guests filled the hall.

22:11 "Now the king came to view the guests,
And he saw a man in there
Who was in improper attire.*
No wedding clothes, did he wear.

22:12	"And the king said to him, 'Comrade,
	How have you entered this place
	Without possessing wedding clothes?'
	The man argued not his case.
22:13	"The king then said to the servants,
	'Tie up both his hands and feet.
	Throw him out into the darkness.
	There'll be weeping and gnashing teeth.'
22:14	"For many are called, but few are chosen."
22:15	Then the Pharisees went their way
	And planned together to trap Him
	In some word that He might say.
22:16	They sent with the Herodians
	Their disciples to Him to say,
	"Teacher, we know that You're truthful,
	And You truthfully teach God's way.
	"We know it matters not to You
	About anyone's *critique,
	For You're completely impartial.
	Any favors, You don't seek.♦
22:17	"Therefore, tell us what do You think?
	Is it permitted to pay
	A personal tax to Caesar,
	Or would this not be okay?"
22:18	But Jesus perceived their intent
	As being wicked and said,
	"Why do you test Me, hypocrites?
22:19	Show me the coin. *Go ahead.

	"Show me the coin that's for the tax."
	A denarius, they brought.
22:20	"Whose image and label is this?"
	An answer from them He sought.

22:21	They said, "Caesar's." Then He replied,
	"So that you won't be at odds,*
	Give to Caesar what is Caesar's,
	And give to God what is God's."

22:22	When they heard this, they were amazed,
	And left Him, going away.
22:23	Some Sadducees came up to Him
	To question Him that same day.

	These say there's no resurrection.
22:24	They asked, "Teacher, Moses said,
	'If a man dies without children,
	Then his brother has to wed.

	"'Being the closest relative,
	The widow, he must marry
	And raise offspring for his brother.'
	So answer this, our query:*

22:25	"Seven brothers were among us.
	One married, then lost his life.
	Because he produced no children,
	To his brother, he left his wife.

22:26	"The same happened to the second.
	To the third, this did befall.
	The same happened through the seventh.
22:27	Then the wife died last of all.

22:28	"So then, in the resurrection, The woman will be whose wife, Which one of the seven brothers? For they all had her *in life."
22:29	In reply, Jesus said to them, "Yourselves you always defraud Since you do not know the Scriptures Or even the power of God.
22:30	"For in the resurrection life, People don't marry *their love. They are not given in marriage But are like angels above.[127]
22:31	"Now, about the subject matter Of the raising of the dead, What was spoken to you by God, Have you all not ever read?
22:32	'I am the God of Abraham, Isaac, and Jacob.' He said. So, He's the God of the living And not the God of the dead."
22:33	After the crowds heard this teaching, . At His words they were amazed, But out of the Sadducees' mouths,* No rebuttal could be phrased.*
22:34	This muzzling of the Sadducees Was by the Pharisees heard. They gathered themselves together
22:35	To test Jesus *with some word.

	One of them who was a lawyer
	This question to Him disclosed,
22:36	"Teacher, what's the great commandment
	In the Law *as You've supposed?"

22:37 He told him, "'Love the Lord your God
With your heart fully resigned,
And with the fullness of your soul,
And with your entire mind.'

22:38 "This commandment is the great one.
As foremost it is reckoned.
22:39 And 'Love your neighbor as yourself'
Is like it and is second.

22:40 "For the whole Law and the Prophets
On these two commands are hung."
22:41 The Pharisees still were gathered.
So, a question, Jesus flung.

22:42 "What do you think about the Christ,
Whose son is He?" He inquired.
They said to Him, "David's, *of course."
22:43 He said, *"His words are inspired.

"How does David in the Spirit
In a Psalm in which he wrote*
Call the Christ his personal Lord?
His words to you, I now quote.*

22:44 "He said, 'The LORD said to my Lord,
*At My right hand take Your seat
Until I put Your enemies
Completely beneath Your feet.'*

22:45	"Therefore, if David calls Him 'Lord', This Christ who was yet to come,* Tell Me,* how is it possible For the Christ to be his son?"
22:46	No one could answer Him a word As to the question He shared.* From that day on, to question Him, Not one of them even dared.

23:1	To the crowds and His disciples, Jesus with these words then hit,
23:2	"Both the scribes and the Pharisees In the seat of Moses sit.
23:3	"Therefore, practice and keep all things, Whatever to you, they teach, But stop doing the works they do. They don't practice what they preach.
23:4	"But they bundle up heavy loads That are very hard to bear And lay it on people's shoulders, Yet that load, they do not share.*
	"They don't want to lift a finger To help move the heavy load,
23:5	For they do all their works for men. Attention, they want bestowed.

"They broaden their phylacteries,
And their tassels, they extend.
23:6 They love to be the honored guest
At the dinners *they attend.

"The chief seats in the synagogues,
They all love to occupy.
23:7 They love greetings in the markets,
And love to be called, "Rabbi."

23:8 "But don't let the title Rabbi
Be placed on you by others,
For one person is your teacher,
And all of you are brothers.

23:9 "Don't call anyone your father
Who upon this earth abides,
For one person is your Father,
He who in heaven resides.

23:10 "Don't let anyone call you guides
Since Christ is the only One,
23:11 But the greater among you all,
Your servant, must first become.

23:12 "Now, whoever exalts himself,
Will be humbled *and not praised.
And whoever humbles himself,
Will be exalted, ♦yes, raised.

23:13 "Woe to you, scribes and Pharisees,
You're hypocrites, *as I call,
Since you shut out heaven's kingdom
Before the presence of all.

"For you yourselves aren't getting in,
And you are not permitting
Those to enter who would enter.
Woe to you for forbidding.[128]

23:15 "Woe to you, scribes and Pharisees.
You're hypocrites, *I assert,
Because you traverse sea and land
To make a single convert.

"When it happens that a convert,
You successfully acquire,
You make him two times what you are,
The son of Gehenna's fire.

23:16 "Woe to you blind leaders who say,
'If by the sanctuary
One decides to make an oath,
No weight, does that oath carry.

"'However, if someone decides
By the sanctuary's gold
To make an oath *of any kind,
To that oath one has to hold.'

23:17 "You are foolish, and you are blind.
Which is greater of the two,
The gold or the sanctuary
Which sanctifies it *clear through?

23:18 "You say, 'Whoever makes an oath
By the altar, it means nil,
But if by the gift on the altar,
Then that oath you must fulfill.'

23:19	"You are most definitely* blind!
	Which is greater of the two?
	Is it the gift, or the altar
	Which sanctifies it *clear through?
23:20	"So, all who swear by the altar,
	The swearing is really made
	By the altar and by all things
	Which upon it have been laid.
23:21	"If one by the sanctuary
	Swears a particular oath,
	He swears by it and its Dweller.
	It's not either/or. It's both.*
23:22	"And if a person by heaven
	Swears a particular oath,
	He swears not only by God's throne
	But by Him who sits there - both.
23:23	"Woe to you, scribes and Pharisees.
	Hypocrisy you project,
	For you tithe mint, dill, and cumin
	Yet weightier things neglect.
	"The weightier things of the Law,
	Mercy, faith, and equity,
	You should do without neglecting
	The others. ♦But you can't see!
23:24	"You're blind guides who strain out the gnat
	Yet swallow the camel whole.
23:25	Woe to you scribes and Pharisees,
	Hypocrites *down to your soul!

"Why?* Because you cleanse the outside
Of both the plate and the cup,
But with greed and self-indulgence,
On the inside, they're filled up.

23:26 "Blind Pharisees! First, you must cleanse
The inside of the cup, *I tell,
In order that it might become
Clean on the outside as well.

23:27 "Woe to you scribes and Pharisees.
In hypocrisy, you abide
Because you are like whitewashed tombs
Which appear fine on the outside.

"On the outside, they look lovely,
But the inside *is unseen,
Full of the bones of dead people
And everything that's unclean.

23:28 "So also, you appear righteous
To the people *whom you guide,
But you're full of hypocrisy
And of lawlessness inside.

23:29 "Woe to you scribes and Pharisees.
You're hypocrites, and here's why:
You build the prophets' tombs and adorn
The graves where the righteous lie.

23:30 "You say, 'If we were in the days
Which our ancestors were from,
We would never have shared with them
In the prophets' martyrdom.'

23:31	"You're witnesses against yourselves
	Of who you are *in your heart,
	Sons of those who killed the prophets.
23:32	Finish your ancestors' part.
23:33	"You brood of venomous vipers,
	You snakes *(yes, these are your names),
	How might you run from the judgment
	Of Gehenna's awful flames?
23:34	"For this reason, take careful note.
	I'm sending before your face
	Prophets, scribes, and those who are wise.
	What will you do in this case?*
	"Some, you will kill and crucify.
	Some, you'll whip *without pity,
	Doing this in your synagogues,
	Hunting from city to city.
23:35	"This is so that all of the blood
	Will then come upon your head
	That has been poured out on the earth
	Which from the righteous were shed.
	"Starting with the blood of Abel
	Who was righteous *in God's eyes.
	His blood was poured out on the ground*
	Because him, you did despise.*
	"Ending with Zacharias's blood.
	(He was Barachiah's son).
	'Tween the altar and sanctuary
	His murder by you was done.

23:36	"I am telling you all the truth In this, My declaration.* Every one of these things will come Upon this generation.
23:37	"Jerusalem, Jerusalem, The prophets, you put to death. You stone those who are sent to her. You have snatched from them their breath.♦
	"How often I wished to gather Your own children as a hen Gathers her young under her wings, But you were unwilling then.
23:38	"Behold, your house is being left To you in desolation.
23:39	For I am telling you *the truth. I'm leaving your habitation.*
	"You will not see Me from now on 'Til you say *in one accord, 'How blessed is the person who comes In the name of the Lord.'"

24:1	Then Jesus was proceeding on, Leaving from the temple courts. His disciples came to show Him The temple buildings *of sorts.

24:2	But in reply to them, He said,
	"As to these things that you view,
	No stone will stand on another
	That won't be toppled. It's true."
24:3	As He sat on Mount Olivet,
	The disciples privately came
	To ask Jesus *these three questions
	About His prophetic claim.*
	"Tell us when these things will occur,
	The stones in a toppled stage,*
	And what's the sign of Your coming
	And of the end of the age?"
24:4	Jesus said in reply to them,
	"Don't be duped by any scam,
24:5	For many will come in My name,
	Saying, 'Christ, that's who I am.'
	"These false christs will deceive many,
24:6	But of wars you'll be hearing,
	As well as rumors of battles,
	But see that you're not fearing.
	"For all these things have to happen,
	But the end is not yet come,
24:7	For nation will war with nation
	And kingdom against kingdom.
	"There'll be famines in every place
	And great shakings of the earth,
24:8	But all these are the beginning,
	The start♦ of the pains of birth.

24:9   "At that time they'll put you to death,
        Handing you to tribulation.
        Due to My name, you'll be hated
        By every single nation.

24:10   "At that time, many will be made
        To stumble ◆and fall away,
        And they will hate one another.
        One another, they'll betray.

24:11   "Many false prophets will arise,
        And many, they will mislead.
24:12   The love of many will grow cold
        Since sin continues to breed.

24:13   "However, the one who endures,
        Who remains◆ until the end,
        That is the one who will be saved.
        For how long must you contend?*

24:14   "This good news about the kingdom
        Throughout the world will be preached
        As a witness to all nations,
        And then the end will be reached.

24:15   "Therefore, take action when you see
        What's called 'the abomination'
        Standing firm in the holy place,
        The one causing desolation.

        "It was through the prophet Daniel
        That was spoken this event.
        Let the one reading understand
        As to what was really meant.*

	"So when this abomination*
	In the holy place you see,*
24:16	At that time, into the mountains,
	Let those in Judea flee.

24:17	"If anyone is on the roof,
	Don't let that one go back down
	To gather up things from his house.
	Immediately, leave this town.*

24:18	"If anyone is in the field,
	Do not let that one return
	In order to retrieve his coat
	As a matter of concern.*

24:19	"But it will be a woeful time
	For those pregnant in those days,
	Also for those who are nursing
	Their precious little babes.*

24:20	"Keep on praying concerning this
	That it won't be wintertime,
	Or it won't be on a Sabbath
	That you'll have to run and climb.[129]

24:21	"For at that time, there will occur
	A massive tribulation,
	A kind which has not yet happened
	Since the start of creation.

	"And such kind of tribulation
	Won't ever again occur,
24:22	And if those days were not shortened,
	No flesh would be saved for sure.

> "However, for the elect's sake
> And for their preservation,*
> There will be abbreviated
> Those days *of tribulation.

24:23 > "If any tells you in that time,
> 'The Christ is right here, behold!'
> Or 'Take a look! He's over there!'
> Do not believe what you're told.

24:24 > "Because false christs and false prophets
> Will arise and will give out
> Fantastic signs and great wonders,
> But deception it's about.

> "They do these great signs and wonders
> For the purpose, if perchance,
> To deceive even the elect.
24:25 > Look! I've told you in advance.

24:26 > "Therefore, don't go if they tell you,
> 'He's in the desert, behold!'
> Or 'Look! He's in the inner rooms.'
> Do not believe what you're told.

24:27 > "For as lightning comes from the east
> And flashes into the west,
> So too, the Son of Man's coming
> In this way will manifest.

24:28 > "Wherever the dead carcass is,
> Vultures will be gathered there.
> So, of the Son of Man's coming*
> Everyone will be aware.*

24:29   "But after the tribulation
Of those days *which I did cite,
Instantly, the sun will grow dark,
And the moon won't give its light.

"The stars, they will fall from the sky.
Heaven's powers will be shaken.
24:30   Then the Son of Man's sign will shine,
And it won't be mistaken.*

"In the sky, His sign will appear.
All earth's tribes will mourn at the sight
Of the Son of Man on heaven's clouds
Coming with great glory and might.

24:31   "With trumpet blast, He'll send His angels
To gather from the four winds
His elect from all the boundaries,
As far as the sky extends.

24:32   "Learn the lesson of the fig tree:
Whenever its leaves appear
With its branch already tender,
You know that summer is near.

24:33   "So also, whenever you see
These things *of which I foretold,
You know it is[130] near, at the doors.
24:34   This truth to you, I unfold:

"This generation won't pass by
Until all these things transpire.
24:35   Heaven and earth will pass away,
But My words will never expire.

24:36   "Now, concerning that day and hour,
         By nobody is it known,
         Not heaven's angels, not the Son,
         But just the Father alone.

24:37   "For as the days of Noah were,
         The Son of Man's coming will be,
24:38   For in those days before the flood,
         They ate and drank *merrily.

         "They were entering marriages.
         Into marriage, they were giving.
         'Til the day Noah entered the ark,
         This was how they were living.*

24:39   "They did not know 'til the flood came
         And carried them all away.
         Likewise, the Son of Man's coming
         Will be *on that hour and day.

24:40   "Then there'll be two men in the field -
         One snatched and one forsaken.
24:41   Two women grinding at the mill –
         One left and the other taken.

24:42   "Therefore, keep on staying alert
         Because you don't really know
         On which day your Lord is coming.
24:43   Keep understanding this though:

         "If the house owner knew the time
         The thief was coming *to raid,
         He would watch and not let the thief
         Approach his house to invade.

24:44	"For this reason, so also you From readiness do not shrink[131] Since the Son of Man is coming At an hour you do not think.
24:45	"So, who's the wise and faithful slave Whom the master has assigned Over his household to serve food To them as properly timed?
24:46	"That slave is blessed when his lord comes And finds him doing as charged.
24:47	Truly, over all the lord owns, He'll make his slave's care enlarged.
24:48	"If that bad slave says in his heart, 'To delay, my lord resigns.'
24:49	And starts to beat his fellow slaves, And with drunks, he drinks and dines -
24:50	"The lord of that slave will arrive On a day he won't expect And at an hour he won't realize,
24:51	And him the lord will dissect. "Along with all the hypocrites, His portion will be assigned. In that place, eyes will be weeping. Teeth will continue to grind.

25:1	"Heaven's kingdom will then be like Ten virgins who did arise With their lamps to meet the bridegroom.
25:2	Five were foolish. Five were wise.
25:3	"When the foolish ones took their lamps, To take oil, they did not,
25:4	But the wise ones took with their lamps Oil in the flasks they brought.
25:5	"But when the bridegroom had delayed, Open eyes, they could not keep.* They became extremely drowsy, And soon they fell fast asleep.
25:6	"Now, in the middle of the night A cry through the air rang out. 'See, the bridegroom! Come to meet him.'
25:7	Those virgins ◆were stirred about.
	"They all got up and trimmed their lamps.
25:8	The foolish said to the wise, 'Give us some of your oil because Our lamps have burned its supplies.'
25:9	"But the wise answered by saying, 'There won't be enough supply For you and us. Instead, you go And oil from the merchants buy.'

25:10	"Now, while they were away buying,
	The bridegroom came *into sight.
	Those ready entered the feast with him,
	And the door was shut up tight.
25:11	"Later, the other virgins came.
	'Lord, open to us *the hall.'
25:12	He answered, 'Truly I tell you,
	I do not know you at all.'
25:13	"Therefore, ♦in light of what I've said,
	On the alert, you must stay
	Since you don't know *of the return,
	Neither the hour nor the day.
25:14	"For the kingdom is like a man
	Traveling to a distant land.
	He called his own slaves, and to them
	His possessions, he did hand.
25:15	"Five talents to one, two to the next,
	And one to the last he gave.
	He distributed the talents,
	Matching the skill of each slave.
	"Then the man went on his journey.
25:16	As soon as he went *out the door,
	The one who received five talents
	Leveraged it and gained five more.
25:17	"Likewise, the one who received two
	Gained another two talents worth.
25:18	But the one who received just one
	Hid his lord's silver in the earth.

25:19   "After a lengthy time had passed,
　　　　　The lord of those slaves returned,
　　　　　Deciding to settle with them
　　　　　To see how much they had earned.

25:20   "The one who received five talents
　　　　　Approached *to give an account
　　　　　And brought to him five more talents,
　　　　　Thus doubling the amount.*

　　　　　"He said, 'Lord, you entrusted me
　　　　　With five talents of your own.
　　　　　Look, here's an additional five
　　　　　Which my investment* has grown.'

25:21   "His lord said to him, 'You did well.
　　　　　You're a good and faithful slave.
　　　　　You proved yourself to be faithful
　　　　　With the little bit *I gave.

　　　　　"'You were faithful with a little
　　　　　That to your skill did accord.[132]
　　　　　You'll be set over many things.
　　　　　Enter the joy of your lord.'

25:22   "The one who received two talents
　　　　　Approached *to give an account.
　　　　　'Look, lord, you gave me two talents.
　　　　　I add two to that amount.'

25:23   "His lord said to him, 'You did well.
　　　　　You're a good and faithful slave.
　　　　　You proved yourself to be faithful
　　　　　With the little bit *I gave.

"'You were faithful with a little
That to your skill did accord.¹³³
You'll be set over many things.
Enter the joy of your lord.'

25:24 "He who had received one talent
Came up to his lord and said,
'Lord, I've known you as a hard man,
And I became full of dread.¹³⁴

"'I've known you as a man who reaps
Where sowing was not your deed
And who gathers from the places
Where you did not scatter seed.

25:25 "'After you left, I was afraid.
Not wishing for you to lack,*
I hid your talent in the earth.
Look, what's yours, you now have back!'

25:26 "In reply, his lord said to him,
'You wicked and lazy slave,
You knew me to be a hard man*
When that one talent I gave.*

"'You've known me as a man who reaps
Where sowing was not my deed
And who gathers from the places
Where I did not scatter seed.

25:27 "'You should have given the silver
To the bankers *to invest
That when I came, I would have gained
What is mine with some interest.

25:28　"'Therefore, take the talent from him,
　　　　This wicked and lazy slave.*
　　　　Give it to him with ten talents
　　　　Who faithfully did behave.'*

25:29　"For to all who keep on having
　　　　(Since in faithfulness they're found)*
　　　　Certainly* more will be given,
　　　　And they will surely abound.

　　　　"But from the one who does not have
　　　　(Since faithfulness he's forsaken)*
　　　　Even what he happens to have
　　　　Will surely from him be taken.

25:30　"Cast into the outer darkness
　　　　Any worthless slave *you find.
　　　　In that place, eyes will be weeping.
　　　　Teeth will continue to grind.

25:31　"Whenever the Son of Man comes
　　　　In His glory *to be shown
　　　　And all the angels come with Him,
　　　　He'll sit on His glorious throne.

25:32　"All the nations will be gathered
　　　　In the presence of the Son,
　　　　And He will, from one another,
　　　　Separate them, every one.

　　　　"He will separate the nations
　　　　As the shepherd would divide
　　　　All the sheep from among the goats,
　　　　Placing them on either side.*

25:33	"He'll stand the sheep on His right side. On His left, the goats He'll display.
25:34	Then to the sheep on His right side, The King to these ones will say:

"'Come and inherit the kingdom
Which for you has been prepared
Since the foundation of the world.
Blessed by My Father you're declared.

25:35	"'For when you saw Me in hunger, You gave Me some food to eat. When you saw that I was thirsty, With drink My thirst you did treat.

"'When I was a stranger to you,
To gather Me in, you chose.

25:36	When you saw that I was naked, You put around Me some clothes.

"'When you saw that I was sickly,
You tended to Me with care.
When you heard that I was in jail,
You came to visit Me there.'

25:37	"Then the righteous will say to Him, 'Lord, *when did this we complete? When did we see You in hunger And give You some food to eat?

"'Or when did we see You thirsty
And give You drink *unbeknown?

25:38	When did we see You a stranger And take You into our home?

	"'Or when did we see You naked
	And around You put some clothes?
25:39	When did we see You sick or jailed
	And to visit You, we chose?'

25:40 "The King will say, 'When you did it
(This is the truth that I tell)
To one of the least of My brothers,
You did it to Me as well.'

25:41 "Then He'll say to those on His left,
'Go from Me, you who've been cursed,
Into the everlasting fire
Made ready for demons first.*

"'For the devil and his angels,
This abode* has been prepared,
And now it is the place for you.*
With demons it will be shared.*

25:42 "'For when you saw Me in hunger,
You gave Me no food to eat.
When you saw that I was thirsty,
My thirst, you refused to treat.

25:43 "'When I was a stranger to you,
Not a welcome, did you share.
When you saw that I was naked,
You gave Me no clothes to wear.

"'When you saw that I was sickly
Or heard that I was in jail,
You did not come to visit Me.
To care for Me, you did fail.'◆

25:44	"Then they'll answer and say to Him, 'Lord, *when did this all take place? When did we see You hunger or thirst Or You as a stranger, face? "'Or when did we see You naked Or sick or in a jail cell And not respond by serving You? When did this take place? Please tell.'*
25:45	"Then He'll say, 'When you did nothing (This is the truth that I tell) To one of the least of My brothers, You did nothing to Me as well.'
25:46	"Into eternal punishment, These will depart *for their sin. However, everlasting life, The righteous will enter in."

26:1	When Jesus finished all these words, To His disciples He said,
26:2	"You know that the Passover feast Is just two more days ahead. "The Son of Man will be betrayed, Delivered up at that time♦ In order to be crucified. Yes, His death they will assign."*

The Poetic Scriptures of Six Writers

26:3   Then the elders of the people
           And the chief priests *with one aim
           Were gathered in the high priest's court.
           Caiaphas was that priest's name.

26:4   They plotted ♦and planned together
           So that in a cunning way
           They could grab and arrest Jesus
           And put Him to death *someday.

26:5   But they were saying, "We must not
           At the feast bring this about.
           Otherwise, among the people,
           A great uproar might break out."

26:6   Now, Jesus came to Bethany,
           To Simon the leper's home.
26:7   A woman came before Jesus
           With a jar that she did own.

           It was made of alabaster,
           Costly perfume in it stored.
           While He reclined at the table,
           On His head the scent, she poured.

26:8   But the disciples, seeing this,
           Were outraged. "Why waste?" they said,
26:9   "It could have been sold for a lot,
           Given to the poor instead."

26:10 Knowing this, Jesus said to them,
           "For what cause do you proceed
           To make trouble for this woman?
           She did to Me a good deed.

26:11	"For you always have around you Those who are in poverty. However, *My time here is short. You will not always have Me.
26:12	"For when this one took this perfume And upon My body placed, She prepared me for burial. The perfume, she did not waste.*
26:13	"Wherever this gospel is preached Throughout the whole world, I tell, Truly, what she did will be told In memory of her as well."
26:14	Now, at that time, one of the Twelve (Judas was that person's name, Also called the Iscariot), Before the chief priests, he came.
26:15	He said, "What will you give to me So Him to you, I'll betray?" Weighing out thirty silver coins, The chief priests gave him his pay.
26:16	From that very moment of time, This traitor* began to seek A decent opportunity To betray Jesus *that week.

26:17	The first day of the festival,
	The Feast of Unleavened Bread,
	The disciples came to Jesus
	Asking Him *where to be fed.
	"Exactly where do You desire
	That we make preparation
	For You to eat the Passover?
	What is Your declaration?"*
26:18	He said, "Go into the city.
	To a certain man appeal
	By telling him *these very words
	Which to you I now reveal.*
	"'The teacher says, *My time is near.*
	In your presence, ◆*I will dine.*
	I'll be eating the Passover
	With these disciples of Mine.'
26:19	The disciples did as ordered.
	Obeying, they did prepare
26:20	The Passover, and that evening
	He reclined with the Twelve there.
26:21	While they were eating, Jesus said,
	"The truth to you all I tell.
	One of you here will betray Me."
26:22	To extreme sorrow they fell.

| | Each one started saying to Him,
| | "Lord, I'm not the one, am I?"
| | As they were speaking one by one,♦
| **26:23** | He gave to them this reply:

| | "The one who dipped along with Me
| | His own hand into the bowl,
| | That's the one who will betray Me.
| **26:24** | Woe to that man's *very soul.

| | "Although it's been written of Him
| | That the Son of Man must go,
| | To the man by whom He's betrayed
| | Comes the pronouncement of woe.

| | "It would be good if he weren't born."
| **26:25** | Judas, the traitor, broke in,
| | "Rabbi, I'm not the one, am I?"
| | He told him, "You have spoken."

| **26:26** | While they ate, Jesus took some bread
| | And gave thanks. Then it, He broke.
| | He gave it to the disciples.
| | "This is My body." He spoke.

| **26:27** | "Take. Eat it." And then He gave thanks
| | After He reached for a cup.
| | He then gave it to them and said,
| | "Drink from it. You all must sup.

| **26:28** | "For this is My covenant blood.
| | The new covenant begins.[135]
| | My blood is poured out for many
| | For the forgiveness of sins.

26:29   "But I tell you, from this time on
        That from this fruit of the vine,
        I by no means may drink at all
        Until *this appointed time:

        "That day in My Father's kingdom
        When I drink it new with you."
26:30   They (after singing together)
        Up Mount Olivet withdrew.

26:31   Then Jesus told them, "All of you
        On this particular night
        Will be caused to trip over Me,
        For it's written *which I cite:

        "'I'll strike down and kill the shepherd'
        (The speaker is the Lord God),*
        'And as for the sheep of His flock,
        They will be scattered abroad.'

26:32   "But after I'm resurrected,
        Of you, I will go ahead
        Into the region, Galilee."
26:33   But to Him, Peter then said:

        "If every person will be caused
        To stumble and trip over You,
        I myself will never ever
        Be made to stumble. *It's true!"

26:34   Jesus told him, "Here is the truth:
        On this particular night
        Before a cock is made to crow,
        Thrice you'll deny Me *outright."

26:35   "Even if I must die with You,"
            Peter to Him did exclaim,
            "I will by no means deny You."
            The rest of them said the same.

26:36   To a place called Gethsemane,
            With them all, Jesus then strolled.
            "Sit here while I go there and pray."
            To His disciples, He told.

26:37   He took the two sons of Zebedee,
            And Peter, He also brought.
            He started to be deeply grieved
            And to be very distraught.

26:38   "My soul is to the point of death,
            Heavy with grief." He did say.
            "Stay here and keep awake with Me."
26:39   He went a short ways away.

            He fell to the ground on His face.
            "My Father," He began to pray,
            "If it is at all possible,
            From Me let this cup pass away.

            "However, I am not praying
            To insist on My own will,
            But I am really asking this,
            That it be Yours, You fulfill."

26:40	He found His disciples sleeping. Peter, He began to scold, "So, could you men not stay awake For one hour with Me as told?
26:41	"That you don't fall to temptation, To watch and pray always seek. Indeed the spirit is willing, But the flesh is very weak."
26:42	Again, leaving a second time, He prayed, "If this can't pass by Unless I drink it, My Father, Then let Your own will apply."
26:43	He again found them sleeping. Heavy eyes, they could not bear.
26:44	He then left to pray a third time And again said the same prayer.
26:45	He then came to the disciples And told them, "Are you still here Sleeping and getting rest again? Behold, the hour has drawn near. "The Son of Man is being betrayed Into sinners' hands, and lo!
26:46	He who betrays Me, has drawn near. Now get up. Let us all go!"
26:47	Judas, one of the Twelve approached While Jesus gave this command. A large crowd accompanied him With both swords and clubs *in hand.

	The chief priests and the people's elders
	Sent along this multitude.
26:48	The one who was betraying Him,
	Gave them a sign *to be viewed.

	He told them, "Whomever I kiss,
	That is the One you must take."
26:49	As soon as he came to Jesus,
	His signal, he then did make.

	He said, "Joyous greetings, Rabbi."
	And then Him, Judas did kiss.
26:50	But Jesus said to him, "Comrade,
	For what are you doing this?"

Then the large multitude approached
As soon as they saw the sign.
They laid their hands upon Jesus
And captured Him *at that time.

26:51 Yet one of the ones with Jesus
Drew his sword, *showing no fear.
He struck the slave of the high priest,
Severing the slave's right ear.[136]

26:52 Jesus told him right then and there,
"Put your sword back in its place,
For all will perish by a sword
Who taking a sword embrace.

26:53 "Or do you think I cannot call
On My Father who'll provide
More than twelve legions of angels
Right now to stand by My side?

26:54	"So, in light of what I can do,
	Why should you cause such a stir?*
	How might the Scriptures be fulfilled
	That say these things must occur?"
26:55	At that time, Jesus told the crowds,
	"As against a thief, you came,
	Having your swords and clubs *in hand.
	To capture Me was your aim.
	"Every day in the temple courts
	I was sitting as I taught,
	Yet did you try to capture Me?
	To attempt this,* you did not.
26:56	"But this whole thing has come about
	So that there might be fulfilled
	What the prophets in the Scriptures
	Foretold *as God has willed."
	At that time, all the disciples
	Left Him and ran *from that spot.
26:57	Now, to Caiaphas the high priest,
	By His captors, He was brought.
	The scribes and the people's elders
	Were already gathered there,
26:58	But Peter was following Him
	From a distance *with great care.
	Going as far as the high priest's court,
	Peter made his way inside
	And was sitting with the guards
	To see the outcome applied.

26:59	The chief priests and the whole Council Were seeking testimony Against Jesus to put Him to death Though the witness was phony.
26:60	Although many false witnesses Came forward *to testify, They did not find any to use. Then later these two came by.
26:61	They said, "This One said, 'To tear down God's sanctuary I can, And I'm able to rebuild it Over a three-day span.'"
26:62	The high priest stood and said to Him, "Is there nothing to reply? What are these charges against You Which these two men testify?"
26:63	But Jesus was staying silent. The high priest to Him replied, "Under oath by the living God, I place you. *It's now applied.
	"Tell us if You're the Christ, God's Son."
26:64	"You said it." to them He told. "However, I am telling you, From now on this, you'll behold:

"You'll see the Son of Man sitting
On the Powerful One's right.
Coming on the clouds of heaven,
The Son of Man, you will site."◆

26:65 Then the high priest tore his garments.
"He has blasphemed!" was his cry.
"What need do we continue to have
For more to testify?

"Look, now you've heard the blasphemy.
26:66 What do you think *should be done?"
They then replied to the question,
"Death is deserved by this One."

26:67 At that time, they spit on His face
And with their fists gave Him blows
And slapped Him while they were saying,
26:68 "Prophecy to us, disclose.

"O Christ, prophesy to us now.
Who hit You, *and who did that?"
26:69 Now Peter was in the courtyard.
In the outside air, he sat.

One servant girl came up to him.
She said, "You accompanied
Jesus of Galilee also."
26:70 But Peter did not concede.

He denied it in the presence
Of everyone with a shout.
"I do not have any knowledge
Of what you're talking about!"

The Poetic Gospel of Matthew

26:71 He went to the courtyard's gateway.
A different girl saw him there.
"He was with Jesus of Nazareth."
To others, she did declare.

26:72 He denied it a second time
But by an oath which he swore.
"I do not even know the Man."
He denied it as before.*

26:73 A short time later, bystanders
Came up to Peter to say,
"Surely you're also part of them.
Your accent gives you away."

26:74 Then promising to curse himself,
Peter began *to explode.
"I do not even know the Man!"
A cock immediately crowed.

26:75 Peter then remembered the word
Jesus had spoken *that night.
"Before a cock is made to crow,
Thrice you'll deny Me *outright."

Peter then went through the gateway,
And to the outside he stepped.
Sorrow filled his entire being.♦
In deep agony he wept.

27:1	Now, when the morning had arrived,
	The chief priests, each one of them,
	Along with the people's elders
	Came together to condemn.
	They all plotted against Jesus
	So that death, He'd meet *that day.
27:2	Then after they tied Jesus up,
	From there* they led Him away.
	They handed Him up to Pilate,
	The governor Rome did send.[137]
27:3	Judas, the one who betrayed Him,
	Saw that Jesus was condemned.
	At that time, he felt such regret
	That he instantly returned
	To the high priests and the elders
	The thirty coins *which he earned.
27:4	He said to them, "I've greatly sinned.
	Innocent blood I've betrayed."
	They said, "You see to this yourself.
	What is that to us? *You're paid."
27:5	Then Judas threw the silver coins
	Into the sanctuary.
	He went away and hung himself.
	His guilt, he could not carry.*

The Poetic Gospel of Matthew

27:6 The high priests took the silver coins
And said, "These we cannot place
Into the temple treasury.
It's unlawful in this case.

"For it is the price paid for blood."
27:7 Then after they counseled more,
They bought with it the Potter's Field.
Burial it would be for.

It would be a burial plot
For strangers' bodies to lay.
27:8 Therefore, that field came to be called
The Field of Blood to this day.

27:9 What was spoken through the prophet
At this time became fulfilled.
The prophet Jeremiah spoke
These words the Spirit instilled:*

"Thirty silver coins was the price
Israel's sons on Him had sealed.
27:10 As the Lord had commanded me,
I paid for the Potter's Field."

27:11 Now, Jesus stood before *Pilate
And leaders who would accuse.[138]
The governor questioned Jesus,
"Are You the King of the Jews?"

	But Jesus said, "It's as you've said."
27:12	And in each accusation
	Made by the chief priests and elders,
	He gave no explanation.

27:13 At that time, Pilate said to Him,
"You're ears, aren't You applying
To the many things against You
These men are testifying?"

27:14 Yet Jesus did not answer him,
Not even a single word.
The governor greatly marveled
As a result of what occurred.

27:15 Now, at the feast, the governor
Was accustomed to set free
To the crowd just one prisoner,
Whomever they wished him to be.

27:16 Now, at that time, they were holding
A person who had gained fame,♦
A notorious prisoner.
Barabbas was this man's name.

27:17 Therefore, since the crowd was gathered,
Pilate hoping they'd be enticed[139]
Asked, "Whom should I release to you,
Barabbas or Jesus called Christ?"

27:18 For he knew they handed Him up
Due to envious intent.
27:19 While sitting on the judgment seat,
This word, his wife to him sent:

"Do nothing to that righteous Man
Because in a dream today
I suffered much because of Him."
So the crowd, he hoped to sway.*

27:20 But the chief priests and the elders
In the crowds' mind had instilled
To ask that Barabbas be freed
And for Jesus to be killed.

27:21 The governor said to the crowd,
"Your discussion now must cease.*
Which of these two do you desire
That to you all I release?"

They shouted the name, "Barabbas."
27:22 Then Pilate to them replied,
"What should I do to Him called Christ?"
They said, "Have Him crucified."

27:23 He said, "Tell me the reason why?
What evil has He applied?"
But with greater force, they shouted,
"Let this Man be crucified."

27:24 Pilate saw that he was gaining
Nothing *for Jesus's case,
But instead a great upheaval
Was beginning to take place.

So after he took some water
(As a symbol this was meant),*
He washed his hands before the crowd,
Saying, "I am innocent."

	"I'm innocent of this Man's blood.
	You must see *it's on your head."
27:25	"His blood on us and our children!"
	To him all the people said.

27:26	He released to them Barabbas,
	But on Jesus, he applied
	A scourge before giving Him up
	So as to be crucified.

27:27	The soldiers of the governor
	Took Jesus inside their base.
	They gathered the entire cohort[140]
	Against Him *so to disgrace.

27:28	They put a scarlet robe on Him
	After stripping off His clothes.
27:29	Then on His head they placed a wreath
	Which from thorns they did compose.

	They put a reed in His right hand
	And before Him bowed their knees.
	They shouted, "Hail, King of the Jews!"
	Mocking Him *as they would please.

27:30	They spit on Him, then took the reed.
	On His head, they gave Him blows.
27:31	Their mocking done, they stripped the robe
	And on Him put His own clothes.

	At that time, they led Him away
	So that He'd be crucified.
27:32	But as they were on their way out,
	A man from Cyrene they eyed.

　　　　　　He was a Jew* known as Simon.
　　　　　　This man, they forcefully made
　　　　　　To carry the cross of Jesus.
　　　　　　On Simon, the cross was laid.*

27:33　　　They arrived at the location,
　　　　　　Golgotha, as it was named,
　　　　　　A word that means "Place of the Skull,"
　　　　　　The Aramaic explained.*

27:34　　　They gave Jesus some wine to drink
　　　　　　Mixed with an herb known as gall.
　　　　　　After He took a little taste,
　　　　　　He wanted no drink at all.

27:35　　　After they crucified Jesus,
　　　　　　His clothing, *they did not spare.
　　　　　　Casting lots, they divided them.
27:36　　　Then they sat guarding Him there.

27:37　　　They also placed over His head
　　　　　　This charge written *on a sign:
　　　　　　"This is Jesus, King of the Jews."
　　　　　　Therefore, all could read His crime.*

27:38　　　Along with Him were crucified
　　　　　　Two men convicted of theft.
　　　　　　One was crucified on His right
　　　　　　And the other, on His left.

27:39　　　Now those who were passing by Him,
　　　　　　Contempt, they were displaying.♦
　　　　　　They were speaking evil of Him,
　　　　　　Shaking their heads and saying:

27:40	"You who'd raze the sanctuary
	And in three days restore somehow,
	If You're God's Son, then save Yourself.
	Come down from this cross *right now."
27:41	In the same way, the chief priests too,
	With the elders and the scribes
	Were saying of Him on the cross
	With taunting and♦ mocking cries:
27:42	"He saved others. As for Himself,
	He cannot save anyhow.
	He's Israel's King. Therefore, let Him
	Come down from the cross right now.
	"If He does, we'll believe in Him.
27:43	If trust in God He's retained,
	Let God save Him now if He wants,
	For 'I'm God's Son,' He's proclaimed."
27:44	Now, the thieves crucified with Him
	Were insulting Him the same,
27:45	But from noon until three o'clock,[141]
	Darkness on all the earth came.
27:46	Around three o'clock, Jesus cried,
	"Eli!" in a clear, loud tone.
	"Eli, lema sabachthani?"
	The meaning needs to be known.*
	Its meaning is, "My God, My God,
	Why Me, have You forsaken?"
27:47	Now some of the ones standing there
	Heard him *yet seemed mistaken.[142]

	Some said, "He's calling Elijah."
27:48	Instantly, one of them raced,
	Took a sponge, filled it with sour wine,
	And it on a reed, he placed.

	He began to give Him a drink.
27:49	This, the rest did not condone.
	"Let us see if Elijah comes
	And saves Him. Leave Him alone."

27:50	But Jesus after He cried out
	Once again with a loud voice,
	Let His spirit leave *His body.
	He laid down His life by choice.[143]

27:51	And note, the sanctuary's veil
	From top to bottom was split,
	Divided into two pieces,
	And the earth shook quite a bit.

	The rocks were also split by this.
27:52	The tombs, they were opened wide,
	And there were raised many bodies
	Of holy ones who had died.

27:53	After the Lord's resurrection,
	They rose from those tombs *of stone.
	They entered the holy city
	And to many were made known.

27:54	The centurion and his men
	Who over Jesus kept guard
	Saw the earthquake and the events,
	And terror hit them all hard.

The Poetic Scriptures of Six Writers

"This truly was the Son of God."
All of them began to say.
27:55   Now, many women were present,
Observing from far away.

These women had followed Jesus
All the way from Galilee
For the purpose of serving Him.
27:56   Now among them were *these three:

Mary Magdalene, and Mary
(Mother of Joseph and James),
And the mother of Zebedee's sons
(James and John were their names).*

27:57   A man came when evening arrived.
Joseph was what he was named.
He was from Arimathea.
Many riches, he had gained.

He was a disciple of Jesus,
But this had not been revealed.[144]
27:58   After coming before Pilate,
For Christ's body he appealed.

That the body be given him,
Pilate charged it be allowed.
27:59   Joseph took and wrapped the body
In a clean fine linen shroud.

27:60	He placed it in his own new tomb
Which he had carved in the rock.
He rolled a huge stone to the tomb
So the entrance, it would block.
27:61	Then after this, he went away.
Now, both Mary Magdalene
And the other Mary were sitting
Across from the tomb *unseen.
27:62	On the next day, the one after
The day of preparation,
The chief priests and the Pharisees
Were all in congregation.
27:63	Standing before Pilate, they said,
"Sir, we clearly recollect
The deceiver, while still alive,
Proclaimed He would resurrect.*
27:64	"'After three days, I will be raised.'
The deceiver did assure.
So, charge that until the third day
The gravesite be made secure.
	"Otherwise, His own disciples
Might come and steal Him away.
'He has been raised up from the dead!'
To the people, they will say.
27:65	"Then the last deception will be
Worse than the first one, *for sure."
Pilate said, "Go. You have your guard.
As you know, make it secure."

27:66 After they proceeded from there,
They secured the tomb much more
By setting along with the guard
A seal on the tomb's stone door.[145]

28:1 Now, after the Sabbath ended,
The next day's light coming soon,
Mary Magdalene came to see
With the other Mary the tomb.

28:2 Behold, a great earthquake occurred,
For an angel came to the cave.
The Lord's angel came from heaven
And rolled the stone from the grave.

Now, he was sitting on the stone,
28:3 And lightning, he resembled.
His apparel was white as snow,
28:4 And the guards feared and trembled.

They all were so afraid of him
That they became as though dead.
28:5 In response to the women's *fear,
This angel of the Lord said:

"Stop being afraid, for I know
That Jesus you're looking for,
That One who had been crucified.
28:6 He is not here anymore.

| | "Come and see where He was lying.
| | He was raised just as He said.
| **28:7** | Go quickly. Tell his disciples
| | That He was raised from the dead.

| | "Into the region, Galilee,
| | He goes before you, behold.
| | There you will view Him with your eyes.
| | Take note of what I have told."

| **28:8** | And leaving at once from the tomb
| | With fear yet with joy so great,
| | They both ran to His disciples
| | So as this news to relate.

| **28:9** | But suddenly, Jesus met them.
| | "Greetings!" to them Jesus said.
| | They came before Him, grabbed His feet,
| | And worshipped Him *but in dread.

| **28:10** | Then Jesus told them, "Stop fearing.
| | Go to My brothers and share
| | That they must go to Galilee,
| | For they all will see Me there."

| **28:11** | While the women were proceeding,
| | To the city there did race
| | Some of the guard who went and told
| | The chief priests all that took place.

| **28:12** | After gathering with the elders,
| | Taking their words into account,
| | They gave silver to the soldiers,
| | A considerable amount.

28:13 They said, "You are to say these words:
       'The disciples came at night
       And stole Him while we were sleeping.'
       The governor *won't indict.

28:14 "For if this should be heard by him,
       His persuasion, we'll hurry
       So that he will not indict you.[146]
       We'll keep you free from worry."

28:15 So, after taking the silver,
       Their counsel, they did obey,
       And this message was widely spread
       Among the Jews to this day.

28:16 Now the eleven disciples
       Proceeded to Galilee,
       To a designated mountain
       Where Jesus told them He'd be.

28:17 After His followers[147] saw Him,
       They fell down upon their knees,♦
       And they began to worship Him,
       With doubt among some of these.

28:18 Then Jesus came closer and said
       To them *with the eleven,
       "All authority is now Mine
       On the earth and in heaven.

28:19 "Therefore, make into disciples
       All the nationalities,
       As you are proceeding about,
       Baptizing each one of these.

"Baptizing them into the name
Of the Father and of the Son,
Also of the Holy Spirit,
And teaching them, every one.

28:20   "Teaching them to keep all the things
Which to you I did mandate.
Behold, I'm with you all the days
'Til the ages terminate."

THE POETIC GOSPEL OF MARK

1:1 The Beginning of the Gospel
About Jesus Christ, God's Son.
That is the title of this book.[148]
The gospel has just begun.✦

1:2 As is written in Isaiah,
The prophet *who this foretold,
"I am sending before Your face
My messenger. Behold!

"That person will prepare Your way.
1:3 In the desert, his voice will state,
Crying out, 'Prepare the Lord's way.
Keep making His pathways straight.'"

1:4 John arrived in the desert place.
A baptism he proclaimed,
One of repentance so that sins
Be forgiven, ✦not retained.

1:5	Now all the Judean country,
	And all Jerusalemites
	Were going out to where John was,
	Yes, all these Israelites.*

        They were being baptized by him
        While all their sins they confessed.
        In the Jordan, they were baptized,
1:6   And this was how John had dressed:

        He had clothed himself with garments
        Crafted out of camel's hair,
        And a belt made out of leather
        Around his waist he would wear.

        A simple* diet of locusts
        And wild honey was his food,
1:7   And he was proclaiming these words,
        Saying *to the multitude:

        "After me, there is One coming
        Who is mightier than I.
        His sandal strap I'm unworthy
        To stoop so as to untie.

1:8   "I myself have baptized you all
        In water *for all to view.
        However, in the Holy Spirit,
        He Himself will baptize you."

1:9   From Nazareth of Galilee,
        Jesus arrived in those days.
        In the Jordan, He was baptized
        By John *who of Him had phrased.

The Poetic Gospel of Mark

1:10 As He came up from the water,
He instantly viewed above
The sky splitting and the Spirit
Descending on Him like a dove.

1:11 Then a voice sounded from heaven,
The Scriptures being cited,[149]
"You are My Son I dearly love.
In You I am delighted."

1:12 Immediately, the Spirit
Drove Him out from there a ways,
Deeper into the desert place.
1:13 He was there for forty days.

While in that place, He was being
Tempted by Satan *to sin,
And He was with wild animals,
Yet angels were serving Him.

1:14 Now after John was arrested,
Jesus entered Galilee,
Preaching the gospel about God
1:15 While giving this constant plea:

"The time of fulfillment has come,
And God's kingdom has drawn near.
Keep repenting and believing
In this gospel *that you hear."

1:16	Along the sea of Galilee, Jesus was making His way. He saw two men casting a net Into the water one day. Simon and his brother Andrew, On these two His eyes were laid.* They were casting into the sea Because fishing was their trade.
1:17	Jesus told them, "Come follow Me. I'll make you fishers of men."
1:18	And instantly, leaving their nets, They followed Jesus right then.
1:19	And going a little farther, Zebedee's sons He did note, James along with his brother John Mending their nets in the boat.
1:20	At once He called them, and they left The boat* and all those within (Their father with the hired hands) And went away after Him.
1:21	Then they entered Capernaum, And on the Sabbath, straightway, He went into the synagogue And began teaching *that day.
1:22	They were amazed at His teaching, For His teaching He expressed As one having authority And not as the scribes possessed.

1:23	Suddenly, in their synagogue,
	There was a man who cried out.
	In him was an unclean spirit.
	These words he began to shout:
1:24	"What's there, Jesus of Nazareth,
	Between us and You to be done?
	Have You come to destroy us now?
	I know You are God's Holy One."
1:25	Jesus rebuked him by saying,
	"Quiet! From this man come out."
1:26	The unclean spirit convulsed him
	And left with a mighty shout.
1:27	Now, everyone was so amazed
	That questions began to spew.
	Among themselves, they asked, "Who's He?
	What is this teaching that's new?
	"For it is with authority
	That He makes such a demand
	To the spirits that are unclean,
	And they obey His command."
1:28	Instantly, the report of Him
	Spread in every direction,
	Into the whole of Galilee
	And each surrounding section.
1:29	They went out from the synagogue
	And instantly traveled on
	To the house of Simon and Andrew
	Along with James and John.

The Poetic Scriptures of Six Writers

1:30   The mother-in-law of Simon
        Was lying with a fever great.
        They told Him immediately
        About her *serious state.

1:31   After coming into her *room
        And grabbing her by the hand,
        He raised her up. The fever left.
        Then to serve them she began.

1:32   When evening came, after sunset,
        To Him they brought ◆the distressed,
        Everyone who had illnesses
        And all the demon-possessed.

1:33   The entire city had gathered
        At the door *to watch Jesus.
1:34   He healed those who were afflicted
        With various diseases.

        Jesus cast out many demons,
        But to speak they did not do,
        For Jesus did not allow it
        Since His identity they knew.

1:35   Rising early in the morning
        While the deep darkness still loomed,
        He went into a desert place
        Where in prayer He was consumed.

1:36	Simon and the people with him His whereabouts did pursue.
1:37	At last, they found Him and told Him, "Everyone is seeking You."
1:38	He said to them, "Let's go elsewhere, To the nearby towns, *each one, So that I might preach there as well, For that is why I have come."
1:39	And He went throughout Galilee Spreading His message about, Wherever they had synagogues, And casting the demons out.
1:40	A leprous man came before Him, Urging Him while on his knees, Telling Him, "If You are willing, You can cleanse me *of disease."
1:41	And moved with deep-felt compassion And extending out His hand, He touched and told him, "I'm willing. Become clean *as I command."
1:42	The leprosy vanished from him. He was cleansed without delay,
1:43	But Jesus sternly warned the man And at once sent him away.
1:44	He said to him, "See that you say Nothing to anyone though, But to the priest bring offerings As yourself to him you show.

"Offer what Moses commanded
In the laws of ceremony[150]
For the uncleanness which you had
To them as a testimony."

1:45   Instead, he went out and began
To talk about it a lot
And to spread around the report.
To travel, Jesus could not.

He could not enter a city,
But outside He had to stay
In the desert since from all sides
To Him they were making their way.

2:1   Days later, to Capernaum
Jesus returned once again.
It was heard *by the residents
That He was at home right then.

2:2   So many people were gathered
That they could make room no more
For additional arrivals,
Not even before the door.

He was speaking the word to them
2:3   When some people had started
To bring Him a paralyzed man.
By four men he was carted.

2:4	Yet because they were unable
	To reach Jesus through the horde,
	They carefully unroofed the roof,
	Digging through above the Lord.
	They lowered the paralyzed man
	As he lay upon his bed.
2:5	Jesus seeing the faith they had
	To the paralytic said:
	"Child, your sins have been forgiven."
2:6	Now, some scribes were sitting there
	And were discussing in their hearts,
	Of which Jesus was aware.[151]
2:7	"Why does this Man speak in this way?
	It's blasphemy which He's jawed.
	Who is able to forgive sins?
	Only one can, and that's God!"
2:8	Instantly, Jesus said to them
	(For in His spirit He knew
	They were talking within themselves),
	"Why in your hearts take this view?
	"To speak to this paralyzed man,
2:9	Which is the easier talk:
	'Your sins are forgiven' or to say,
	'Rise up, take your bed, and walk'?
2:10	"That you may know the Son of Man
	Has the right on earth *any day
	To forgive sins –" Jesus then turned
	To the paralyzed man to say:

2:11	"I tell you, get up! Take your bed. Go home. *You can walk about."
2:12	He got right up and took his bed And before all walked right out.
	This caused all to be astounded, And God, they all did adore While saying to one another, "We've never seen this before."

2:13	Again He went along the sea, And the whole crowd *from before Was coming into His presence. So, He was teaching them *more.
2:14	While Jesus was walking along, Alphaeus's son caught His eye. He was sitting at a tax booth. The man was known as Levi.
	Jesus said to him, "Follow Me." He rose and followed behind.
2:15	Then Jesus came to Levi's house, And with Levi, Jesus dined.
	Now tax collectors and sinners In large number also ate With Jesus and His disciples, For His following was great.

2:16	When the scribes of the Pharisees
Saw His association
With sinners and tax collectors,
They sought an explanation.*
	So they questioned His disciples,
"Tell us why He is eating
With tax collectors and sinners?
An answer we are needing?"*
2:17	When hearing this, Jesus told them,
"The strong have no need at all
Of a physician, just the sick.
So, what people must I call?*
	"I came not to call the righteous.
For that work I was not sent.*
I have come to call the sinners.
I have called them to repent."[152]
2:18	Now, on this day,* John's disciples
And Pharisees were fasting.
So, they[153] came before His presence.
This question they were asking:
	"Why do the disciples of John
And those of the Pharisees
Practice fasting but Yours do not.
Provide us the reason, please."*
2:19	Jesus said, "Can the bridegroom's guests
Fast while the bridegroom is there?
As long as the bridegroom's with them,
They can't fast. There's no despair.[154]

2:20	"But days will come when the bridegroom
From them will be snatched away.
At that time, they'll be in despair.*
Then they will fast in that day.
2:21	"Nobody sews an unshrunk patch
On a garment that is old,
For as it shrinks, the garment tears,
And a worse tear will unfold.
2:22	"Also, nobody pours new wine
Into wineskins that are old,
Or else the wine will burst the skins.
New wine, old skins can't hold.*

"The wine is lost, the wineskins too.
They're ruined as expected.*
Pour new wine into fresh wineskins,
And both are then protected."[155] |
| 2:23 | On the Sabbath, He was passing
Through the planted fields' terrain.
His disciples began to make
A path, picking heads of grain. |
| 2:24 | The Pharisees were telling Him,
"Look *at what we are viewing.
What's unlawful on the Sabbath,
Why are these men now doing?" |
| 2:25 | To them He said, "Have you not read
What David did when in need,
When he hungered and those with him, |
| 2:26 | How he entered God's house *with speed? |

"Now Abiathar was high priest
When this incident took place.
He began eating the showbread,
Usually a deed of disgrace.*

"For it's unlawful to eat it
Except for the priests alone,
Yet he gave it to those with him.
To eat it, he did condone."*

2:27   He was also saying to them,
"The Sabbath was created
For the benefit of mankind.
For mankind's sake He made it.*

"Mankind was not created for
The Sabbath *in any way.
2:28   So then, the Son of Man is Lord
Even of the Sabbath day."

3:1   Proceeding from there,[156] once again
To the synagogue He went.
A man was there who had a hand
That was shriveled up ♦and bent.

3:2   The Pharisees were watching Him,
Keeping Him within their views,
To see if He would heal the man
So that Him, they might accuse.

The Poetic Scriptures of Six Writers

3:3 To the man with the shriveled hand,
He said, "Stand up in our midst."
3:4 Then to them Jesus posed a choice
As to what they would insist.*

"Is it lawful on the Sabbath
To do good or to do ill?
Is it lawful on the Sabbath
To save a life or to kill?"

But they all were keeping silent.
3:5 With anger He looked around
Although He was very much grieved
At the hardened hearts He found.

He told the man, "Stretch out your hand."
He stretched it out *toward the Lord,
And right then his shriveled up hand
Became completely restored.

3:6 When the Pharisees went from there,
At once they began to plot
With the Herodians against Him.
His destruction was their thought.

3:7 Yet Jesus with His disciples
Retreated back to the sea.
A very large crowd gathered there
Which had come from Galilee.

From Judea, Jerusalem,
3:8 Around Tyre and Sidon as well,
Idumea, and past the Jordan
The crowd continued to swell.

	Since they heard all He was doing,
	Before Him the crowd had come.
3:9	He instructed His disciples
	To reserve a boat, *just one.

	Because the crowd was very large,
	He had a boat placed in a spot
	So they would not press in on Him,
3:10	For healing to many He'd brought.

These healings had caused everyone
Flogged with maladies as such
To fall on Him *in any way
So that Him, they might just touch.

3:11   Demons[157] seeing Him cried, "You're God's Son!"
        As before Him, they would fall.
3:12   Yet many times He would warn them
        Not to make Him known at all.

3:13   He went up into the mountain
        And called to Himself by name
        Specific ones whom He would want,
        And before Him they then came.

3:14   He produced twelve to be with Him,
        To send them to preach about
3:15   And have power over demons
        In order to cast them out.

3:16   These are the twelve: Simon Peter
        (Peter was the name He laid
        Later upon Simon because
        Of the confession he made);[158]

3:17	Then James, the son of Zebedee,
	And John, the brother of James
	(Boanerges or Sons of Thunder,
	Their Jesus-given nickname);
3:18	Andrew *who was Peter's brother;
	Philip and Bartholomew;
	Thomas and Simon the Zealot;
	And the taxman named* Matthew.
	Then James the son of Alphaeus;
	Thaddaeus *and the traitor
3:19	Known as Judas Iscariot
	Who betrayed Jesus later.

3:20	Jesus returned home, and again
	There gathered a multitude
	So that He and His disciples
	Could not even eat their food.
3:21	Now after His family heard this,
	They came out to grab Him quick,
	For they were saying, "He's crazy!
	In His mind, He must be sick!"♦
3:22	Scribes came from Jerusalem saying,
	"He has Beelzebul *no doubt.
	By the ruler of the demons
	He casts all the demons out!"

3:23	Summoning them, in parables
To them He began to speak.
"How can Satan cast out Satan?
Would that not then make him weak?*
3:24	"If a kingdom is divided
Against its very domain,
It then would be impossible
For that kingdom to remain.
3:25	"If a household is divided
Against its very own clan,
It then would be impossible
For that same household to stand.
3:26	"If Satan stands against himself
As one who is divided,
Then he cannot possibly stand,
But his end, he's provided.
3:27	"One can't enter a strong man's house
And steal the things he does own
Unless he binds the strong man first,
And then he'll plunder his home.
3:28	"All sins of the sons of mankind
Will be forgiven, it's true,
Even all of their blasphemies,
Whatever evil they spew.
3:29	"But whoever speaks blasphemy
Against the Holy Spirit
Will not ever have forgiveness.
God will not ever clear it.*

	"But this person is liable
	For an everlasting sin."
3:30	He said this since they were saying,
	"An unclean spirit's in Him."
3:31	His mother and His brothers came
	And sent, while standing outside,
	Word to Him that upon them
	His attention be applied.
3:32	The crowd sitting around Jesus
	Was saying to Him, "Behold,
	Outside Your mother and brothers
	Are seeking You *we are told."
3:33	And in reply, to them He said,
	"Who's My mother and brothers?"
3:34	Eyeing the crowd encircling Him,
	He said pointing to others:[159]
	"Lo! My mother and My brothers.
	Those relations these fulfill.*
3:35	My mother, brother, or sister
	Is the one who does God's will."

4:1	Once again, He began to teach
	At a place beside the sea.
	A crowd was gathered before Him.
	'Twas as large as it could be.

The Poetic Gospel of Mark

        So, in a boat on the water
        He climbed, and then He sat down.
        The entire crowd was seated
        Beside the sea on the ground.

4:2   He was teaching them many things,
        In parables, although.
        As He taught, He told them, "Listen.
4:3   The sower went out to sow.

4:4   "It happened that in his sowing
        Some seeds fell beside the road.
        The birds then came, and they consumed
        All of these seeds that he sowed.

4:5   "Other seeds fell on rocky earth
        Where not much soil was around.
        Shoots sprang up immediately,
        For soil lacked depth in that ground.

4:6   "When the sun rose up *in the sky
        And shined upon every shoot,*
        They were scorched and withered because
        None of them had any root.

4:7   "And other seeds fell among thorns,
        And although these ones took root,*
        The thorns sprang up and choked them out,
        And they did not produce fruit.

4:8   "Other seeds fell on healthy ground
        And began producing fruit,
        Multiplying themselves much more.
        For these seeds the soil did suit.[160]

"Some seeds multiplied thirty times,
Some sixty times *in that year.
Some multiplied one hundred times.
4:9 Those with hearing ears now hear."

4:10 Then the Twelve with those around Him
Were asking Him *to make known
The meaning of the parables
As soon as He was alone.

4:11 He began explaining to them,
"It's been given you to know
The mystery of God's kingdom,
But to those outside, *not so.

"To them, it's all in parables
4:12 That when these words they receive,
Although seeing, they might still see
Yet the meaning not perceive.

"Although hearing, they might still hear
Yet not really comprehend.
Otherwise, they might turn, and then
Forgiveness, God would extend.[161]

4:13 "The meaning of this parable,
Of it are you not aware?
Then how will you all understand
All the parables I share?

4:14 "The sower sows the word *of God,
4:15 And there alongside the road
Are those on whom the word is sown.
What happens with what's bestowed?*

"Satan comes immediately
Whenever they hear the word
And snatches what was sown in them,
The message which they had heard.♦

4:16 "And there upon the rocky ground
Are those on whom seed is sown.
They at once receive it with joy
As they hear the word made known.

4:17 "Yet they have no root in themselves
But are just temporary.
When trouble¹⁶² comes due to the word,
To fall, they do not tarry.

4:18 "And others correspond to where
The seeds are sown among thorns.
These are the ones who hear the word,
Yet choking later on forms.

4:19 "The anxieties of this world,
The deceit of wealth's pursuit,
And the lusts of everything else
Keep the word from bearing fruit.

4:20 "And there upon the healthy ground
Are those where the seeds were sown.
They hear the word and welcome it.
For fruit-bearing, they are known.

"Not everyone produces fruit*
To the same degree. Behold!*
Some produce thirty times as much,
Some sixty, some a hundredfold."

4:21 He continued speaking to them,
"Is any lamp ever brought
To be put under a basket
Or under a bed? It's not!

"Is not the purpose of a lamp
That's brought into any place
That it be put on a lampstand?
Well, of course, *in every case![163]

4:22 "For there's nothing which is hidden
So that it not be revealed.
Also, nothing becomes secret
But that it be unconcealed.

4:23 "If anybody has an ear,
Let him continue to hear.
Let him pay careful attention♦
With a listening ear."*

4:24 He continued speaking to them,
"What you hear, carefully view.
Your standard of measure will be
Measured and added to you.

4:25 "For he who has will receive more,
And he who has nothing, per say,
Even what he believes[164] he has
From him will be snatched away."

4:26 He continued speaking to them.
"God's kingdom can be compared
To a farmer who scattered seeds
On the ground *which he prepared.

4:27	"He sleeps and rises night and day,
	And the seeds sprout up and grow.
	How the seeds can do such a thing,
	He himself does not know.
4:28	"For the earth automatically
	Produces the fruit *to eat.
	First comes the blade, then next the head,
	And last in the head full wheat.
4:29	"But as soon as the wheat ripens,
	He sends the sickle with one
	To harvest all the ripened wheat
	Because harvest time has come.
4:30	"To what might we compare God's kingdom?"
	Jesus continued to state.
	"Or what parable might we use
	In order to illustrate?
4:31	"Let us use a mustard plant's seed
	Which when sown on the land,
	Though smaller than all seeds on earth,
4:32	Grows massively to stand.
	"It grows larger than all the plants
	With very large branches made
	So that all the birds of the sky
	Can make their nest in its shade."
4:33	He was speaking to them the word
	As they were able to hear
	With many parables like these,
	But the meaning was unclear.*

The Poetic Scriptures of Six Writers

4:34   For to speak without parables
       To the crowd, He would refrain.
       But all things to His disciples,
       He would privately explain.

4:35   When evening came on the same day
       These parables were supplied,*
       To His disciples Jesus said,
       "Let's sail to the other side."

4:36   The disciples then left the crowd
       And in the boat where He sat
       Proceeded to take Him across.
       But more boats came than just that.

4:37   A storm arose with gale force winds.
       The waves were constantly spilling
       Into the boat so that the boat
       Already was quickly filling.

4:38   Now, in the stern He was sleeping.
       On a pillow, He was lying.
       They stirred Him up and cried, "Teacher!
       Don't You care that we are dying?"

4:39   He rebuked the wind and the sea
       Just as soon as He was stirred.
       "Silence. Be still!" And the wind stopped,
       And a great calm then occurred.

4:40	Jesus asked them, "Why be timid?
	Don't you have any faith yet?"
4:41	They were completely terrified.
	With great fear, they were beset.

They were asking one another,
"Who then must this person be
That nature itself♦ obeys Him,
Even the wind and the sea?"

5:1	Into the Gerasene region
	They came, once they crossed the sea.
5:2	When Jesus stepped out of the boat,
	A man met Him instantly.

An unclean spirit, this man had.
He came from among the graves.

5:3 He had made his own living space
There among the tombs ♦or caves.

No one could bind him anymore,
Not even if he was chained

5:4 Because with shackles and with chains
He often had been restrained.

However, he had by himself
Broken the chains *into two
And torn the shackles to pieces.
So him, no one could subdue.

5:5	And throughout every day and night,
	He was at this place of bones
	Or in the mountains crying out
	And cutting himself with stones.
5:6	Seeing Jesus from a distance,
	He ran and before Him, fell.
5:7	Then in a voice extremely loud,
	These words he began to yell:
	"Jesus, Son of the Most High God,
	With You I've nothing to do.
	Do not come here to torment me.
	By God, I am begging You."
5:8	For He had said, "Unclean spirit,
	Exit the man *whom you pain."
5:9	He had also asked the spirit,
	"Tell Me,* what is your name?"
	He told Him, "Since we are many,
	The name I have is Legion."
5:10	He begged Him greatly that He not
	Send them out of the region.
5:11	Now there was a large herd of pigs
	Toward the mountain being fed.
5:12	"Send us into the herd so that
	We may enter them," they pled.
5:13	He allowed them to do just that,
	And after they all came out,
	The demons[165] went into the pigs,
	Two thousand of them about.

The herd of pigs rushed down the slope
Into the waters below,
And in the sea all the pigs drowned,
Two thousand of them or so.

5:14 Those feeding them sprinted about
And reported what they eyed
To the people in the city
And out in the countryside.

Then they came to see *for themselves
What had really taken place.
5:15 They came to Jesus, and they saw
The demoniac face to face.

This man who had Legion inside,
They saw sitting, fully dressed.
He appeared to be sound in mind,
No longer demon-possessed.*

They all became very afraid,
5:16 And those who witnessed this deed
Performed on the demoniac
Disclosed it fully *with speed.

They also told about the pigs
When Jesus gave His orders.*
5:17 The people started to beg Him
To exit from their borders.

5:18 When Jesus climbed into the boat,
The man who had been possessed
Wanted to accompany Him.
And begging, for this he pressed.

5:19	Yet this, Jesus did not allow
	But told him, "Go to your home.
	Tell them all the Lord's done for you,
	How mercy to you He's shown."
5:20	He left and in Decapolis
	Started to proclaim *the word
	Of all that Jesus did for him.
	Everyone marveled *who heard.

5:21	After Jesus had in the boat
	Crossed over the sea once more,
	A large crowd gathered around Him.
	Now, He was right on the shore.
5:22	One of the synagogue leaders
	Whose name was Jairus appeared.
	He saw Jesus, fell at His feet,
5:23	And in begging persevered.
	"My little daughter is near death."
	His plea he began to give.
	"Come and lay Your hands upon her
	So she may be healed and live."
5:24	Then He departed with Jairus.
	The crowd which was very great
	Followed Him, pressing in on Him.
5:25	But one had a bloody state.*

	A woman had for twelve long years
	Constant bloody emissions.
5:26	She had suffered to great degrees
	Under many physicians.

She had spent all her resources
Without improvement to show.
On the contrary, she had come
To an even worse blood flow.

5:27   Because she heard about Jesus,
       Behind Him she made her way
       Through the crowd and touched His garment,
5:28   For to herself* she did say:

       "Even if I touch His garment,
       I'll be saved from this ordeal."
5:29   Immediately, her blood flow stopped,
       And she felt her body heal.

5:30   Jesus realizing in Himself
       That power out of Him rose
       Turned around at once in the crowd
       And questioned, "Who touched My clothes?"

5:31   His disciples were telling Him,
       "This crowd You can plainly see
       That they are pressing in on You,
       And You're asking, 'Who touched Me?'"

5:32   He was looking around to see
       Who had accomplished this touch.
5:33   The woman knew what befell her.
       So she feared and trembled much.

Then she came and fell before Him.
The truth to Him, she then told,
The whole truth, ◆leaving nothing out.
All details she did unfold.◆

5:34   But He said to her, "O daughter,
Your faith, it has made you well.
Go in peace. Stay healthy and free[166]
From the plague which on you fell."

5:35   While He was speaking, a group came
From the synagogue leader's home,
Saying, "Why bother the teacher still?
Your girl died. ◆Leave Him alone."

5:36   But when overhearing this news
Which was told, Jesus then said
To the leader, "Stop your fearing.
Just keep believing *instead."

5:37   He did not allow anyone
With Him to continue on,
Save Peter, James, and James's brother
Who goes by the name of John.

5:38   They proceeded into the house
Of Jairus,[167] and Jesus saw
People there weeping and wailing
With much chaotic hoopla.[168]

5:39   Upon entering, He told them,
"Why be chaotic and weep?
For the little child did not die,
But she is only asleep."

5:40	They began to ridicule Him, But He threw out everyone, Save the child's father and mother And those who with Him had come.
5:41	They entered the room where she was. He grabbed the little child's hand. He said, "Talitha, koum!" which means "Little girl, I tell you, stand!"
5:42	Immediately, the little child Because she was twelve years old Arose and was walking around. Excitement they could not hold.
5:43	They were overflowing with awe, Yet He pushed them to exclude Anyone from learning of this Then told them, "Give her some food."

6:1	Jesus then went out from that place And came to His own hometown. His disciples followed Him there.
6:2	Then the Sabbath came around. In the synagogue, He began To teach all the people there. Many who heard Him were amazed. Questions they began to air.

"From where did these things come to Him?
What's this wisdom He's acquired?
And why is it that by His hands
Such miracles have transpired?

6:3 Is this One, not the carpenter?
Is not Mary His mother?
And are not James, Joses, Judas,
And Simon each His brother?

"Aren't His sisters here before us?
So, from where have extended
All these things to this one person?"[169]
In Him, they were offended.

6:4 "A prophet is not dishonored,"
To these people Jesus told,
"Save in his town by relatives
And by those in his household."

6:5 Except on a few who were sick,
No miracle could He enact.
He laid His hands on just these few,
6:6 Being shocked by the faith they lacked.

Jesus began going around
To the villages to teach.
He made His way in a circle
So each village He would reach.*

6:7 He summoned the Twelve and began
To send them all out by twos,
And over the unclean spirits
He gave them power to use.

6:8 "Take nothing for the road," He charged,
"Except just the staff you hold -
No bread, no bag, and in your belt
Not any silver or gold.

6:9 "But wear the same pair of sandals
As on the road you proceed,*
And do not bring two sets of clothes.
You are wearing all you need."*

6:10 He was also saying to them,
"In each town, no matter where,
Stay in the house you first enter
'Til the time you leave from there.

6:11 "If a town listens not to you,
And you, they do not receive,
Then as a witness against them,
Do this thing after you leave:

"Shake the dust from under your feet
That collected from that place."*
6:12 They went out and were announcing
That repentance all embrace.

6:13 Many demons, they were casting out.
With many sick, they were dealing
As they anointed them with oil,
All of which, they were healing.

6:14	Then King Herod heard about this,
	For Jesus's name had spread.
	Some were saying, "John the Baptist,
	He has risen from the dead!
	"That's why there is working in Him
	All these miracles *we see."
6:15	Some other people were saying,
	"Elijah, this One must be."
	And still others were concluding
	From His miraculous powers,*
	"He's a prophet similar to
	One of those prophets of ours."
6:16	After Herod heard these reports,
	He began saying *with dread,
	"John whom I decapitated
	Has been raised up from the dead!"
6:17	For Herod had sent and grabbed John
	And jailed him and had him chained
	Because his brother Philip's wife,
	Herodias, he had gained.
	After Herod had married her,
6:18	Him, John would often confront.
	"It's not lawful for you to have
	Your brother's wife." *He was blunt.

6:19   Now, against John, Herodias
Was holding a giant grudge.
She wished to kill him but could not
Because Herod would not budge.*

6:20   For Herod was afraid of John,
For of him he was assured
To be both righteous and holy.
So, his safety he secured.

Many times he became perplexed
Whenever him, he heard,
Yet gladly Herod would listen
To John the Baptist's word.

6:21   One day, opportunity knocked.
On his birthday, Herod then
Threw a feast for his lords and chiefs
And Galilees' leading men.

6:22   Then Herodias's daughter
Entered and danced *before all.
Not only Herod, did she please
But those in the dining hall.

He told the girl, "Request from me
Whatever you desire,
And I will grant you your request.
I will give as you require.♦

6:23   He even made a vow to her,
"I will give what you request,
Up to one-half of the kingdom
Which I myself have possessed.

6:24 She went out and asked her mother,
      "What request should I then list?"
      Her mother replied back to her,
      "The head of John the Baptist."

6:25 She at once rushed back to the king.
      She petitioned, "Here's my wish:
      Bring the head of John the Baptist
      To me right now on a dish."

6:26 Then becoming extremely sad
      Due to the vow he did choose
      And because of those dining there,
      Her, he wished not to refuse.

6:27 He sent an executioner
      To bring John's head as stated.
      The man left, and in the prison,
      John, he decapitated.

6:28 Then the executioner brought
      On a dish the head of John.
      He presented it to the girl.
      The girl gave it to her mom.

6:29 After the disciples of John
      Heard *about John's deathly doom,
      They went and took away his corpse,
      And they placed it in a tomb.

6:30	The apostles came to Jesus,
	Assembling themselves as one.
	They reported all things to Him,
	All they had taught and had done.
6:31	Then He told them, "Rest in private.
	To a deserted place retreat."
	For many were coming and going,
	Leaving no good time to eat.
6:32	So, they went in the boat alone
	To an isolated place,
6:33	Yet the people saw them leaving,
	And many knew them by face.
	The people from all the cities
	Ran together on land *and strived
	To reach the place they were going,
	And before them they arrived.
6:34	When Jesus got out of the boat,
	He saw the large multitude,
	And for them He felt compassion
	Because *of how them, He viewed.
	They were like sheep who did not have
	A shepherd *to be their guide.
	Therefore, to the large multitude
	Many teachings, He applied.

6:35	When it was already quite late,
	To Him His disciples stated,
	"The hour is already quite late,
	And here we're isolated.
6:36	"Release the crowd that they may go
	To the fields and towns about
	And buy for themselves food to eat
	And not have to go without."*
6:37	"You must give them something to eat."
	In reply to them, He said.
	They answered Him, "Two hundred days
	Of wages would buy them bread.
	"Should we go and buy this much bread
	And feed them as You decree?"
6:38	He said to them, "Just how much bread
	Do you have right now? Go see."
	And when they learned how much they had,
	They reported the amount.
	"We have five loaves and just two fish.
	That is all that we could count."*
6:39	He ordered them that all recline
	In groups on the grass of green.
6:40	In groups of hundreds and fifties,
	The crowd on the grass did lean.
6:41	He took the five loaves and two fish
	And looked up into the sky.
	He then gave thanks and broke the loaves
	And handed out the supply.

To the disciples, He would give
As they kept giving out bread,
And He divided the two fish
Among all *'til they were fed.

6:42 Everyone ate and became full.
6:43 So, they gathered, *while still grouped,
The leftover bread and the fish.
Twelve basketsful they recouped.

6:44 There were five thousand men who ate
The loaves of bread *and the fish.
6:45 That His disciples board the boat
Was His immediate *wish.

Jesus forced them to go ahead,
Without a delay allowed,
And cross over toward Bethsaida
While He sent away the crowd.

6:46 After everyone had left Him,
Jesus Himself went away.
He went up into the mountain
In order that He might pray.

6:47 By the time evening had arrived,
The boat was in the sea's midst.
Jesus was alone on the land
6:48 And saw them strain *but persist.

They were rowing against the wind.
He walked toward them on the sea
About the fourth watch of the night
Which was sometime after three.♦

	He was wanting to pass them by,
6:49	But when Jesus, they did spot
	Walking on the sea, they cried out,
	For He was a ghost, they thought.

6:50 They all saw Him and were disturbed,
But He spoke with them right then.
Jesus said, "Be of good courage.
It's I. Fear no more, *O men."

6:51 He climbed into the boat with them.
Then the wind no longer blew.
They were completely astonished,
For they did not have a clue.♦

6:52 They did not understand at all
What had happened in regard
To the loaves *that were multiplied,
But their hearts had become hard.

6:53 They came into Gennesaret
Once they crossed over to shore.
They anchored there and left the boat,
But men knew Him *from before.[170]

6:54 Instantly, they recognized Him.
6:55 'Round that whole country, they ran.
They placed on pallets the ailing.
To bring the sick, they began.

Wherever they heard that He was,
To Him the sick they'd bring out -
6:56 In villages, cities, or fields,
Whatever place in His route.

They put them at the marketplaces
And begged that they'd be assured
To touch the fringe of His garment,
And all who touched Him were cured.

7:1   Now the Pharisees, with some scribes
      Who from Jerusalem came,
      Gathered themselves before Jesus
      So as to accuse and to shame.*

7:2   They saw some of His disciples
      Eating bread with unclean hands,
      That is to say, they were not washed
      As their tradition demands.*

7:3   For Pharisees and all the Jews
      Don't eat, save this condition,
      They wash their clenched[171] hands so to hold
      To the elders' tradition.

7:4   After coming from the market,
      They don't even eat unless
      They immerse their hands in water.
      Many other things *they stress.

      These many things which they observe,
      They received *as down it did pass,
      Such as the immersions of cups,
      And pitchers, and bowls of brass.

7:5	The Pharisees and scribes asked Him, "Why do Your disciples tread Against the elders' tradition And with unclean hands eat bread?"
7:6	He said, "Isaiah prophesied About you hypocrites well. As his words have been recorded, These words to you, I now tell:*
	"'This people honors Me with their lips, But far from Me is their heart.
7:7	They worship in vain, and as doctrines, Man-made commands, they impart.'
7:8	"You hold to human tradition By forsaking God's command.
7:9	God's directives, you displace well That your tradition might stand.
7:10	"'Honor your father and mother.' Moses said this. *Don't defy. He also said, 'He who reviles Father or mother must die.'
7:11	"But you say this: 'If a man says To his father or mother, *Whatever from me you might gain* *Is Corban*[172] **to God, no other* -'
7:12	"You don't let him do anything For his parents any more,
7:13	Rendering void the word of God By your tradition, therefore.

"You pass down this law of Corban,
And so from God's word you drift,*
And you do many things like these."
(The word corban just means gift.)

7:14   After calling the crowd again,
These words to them, He began,
"All of you keep listening to Me
And work hard to understand.

7:15   "Nothing from outside of the man
Which enters him can defile,
But that which goes out of the man
Corrupts the man all the while."[173]

7:17   As soon as He entered the house
Away from the crowded scene,
His disciples were asking Him
What the parable might mean.

7:18   He said to them, "Understanding,
Do you yourselves lack also?
All which enters the man from outside
Can't defile him, don't you know?

7:19   "For it goes not into his heart
But the stomach, ♦then the latrine,
Thus going into the sewer."
(He was making all foods clean.)

7:20   Now, He continued telling them,
"It is the things that proceed
Out of the man that defile him,
Every kind of sinful deed.♦

7:21	"For from within the man's own heart,
	Evil thoughts, out they proceed:
	Fornications, thefts, and murders,
7:22	Adulteries, and forms of greed.
	"Wicked deeds, guile, lewdness, envy,
	Blasphemy, foolishness, pride -
7:23	All these evils defile the man
	As they come out from inside."

7:24	Now, from there He arose and went
	Into the border of Tyre.
	Knowledge of the house He entered,
	He wished that no one acquire.
	Yet to escape people's notice,
	He was unable to do,
7:25	But right away a woman came
	Who was a Greek, *not a Jew.[174]
	Because by an unclean spirit
	Her little daughter was bound,
	She came, once hearing where He was,
	And before His feet fell down.
7:26	Syro-Phoenician was her race,
	But her, this did not bother.*
	She was asking Him to cast out
	The demon from her daughter.

7:27	"First let the children be filled up." He said to her, *which meant "no." "It's bad to take the children's bread And it, to little dogs throw."
7:28	"But Lord!" she answered back to Him, "Even little dogs are able To eat the crumbs of the children Which fall under the table."
7:29	He said to her, "Be on your way Because of the word you said. The demon is gone from your girl. Back to your house, you can head."*
7:30	After she went into her house, Her little daughter she found Lying in bed, and by the demon, No longer was she bound.
7:31	From Tyre's border through Sidon To Galilee's Sea, He went. To the middle of Decapolis, He again made His ascent.[175]
7:32	They brought him a talking deaf man Who was hard to understand. They were begging that upon him He would lay His healing hand.
7:33	Taking him aside from the crowd, Into the man's ears He flung The ends of* His fingers, and next, With His spit He touched his tongue.

7:34	He then looked up into the sky, And very deeply He sighed. He said to the man "Ephphatha" Which means "to open up wide."
7:35	Instantly, his ears were opened. His tongue was fully released. Then he began speaking clearly. His impediment had ceased.♦
7:36	Jesus specifically charged them That to share this they refrain. However, the more He charged them, Then the more they would proclaim.
7:37	"He has performed all things so well." They'd say, overcome with awe. "He even makes the deaf to hear And the mute speak *without flaw."

8:1	In those days, there was once again A large crowd having no food. He called the disciples and said,
8:2	"I pity this multitude.
	"Because for three days already They all with Me have remained, And now they have nothing to eat. To dismiss them,* I've refrained.*

8:3	"If I release them to their home As hungry as they all are, They will surely faint on the way, And some have come from afar."
8:4	His disciples replied to Him, "Just where can anyone head Around here in this desert place To fill these people with bread?"
8:5	"Add up the loaves among yourselves."* To His disciples He said. "How many loaves do you possess?" They voiced, "Seven loaves of bread."
8:6	Then He gave orders to the crowd That they recline on the ground. He took the loaves and then gave thanks. He broke them to pass around. He was giving His disciples Pieces of bread to hand out. In turn, they would take the pieces And give to the crowd about.
8:7	They also had a few small fish. Thanksgiving for these He said. He ordered them to give those out. The crowd ate both fish and bread.
8:8	They ate until they were filled up, And then, *from the multitude Seven large baskets were filled up With all the leftover food.

8:9 As for the number of people,*
     There were four thousand or so.
     Once the leftovers were gathered,*
     Jesus then let the crowd go.

8:10 Then at once, with His disciples
     He boarded the boat and went
     Into Dalmanutha's borders,
     And a short time, there He spent.*

8:11 The Pharisees came and began
     To argue with Him and pressed
     For a sign from heaven by Him
     So that Him, they then might test.

8:12 And then, within His own spirit,
     He gave a tremendous sigh.
     He said, "This generation seeks
     For a certain sign. But why?

     "I'm telling you the truth on this,
     That if this generation
     Will be given a sign by Me –"
     He paused His explanation.[176]

8:13 He left them and boarded again.
     Across the sea they did head.
8:14 But the disciples neglected
     To bring along loaves of bread.

     Except for just one loaf of bread,
     They had no food in the boat.
8:15 He was warning them by saying,
     "Of leaven take careful note.

	"The Pharisees' leaven and Herod's,
	Away from it you must head."
8:16	Among themselves they were saying
	That they had no loaves of bread.

8:17	Aware of this, He said to them,
	"Why are you discussing this,
	Namely, that you've no loaves of bread?
	Is your learning still amiss?

	"Do you still lack understanding?
	Of rocks, do your hearts comprise?
8:18	Are you not seeing or hearing
	Although you have ears and eyes?

8:19	"Don't you recall? Five loaves I broke
	For five thousand *to be fed.
	How many baskets did you fill
	With all the leftover bread?"

	They said, "Twelve." He said, "With four loaves
8:20	The four thousand were then fed.
	By you, how many large baskets
	Were filled with leftover bread?"

	They said to Him, "Seven baskets."
8:21	This question, He then did air:
	"Do you all still not understand
	Of what leaven to beware?"*177

8:22	Next, they came into Bethsaida.
	To Him a blind man, some brought.
	They urged Jesus to touch the man.
	His healing, these people sought.*

8:23	Taking the blind man by the hand,
	Outside the village they paced.
	He spat into both of his eyes,
	And on him His hands, He placed.
	Then Jesus asked him if there was
	Anything that he could see.
8:24	He looked and said, "I'm seeing men
	But each as a walking tree."
8:25	Then He placed His hands on his eyes
	Again, ♦as He did before.
	Then the blind man focused his gaze.
	His sight, Jesus did restore.
	For he was seeing everything
	Clearly as he looked around.
8:26	Jesus sent him straight to his house
	And said, "Don't enter the town."

8:27	Jesus with His disciples went
	To the villages about
	In Caesarea Philippi.
	He questioned them on the route.
	"Who do people say that I am?"
8:28	"John the Baptist, *we've been told.
	Some say Elijah. Others say
	One of the prophets *of old."

8:29	"But who do you say that I am?" This question to all, He did bring. In reply, Peter said to Him, "You're the Christ. ◆You are God's king."
8:30	Then He charged them that about Him They talk to no one at all.
8:31	Then Jesus began to teach them What to Him would soon befall.*
	"The Son of Man must suffer much, Be rejected and killed by scribes And by chief priests and by elders, Yet after three days, He'll rise."
8:32	He was speaking the word plainly. Then Peter took Him aside And proceeded to rebuke Him For the teaching He supplied.*
8:33	He turned and viewed His disciples, Then rebuked Peter and said, "Get behind Me, adversary![178] To opposition, you've sped.◆
	"For you are not thinking at all On the things that are of God. You are only thinking about The things that people applaud."
8:34	Then Jesus called the crowd over To join His disciples there. As to what a follower is,* He was making them aware.*

He said to them, "Let us suppose
My follower one wants to be.
He must deny self, lift his cross,
And continue following Me.

8:35 "For he who wants to save his life,
It's destruction he will pave.
He who destroys his life for Me
Or the gospel, his life he'll save.

8:36 "For what does it profit a man
If the whole world, he acquires,
Yet *at the end of that process,
That man's own life, this expires?

8:37 "Or *to put it another way,
Just what might a person give
As an exchange for his own life?
What is worth more than to live?*

8:38 "For all who are ashamed of Me
And of the words that I say
In the sinful and adulterous
Generation of this day -

"The Son of Man will also be
Ashamed of that one, *I say,
When He comes with holy angels
In His Father's glory *one day."

9:1 He also said, "I speak the truth.
Some standing here this hour
Will not taste death until they see
God's kingdom arrived in power."

9:2	After six days, Jesus then took
	Peter, also James and John.
	He brought them up a high mountain.
	With them, no others had gone.[179]
	He became transformed before them.
9:3	His white clothes shined very bright.
	No launderer on earth could make
	A piece of clothing as white.
9:4	Two men,* Elijah with Moses
	To the disciples appeared.
	They were conversing with Jesus.
	This thought, Peter volunteered:
9:5	"Rabbi, it's good that we are here.
	Three tabernacles will do:
	One for Moses, one for Elijah,
	And let us make one for You."
9:6	For he knew not how to respond,
	For they were all terrified.
9:7	Then a cloud overshadowed them.
	A voice came forth from inside.
	From the cloud these words were given:
	"This person, He is My Son.
	This is He whom I dearly love.
	Listen to Him, everyone."

9:8	Suddenly, as they looked around,
	They could not see anywhere
	Anybody any longer.
	Just Jesus was with them there.
9:9	Now, as they came down the mountain,
	He charged them not to relate
	To anyone the things they saw
	Before a specific date.*
	'Til the time that the Son of Man
	Would resurrect from the dead,
	They were not to tell anyone,
9:10	And they did as Jesus said.
	The phrase "resurrect from the dead,"
	Of its meaning they conversed.
9:11	Then they asked Him, "Why do the scribes
	Say Elijah must come first?"
9:12	"Elijah indeed, coming first,
	Restores all things." Jesus said.
	"But how should what has been written
	Of the Son of Man *be read?
	"He'll suffer much and be despised.
9:13	So, I say, Elijah's come.
	They did to him what they wanted
	As was written of that one."
9:14	When they came to the disciples,
	A large crowd around them, they saw,
	Also scribes arguing with them.
9:15	In seeing Jesus, there was awe.

At once the whole crowd ran to Him,
Giving Him salutations.

9:16 He asked the scribes, "Why with My men
Do you have disputations?"

9:17 One from the crowd replied to Him,
"Teacher, I brought You my son
Who has a spirit within him
That makes him mute, ♦makes him dumb.

9:18 "Wherever the spirit grabs him,
It throws him down to the ground.
He foams at the mouth, grinds his teeth,
And in stiffness he is bound.

"I told those disciples of Yours
To cast it out *of my son.
However, they were unable,
Although they all tried, each one."[180]

9:19 But in response to them, He said,
"O faithless generation,
To remain and put up with you,
What will be the duration?

"Bring this father's son here to Me."
9:20 So, to Him the son, they brought.
As soon as the spirit saw Him,
Its demonic work it wrought.*

The spirit caused him to convulse
As upon the ground he fell.
He began rolling all around,
Foaming at the mouth as well.

9:21   Then He questioned the boy's father,
          "Just how long do you recall
          This thing happening to your son?"
          He replied, "Since he was small.

9:22   "Often this demonic spirit
          Has propelled *my little boy
          Into fire and into waters
          So that him it might destroy.

          "But if there's something You can do,
          Come to our aid, *I implore,
          By demonstrating compassion
          On both of us *and restore!"

9:23   But Jesus told him, "'If You can!'
          To faith you are not cleaving.*
          But everything is possible
          To him who keeps believing."

9:24   Right then, the father of the boy
          Began crying out *in grief,
          "I do believe. *I do believe.
          But please help my unbelief."

9:25   When Jesus saw the crowd running
          Gathering together again,
          He rebuked the unclean spirit,
          Telling it these words right then:

          "You unclean spirit who shuts ears
          And is making this boy dumb,
          You aren't to enter him again.
          I charge you, out of him come."

9:26	With shouting and much convulsing, It came out *as specified. He became so much like a corpse That many were saying, "He died."
9:27	But Jesus *immediately Took hold of him by his hand And proceeded to lift him up. Then to his feet, he did stand.
9:28	After Jesus entered a house Without the public about, His disciples were asking Him, "Why could we not cast it out?"
9:29	He said to them, "That for this kind To come out of anywhere, It is in no way possible Except in the realm of prayer."[181]

9:30	They began, once they left from there, To travel through Galilee, Yet He did not want anyone To learn of where they might be.
9:31	For He was teaching His disciples, And He was saying to them, "The Son of Man is being given Over to the hands of men.

"And they will kill the Son of Man,
Yet though the Son of Man dies,*
Though they kill Him successfully,
After three days, He will rise."

9:32   But they were not comprehending
The message that Jesus taught,
And they were too scared to ask Him.
To question Him, they did not.♦

9:33   They came into Capernaum,
And into the house they went.
He asked them that while on the road
What had been their argument.

9:34   But they were keeping their mouths shut,
For each played a debater
Among themselves while on the road
As to which of them was greater.

9:35   Jesus sat down and told the Twelve,
After to them He did call,
"If one wants to be first, he must
Be last and servant to all."

9:36   He took and stood a little child
In their midst in their session.
Then He took the child in His arms
And to them taught this lesson:

9:37   "Whoever welcomes one of these
Little children in My name,
That person is welcoming Me.
Welcome these children the same.*

        "And if anyone welcomes Me
        (Listen to this truth that I tell),*
        They are not just welcoming Me
        But the One who sent Me *as well."

9:38   "Teacher," John began asking Him,
        We saw someone in Your name
        Casting out demonic spirits,
        And him, we worked to restrain.

        "Since he was not following us,
        This man, we tried to prevent."
9:39   But Jesus said, "Don't hinder him
        Since Me, he does represent.*

        "For no one works a miracle
        In My name who then will do
        An immediate turnaround
        And speak evil of Me too.

        "So, do not try to stop this man,
9:40   For whoever does not stand
        Against us is really for us.
        Therefore, do as I command.*

9:41   "For truly he who gives to you
        A cup of water in accord
        To the name that you are of Christ
        Will never lose his reward.

9:42   "Whoever causes little ones,
        Even if just one of these,
        Who are believers to stumble,
        He's better off in the seas.

"It would be good if a millstone
That by a donkey is run
Had been placed around his own neck
While into the sea he's flung.

9:43 "If your one hand keeps causing you
To stumble *into some wrong,
Then cut it off *from your body.
To you let it not belong.*

"It's good that you enter life maimed
Than to go with the entire
Set of two hands in Gehenna,
Into the undying fire.[182]

9:45 "If your one foot keeps causing you
To stumble into some wrong,
Then cut it off *from your body.
To you let it not belong.*

"It is good that you enter life
In the condition called lame
Than to be thrown with both your feet
Into Gehenna's flame.

9:47 "And if your one eye keeps causing you
To stumble into some wrong,
Then gouge it out *of its socket.
To you let it not belong.

"It's good to enter God's kingdom
As one-eyed *being your name
Than to be thrown with both your eyes
Into Gehenna's flame.

9:48	"For in the words of Isaiah,[183] 'Their maggot, it never dies, And the fire, it is never quenched But continues to agonize.*
9:49 **9:50**	"For all will be salted by fire,[184] And you know that* salt is good, But if salt's no longer salty, How will it salt *as it should? "Keep having salt within yourselves, For you know that salt is good.* Keep the peace with one another, Being salty as you should."*

10:1	Then He arose from there and went Into the Judean land And beyond the Jordan River. The crowds began to expand. They gathered again before Him, And as He had done before, He began teaching them again.
10:2	Then Pharisees took the floor. They began to question Jesus If it was lawful *or not For a man to divorce a wife To test Him in what He taught.

10:3	"Moses told you what?" He replied.
10:4	"Moses allowed," they did say,
	"That one write a bill of divorce
	And then send his wife away."
10:5	Jesus told them, "For your hard hearts
	This command to you, he wrote.
10:6	But from the start of creation
	What God intended, I'll quote.*
	"'As male and female, He made them.
10:7	Due to this, a man must leave
	Both his father and his mother,
	And to his wife he must cleave.¹⁸⁵
10:8	"'The two will then become one flesh.'
	Therefore, a man and his wife♦
	Are not two *separate entities
	But one flesh *while they have life.
10:9	So, in light of what Scripture says,¹⁸⁶
	Whatever God has united,
	Is not lawful for any man
	To have the same divided."
10:10	Inside the house, the disciples
	Were asking Him once again
	About the matter *of divorce.
10:11	So, He said this to the men:
	"Whoever marries another
	After sending his wife away
	Is committing adultery
	Against his first wife, *I say.

10:12   "If a wife marries another
After sending her man away,
She then commits adultery
By her new union, I say."*

10:13   They were bringing Him small children
So that them, Jesus might touch.
But the disciples seeing this
Began to rebuke them much.

10:14   Jesus became irate and said,
When He saw this occurring,
"Let these small children come to Me.
Them, do not be deterring.

"Because God's kingdom is comprised
Of ones who are of such kind.
10:15   I am telling you all the truth
As to whom it is assigned.*

"Anyone who does not receive
The kingdom of God, *I say,
With the mind of a little child,
Will enter it in no way."

10:16   Then the little children, He took
Into His arms ◆and embraced.
He began blessing each of them
As on them His hands, He placed.

10:17　　As He proceeded on the road,
　　　　 Up to Him one person ran
　　　　 And knelt down right in front of Him.
　　　　 To question Him, he began.

　　　　 "Good teacher, what thing should I do
　　　　 So that I might inherit
　　　　 That life which is called eternal?
　　　　 How will this life, I merit?"*

10:18　　Then Jesus answered back to him,
　　　　 "You label Me good, but why?
　　　　 No one is good except for one,
　　　　 And that is God *the Most High.

10:19　　"You know what the commandments are:
　　　　 'Do not murder anyone;
　　　　 Do not commit adultery;
　　　　 Stealing must never be done.

　　　　 "'Don't give a false testimony;
　　　　 No one are you to defraud;
　　　　 Honor your father and mother.'
　　　　 These commandments are from God."*

10:20　　But this man was telling Jesus,
　　　　 "Teacher, since I was a youth,
　　　　 All these commands, I have observed.
　　　　 I am telling you the truth."*

10:21　　Jesus took a good look at him
　　　　 And loved him by this one act[187]
　　　　 Of telling him what was needed.
　　　　 "There is one thing you have lacked.

"Go sell all the things you possess.
Give to those in poverty,
And you'll have treasure in heaven.
Then come here and follow Me."

10:22 But he was saddened by this word
And left there very distressed,
For he was a man of great wealth.♦
Much property, he possessed.

10:23 Jesus said to His disciples
After looking all about,
"The rich will enter God's kingdom
With difficulty *no doubt."

10:24 They were astonished by these words.
Then Jesus again said this:
"To enter God's kingdom, children,
O how difficult it is.

10:25 "It's much simpler for a camel
To go through a needle's eye
Than for the wealthy to enter
The kingdom of the Most High."[188]

10:26 They became greatly astonished
And to one another raved,
"How is it even possible
For anyone to be saved?"

10:27 Then Jesus looked at them and said,
"Impossible with mankind
But not with God because all things
God can do *if so inclined."

10:28	Peter then was saying to Him, "Of us take a careful view. We ourselves have left everything And have followed after You."
10:29	Jesus said, "I tell you the truth. There is no person as such Who's sacrificed and won't receive One hundred times as much.[189]
	"The one who's left parents,[190] or kids, Siblings,[191] or houses, or fields For My sake and the gospel's sake, A great reward, this all yields.*
10:30	"One hundred times the parents and kids, Siblings, and houses, and fields One will gain now in this season. With persecution, it yields.
	"In the next age, eternal life, This person will inherit,
10:31	But many first ones will be last And last ones, first. *I swear it."[192]

10:32	They were traveling on the road, Going up to Jerusalem. Jesus was at the very front. To there He was leading them.

The Poetic Gospel of Mark

           The disciples were astonished,
           And those following were afraid.
           He took the Twelve aside again,
           And to them this, He relayed.

           He began to tell them the things
           That were about to occur
           While being in Jerusalem,
           The things that He would endure.*

10:33   "Look, we're going to Jerusalem,
           But soon after He arrives,*
           The Son of Man will be given
           To the chief priests and the scribes.

           "And they will sentence Him to death.
           To Gentiles Him, they'll betray.
10:34   They will mock Him and spit on Him,
           And will scourge Him *that same day.

           "And last of all, they will kill Him.
           Yes, they will put Him to death,♦
           But after three days, He will rise.
           Yes, He will be given breath."♦

10:35   Now James and John, Zebedee's sons,
           Came before Him and expressed,
           "We wish that You would do for us
           Whatever we might request."

10:36   Jesus replied, "What do you wish
           For Me to do for you two?"
10:37   "Grant us to sit in Your glory,
           Each on either side of You."[193]

10:38 Jesus told them, "What you're asking
       Sinks not into your thinking.
       Are you able to drink the cup
       Which I Myself am drinking?

       "Are you able to be baptized
       With the baptism of this kind,
       The one I'm being baptized with
       As the Father has assigned?"[194]

10:39 They said to Him, "We are able."
       But Jesus to them did tell,
       "The cup I Myself am drinking,
       You also will drink as well.

       "In regards to the baptism
       With which I'm being immersed,
       You'll also be baptized with it.
       Of this you are now well versed.*

10:40 "But to sit on My right or left
       By Me cannot be declared,
       But it is exclusively for
       Those whom it has been prepared."

10:41 When the other ten heard all this,
       They began to be irate
       At James and John *on this matter.
10:42 Jesus called them and did state:

       "The people who are considered
       The rulers of the nations
       Lord it over those whom they rule.
       You know these observations.

	"And those who are considered great
	Exert their authority,
10:43	But as it pertains among you,
	This is not how it's to be.

"All who wish to be great among you
Must as your servant behave.
10:44 All who wish to be first among you
Must be everybody's slave.

10:45 "Even the Son of Man did not
Come to be served by any
But to serve and to give His life
As a ransom for many."

10:46 Next they came into Jericho,
But as He was going out
With His disciples and a big crowd,
A beggar began to shout.*

Bartimaeus, Timaeus's son,
Was this loud beggar's name,*
He was sitting beside the road.
Now his blindness *was his fame.

10:47 He heard that Jesus the Nazarene
Was about to pass right by.
"Jesus, Son of David, pity me!"
The blind man began to cry.

10:48	But in order to silence him,
	Their rebuke, many did pour.
	"Son of David, have mercy on me."
	He shouted out even more.
10:49	Jesus stood still and said, "Call him."
	They called the blind man and said,
	"He's calling you. So now get up.
	Have courage ♦and don't have dread."
10:50	And after throwing down his coat,
	He sprang right up to his feet
	And then made his way to Jesus
	So that Him he might entreat.*
10:51	Jesus said in reply to him,
	"What do you wish that I do?"
	The blind man replied back to Him,
	"Rabbi, that my eyes might view."
10:52	"Go! Your faith has rescued you,"
	Jesus to the blind man told.
	Immediately, he could see
	And followed Him on the road.
11:1	As they approached Jerusalem,
	They stopped about two miles out,*
	At Bethphage and at Bethany
	Nearby Olivet, the Mount.
	He sent two of His disciples,
11:2	Telling them, "Enter the town,
	The one that is opposite you.
	As you enter, *look around.

        "At once, you'll find a colt tied up
        On which no person has sat.
        Untie the colt and bring it here
        From wherever it is at.*

11:3   "If any person says to you,
        'Why this, do you *commandeer?'
        Say, 'The Lord, He has need of it.'
        Right then, he'll send it back here."

11:4   They went and found a colt tied up
        Out in the street by a door.
        As they untied it, standing there
        Were some *who would not ignore.

11:5   These began to question the two,
        "Why this colt do you untie?"
11:6   They told them just as Jesus said.
        So, they let the two pass by.

11:7   They brought the colt before Jesus,
        And their clothes on it, they flung.
        Then Jesus sat upon the colt,
        Never ridden and so young.*

11:8   Many spread their clothes in the road,
        But on the road, others laid
        Leafy branches cut from the fields.
        They all sang in a parade.*

11:9   Those leading and those following
        Were crying out in one accord,
        "Hosanna, how blessed is this One
        Who comes in the name of the Lord!

11:10	"Our father David's kingdom's blessed, The kingdom, Scripture foresees.[195] Hosanna in the highest heights." (Hosanna means 'Save us, please.')*
11:11	Jesus entered Jerusalem. To the temple courts, He went. He looked around at everything Until the day had been spent.*
	Because the evening had arrived And the hour already late, He went to Bethany with the Twelve So as to recuperate.*
11:12	They left the town of Bethany On the following day. Jesus began to hunger much While traveling on the way.*
11:13	Then from a good distance away, A fig tree with leaves, His eye caught. He went to find if there might be Any fruit on it or not.
	After coming to the fig tree, Nothing except leaves, He found, For 'twas not the season for figs.
11:14	He responded with this sound:
	"May nobody eat fruit from you Any longer in this age." The disciples were listening As He with this tree did engage.*

The Poetic Gospel of Mark

11:15   They came into Jerusalem.
        To the temple courts, He went.
        The seller and the buyers there,
        Out of the temple He sent.

        He overturned all the tables
        Of the moneychangers there,
        And the seats of those selling doves,
        He turned over, every chair.

11:16   He was also not allowing
        For anybody to haul
        Merchandise throughout the temple.
11:17   He was teaching this to all:

        "Is it not written that My house
        Will be called a house of prayer
        To all the people of the world?
        But for thieves you've made it a lair."

11:18   The chief priests and the scribes heard this.
        How to destroy Him, they sought,
        But they feared Him since the whole crowd
        Were amazed at what He taught.

11:19   Now, Jesus and His disciples
        Whenever it became late
        Exited outside the city.
        Then for morning, they would wait.*

11:20	It was early in the morning When they saw while passing by, The fig tree completely withered. From the roots up it was dry.
11:21	Peter told Him while recalling What happened the other day,* "Rabbi, look! The fig tree You cursed Completely withered away."
11:22	In reply, Jesus said to him, "Faith in God, keep possessing.
11:23	To you who exercise this faith,* This truth, I am expressing.
	"Whoever says to this mountain, 'Rise! Be thrown into the sea' And does not doubt within his heart But trusts what he speaks will be -
	"If a person of faith does this, Then for him, it will be done.
11:24	Because of this truth I've told you, I tell you another one.*
	"All for which you pray and request, Keep trusting that you've received, And it will be fulfilled for you Because you've truly believed.
11:25	"If you've something against someone Because they've hurt you some way,* Always practice forgiving them Whenever you stand to pray.

"This way your heavenly Father
Will forgive you for your wrongs
As soon as you commit those sins.[196]
Forgiveness to you belongs."♦

11:27   They returned to Jerusalem,
        But the chief priests, elders, and scribes
        (As He walked in the temple courts)
        Approached Him *to criticize.

11:28   They asked, "By what authority
        Do You do such things as these?
        Who gave You this authority
        To practice them. *Tell us, please."

11:29   Jesus told them, "Just one question,
        I will ask you all as well.
        If you answer Me, then My source
        Of authority I'll tell.

11:30   "John's baptism was from what source,
        From heaven or humanity?"
11:31   So, they reasoned among themselves
        As to what their answer should be.*

        "If we say that it's from heaven,
        To us He will then reply,
        'For what reason did you, therefore,
        Not believe him ♦and comply?'

11:32	"But should we say that it's from men?" (Of the crowd they had great fear, For John as a prophet indeed Was what the people held dear).
11:33	They answered Jesus, "We don't know." He said, "Then I won't tell you By what kind of authority That I do the things I do."
12:1	He began telling parables. He told them, "There was a man Who planted a massive vineyard. A wall around it, he ran.
	"The man dug out a trough for wine. A tower, he did erect. He leased it all out to farmers. Then on a journey, he left.
12:2	"Now, in the season of harvest, A slave *whom he selected, He sent to the farmers so that Some grapes might be collected.
12:3 **12:4**	"But seizing him, they beat the slave And with nothing, sent him back. Again, he sent another slave, But this slave, they did attack.♦
12:5	"They beat this one upon the head. They did not give him respect. Again, he sent another one. To kill him, they did elect.

| | "He also sent many others.
| | To some, a beating was done.
| | Others were killed by the farmers.
| 12:6 | Yet he had one left, a son.

| | "This son of his, he dearly loved.
| | He sent him last *to collect.
| | Reasoning to himself,* he said,
| | 'My son, they'll surely respect.'

| 12:7 | "These farmers said among themselves,
| | 'This person, he is the heir.
| | Come now. Let us put him to death.
| | The inheritance, we'll share.'

| 12:8 | "Once they grabbed the dearly loved son,
| | They killed him. Then him, they threw
| | Outside the vineyard *of the lord.
| 12:9 | What will the vineyard's lord do?

| | "He will come against the farmers
| | And destroy them 'til they're dead.
| | He'll give the vineyard to others.
| 12:10 | This Scripture, have you not read?

| | "'A stone the builders rejected
| | Became the capstone that ties.
| 12:11 | By the Lord this has come about.
| | It's marvelous in our eyes.'"

| 12:12 | They sought to grab Him yet feared the crowd,
| | For they knew that what He said
| | In the parable was against them.
| | So, leaving Him, off they sped.

12:13	Some Pharisees and Herodians Were sent to Him with the task Of trapping Him in a statement.
12:14	They came to Him and did ask:
	"Teacher, we know that You're truthful Since favorites You don't play. By no one are You influenced, But in truth You teach God's way.
	"Is it lawful to pay Caesar A personal tax or not? Should we pay, or should we refrain? Enlighten us with Your thought."*
12:15	But He knew their hypocrisy. "Why do you give Me this test? Bring to Me a coin to look at, A denarius." He pressed.
12:16	So, they brought one, and He asked them, "This image and what's inscribed, To what person do these belong?" "Caesar!" to Him they replied.
12:17	Jesus said this, which amazed them, "So that you won't be at odds,* Pay to Caesar what is Caesar's, And pay to God what is God's."

The Poetic Gospel of Mark

12:18   Then to Him came the Sadducees.
(These are the ones who promote
That there is no resurrection).
Moses, they began to quote.*

12:19   "Teacher, Moses wrote down for us
That if a man's brother dies
And leaves a wife yet leaves no child,
That the brother must arise.

"Since he is the dead man's brother,
He must make the wife his mate,[197]
And on behalf of his brother
Offspring, he is to create.

12:20   "Suppose there were seven brothers,
And the first one took a bride.
He did not leave any offspring.
They were childless♦ when he died.

12:21   "Then the second brother took her,
Yet no offspring, did she see.*
He died leaving her childless too,
And then likewise, brother three.

12:22   "All seven did not leave offspring.
Then lastly she died, the wife.
12:23   To which brother will she belong
In the resurrection life?"

12:24   In reply,* Jesus said to them,
"Yourselves, you surely defraud
Since you do not know the Scriptures
Or even the power of God.

12:25   "For when people rise from the dead,
They do not marry *their love.
They are not given in marriage,
But are like angels above.¹⁹⁸

12:26   "About the fact that the dead rise,
Have you not read concerning
The story in the book of Moses
Of the bush *that was burning?

"From the bush* God said to Moses,
'I'm the God of Abraham,
And of Isaac, and of Jacob.'
Notice that He said, 'I am.'

12:27   "He is not the God of the dead
But of those who are alive.
Therefore, you are very deceived,
Thinking the dead don't revive."*

12:28   One scribe who heard them discussing
Saw that He answered them well.
He came and asked, "Of all commands,
Which is the foremost. *Pray tell."

12:29   Jesus answered, "The foremost is:
'With your ears, O Israel, hear.
The Lord our God, the Lord is one.
Love for Him must be sincere.*

12:30   "'You are to love the Lord your God
With all your soul and your heart,
With all your mind and all your strength.
Love Him fully, not in part.*'

12:31	"The second is this: 'As yourself,
	You are to love your neighbor.'
	There is not another command
	Than these two which is greater."
12:32	The scribe told Him, "Well said, teacher.
	You speak the truth that He's one,
	And besides Him there's no other,
12:33	And love for Him must be done.
	"It must be done with the whole heart,
	With all understanding and strength.
	To love one's neighbor as one's self
	Is surely second in rank.*
	"For the commands to love the Lord
	And our neighbor, we must view
	As above all whole burnt offerings
	And every sacrifice too."
12:34	Jesus saw that he answered well
	And replied to him, therefore,
	"From God's kingdom, you are not far."
	To quiz Him, they dared no more.
12:35	As He taught in the temple courts,
	In reply this question, He framed,
	"The scribes say Christ is David's son.
	How can this verse be explained?
12:36	"David himself while inspired
	By the Holy Spirit wrote
	Of his relation to the Christ.*
	His words to you, I now quote.*

"He said, 'The LORD said to my Lord,
*At My right hand take Your seat
Until I put Your enemies
Completely beneath Your feet.'*

12:37 "David himself calls Christ his Lord.
So how is the Christ his son?"
The crowd heard Jesus with gladness
As He addressed everyone.*

12:38 In His teaching He was saying,
"For the scribes, keep watching out.
In their majestic flowing robes
They desire to walk about.

"In the marketplaces they long
For the respectful greetings.
12:39 They long to sit in the chief seats
At the synagogue meetings.

"At meals, they want the honored seats.
12:40 Widows' houses, they devour.
In pretense, they pray. They'll receive
A greater judgment *one hour."

12:41 Opposite the treasury box
Jesus sat so as to view
How into the treasury box
The crowd tossed their revenue.

Many people who were wealthy
Tossed in amounts that were great.
12:42 One poor widow threw in two coins.
One quadrans[199] this does equate.

12:43   Calling His disciples, He said,
"This widow tossed in much more
Than all who put in the treasury.
It's true because she is poor.

12:44   "For they gave from their abundance,
The poor widow, from her need.
She threw in everything she had,
Her whole livelihood *indeed."

13:1   As He went from the temple courts,
To Him one disciple told,
"Teacher, what magnificent stones
And what grand buildings! Behold!"

13:2   Jesus said to the disciple,
"Do you see these buildings grand?
Each stone from them will be brought down.
No stone on a stone will stand."

13:3   When He sat on Mount Olivet
With the temple courts in view,
These men questioned Him privately:
Peter, James, John, and Andrew.

13:4   "Tell us when these things will happen
And what sign is to infer
When all these things *You have spoken
Are just about to occur?"

13:5	"Watch out! Let no one deceive you."
	Jesus began to explain.
13:6	"Many will lead many astray,
	Coming to them in My name.
	"They will say to all, 'I'm *the Christ',
	And these, many will believe.*
	So I repeat,* be on your guard
	So that you, they won't deceive.
13:7	"Now, whenever you hear of wars
	Or news of wars, do not fear,
	For these things are necessary.
	The end is yet to appear.
13:8	"Nation will rise against nation,"
	Jesus went on to explain,*
	"Kingdom will rise against kingdom.
	Conflict will constantly reign.*
	"There will be famines that occur.
	There'll be quakes throughout the earth.
	These things are just the beginning
	Of the labor pains of birth.
13:9	"You yourselves be on the alert.
	They'll hand you to Jewish courts.
	In the synagogues, you'll be flogged.
	You'll be made to give reports.♦
	"Before leaders and kings you'll stand,
	All for the sake of My name,
	As a testimony to them,
	And the gospel, you'll proclaim.*

13:10 "To all the nations of the world,
Every people, tongue, and tribe,♦
The gospel has to first be preached,
And then the end will arrive.²⁰⁰

13:11 "When they put you under arrest
And to trial* lead you away,
Do not worry ahead of time
About the things you might say.

"But the words given you that hour,
Those words are to be testified,
For you are not the ones speaking
But the Holy Spirit *inside.

13:12 "Brother will betray brother to death,
A father, his child as well.
Children will put parents to death
As against them they rebel.

13:13 "You'll be hated by all people
Since for My name you've behaved,
But he who endures 'til the end
Is the one who will be saved.

13:14 "But when the abomination
Of desolation you see
Standing firm where it must not stand,
Let those in Judea flee.

"(Now let the reader understand,
Pertaining to this event
Of the abomination standing,*
As to what is really meant)*

"So, when this abomination*
Of desolation you see,*
At that time, into the mountains
Let those in Judea flee.

13:15 "As for the one on the housetop,
Don't let that one go back down
Or enter and gather up things.
Without delay, leave this town.*

13:16 "As for the person in the field,
Do not let that one return
In order to retrieve his coat
As a matter of concern.*

13:17 "But it will be a woeful time
For those pregnant in those days,
Also for those who are nursing
Their precious little babes.*

13:18 "But keep praying that in winter
This event won't be designed,
13:19 For there'll be a tribulation
In those days of such a kind -

"A kind which has not yet occurred
From the start of God's creation
Until now, and there'll never be
Such kind of tribulation.

13:20 "And if the Lord did not shorten
Those days *of tribulation,
Not a single one would be saved
From annihilation.

"But for the sake of the elect,
For those people whom He chose,
He has shortened the sum of days,
Bringing it to a close.♦

13:21 "If any tells you in that time,
'The Christ is right here, behold!'
Or 'Take a look! He's over there!'
Do not believe what you're told.

13:22 "Because false christs and false prophets
Will arise and will give out
Fantastic signs and great wonders,
But deception it's about.

13:23 "They do all these signs and wonders
For the purpose, if perchance,
To deceive the elect. Watch out!
I've told you this in advance.

13:24 "But this will occur in those days
After that tribulation:
The sun will grow dark, and the moon
Won't give its illumination.

13:25 "The stars will fall down from the sky.
Heaven's powers will be shaken.
13:26 Then they'll see the Son of Man,
And they won't be mistaken.*

"For they'll see coming in the clouds
The Son of Man *in plain view.
He'll come with power that is great,
And He'll come with glory too.

13:27 "Then He'll send angels to gather
The elect from the four winds,
From the borderline of the earth
To as far as the sky extends.

13:28 "Learn the lesson of the fig tree.
Whenever its leaves appear
With its branch already tender,
You know that summer is near.

13:29 "So also, whenever you see
These things *of which I foretold,
You know it[201] is near, at the doors.
13:30 This truth to you, I unfold:

"This generation won't pass by
Until all these things transpire.
13:31 Heaven and earth will pass away,
But My words will never expire.

13:32 "Now, concerning that day or hour,
By nobody is it known,
Not heaven's angels, not the Son,
But just the Father alone.

13:33 "So keep looking and keep watching,
For just when is the season?
You do not know when that time is.
Keep watching for this reason.*

13:34 "It's like a man out on a trip
Who left his house in the hands
Of his slaves, each having a task
To fulfill all his commands.*

	"He also told the gatekeeper
	To keep watch *'til his return.
13:35	Therefore, you keep watching as well,
	For that time, you cannot learn.

"You don't know when the house lord comes,
If it be evening or midnight,
Or if it be when the cock crows,
Or when it just becomes light.

13:36	"This way when he suddenly comes,
	He does not find you asleep.
13:37	So, what I tell you, I tell all.
	In watchfulness yourselves keep."

14:1	Now the feast of the Passover
	And of the Unleavened Bread
	Was only two more days away,
	And some wanted Jesus dead.*

The chief priests along with the scribes
Were seeking out all the while
How they would put Jesus to death
After grabbing Him in guile.

14:2	For they were saying in their plot,
	"We can't at the feast for sure,
	For an uproar by the people
	This possibly might allure."

14:3   And when He was in Bethany
       In Simon the leper's home,
       While He reclined, a woman came
       With a jar that she did own.

       It was made of alabaster.
       In it, pure spikenard was stored.
       She broke the jar. Then on His head
       The costly perfume, she poured.

14:4   Some were saying among themselves
       With much indignation stirred,
       "For what cause has this wastefulness
       Of costly perfume occurred?

14:5   "For more than three hundred denarii,
       This perfume could have been sold
       And distributed to the poor."
       So, her, they began to scold.

14:6   But Jesus said, "Leave her alone.
       Why on her are you so hard?
       She has done a beautiful deed
       By pouring on Me this nard.*

14:7   "The poor, you'll always have with you,
       And whenever you wish to be
       Benevolent to them, you can,
       But you will not always have Me.

14:8   "She used what she held *in her hand.
       For she took it ahead of time
       In preparation for burial
       To anoint this body of Mine.

14:9   "I speak the truth. In the whole world
           Wherever the gospel is spread,
           What this woman has also done
           In memory of her will be said."

14:10 Later, Judas Iscariot,
           One of the twelve, went away
           To the chief priests so that to them
           Jesus, he could betray.

14:11 The ones who listened became glad
           And promised that he'd be paid.
           He was seeking how the betrayal
           Could effortlessly be made.

14:12 The first day of the festival,
           Known as the Unleavened Bread,
           When the Passover lamb was killed,
           The disciples to Him said:

           "What place do You want us to go
           To make the preparation
           That You may eat the Passover?
           Where should be the location?♦"

14:13 He sent two of His disciples,
           And these two, He did direct,
           "Go from here into the city.
           With you, a man will connect.

"A pitcher containing water,
He will be carrying around.
Follow him wherever he goes
Until a dwelling is found.

14:14 "Where he enters, tell its owner,
'The teacher says, *Where's My room*
Where I may eat the Passover
With My own disciples soon?'

14:15 "An upper room that is quite large,
To you he then will reveal,
Fully furnished and made ready.
Prepare for us there the meal."

14:16 The two went out to the city,
Doing as Jesus declared.
They found all just as He told them.
The Passover, they prepared.

14:17 That evening He came with the Twelve.
14:18 He said as they sat and ate,
"One of you who's eating with Me
Will betray Me. Truth, I state."

14:19 They began to be moved with grief
And said to Him one by one,
"Certainly it's not me, is it?"
14:20 But He said to everyone:

"It's one of the twelve *apostles
Who dips with Me into the bowl,
14:21 For the Son of Man must depart
As is said of Him *in God's scroll.

              "But woe to that person through whom
              The Son of Man is betrayed.
              It would have been good for that man
              If he were not born *or made."

14:22   As they were eating, He took bread,
              Gave thanks, and the bread, He broke.
              He gave it to the disciples.
              "This is My body," He spoke.

              "Take and eat it." Then He gave thanks
14:23   After reaching for a cup.
              He then passed it around to them,
              And from it they all did sup.

14:24   He said to them, "This is My blood
              Of the covenant *that's new.
              This blood is poured out for many.
              There's one more truth to tell you.

14:25   "I tell you that from this time on
              That this produce of the vine,
              I by no means will drink from it
              Until *this specific time:

              "That day in the kingdom of God
              When I drink the produce new."
14:26   They (after singing together)
              Up Mount Olivet withdrew.

14:27   Then Jesus told them, "All of you
              Will be caused to trip and fall,
              For it is written in Scripture
              Which I now recite to all:

"'I'll strike down and kill the shepherd.'
(The speaker is the Lord God)*
'And as for the sheep of His flock,
They will be scattered abroad.'

14:28 "But after I'm resurrected,
Of you I will go ahead
Into the region, Galilee."

14:29 But to Him Peter then said:

"Even if everyone is caused
To stumble, ♦to trip and fall,
I will not be made to stumble.
It will not happen at all."♦

14:30 Jesus told him, "Here is the truth:
Today, on this very night,
Before a rooster crows two times,
Thrice you'll deny Me *outright."

14:31 "Even if I must die with You,
You, I'll in no way deny,"
Peter answered insistently.
They all gave the same reply.

14:32 To a place called Gethsemane,
Jesus along with them strolled.
"Sit here 'til I've finished praying,"
To His disciples He told.

14:33	Then He took with Him James and John,
	And Peter, He also brought.
	He began to be deeply grieved
	And to be very distraught.
14:34	"My soul is to the point of death
	Heavy with grief." He did say.
	Remain right here and keep watching."
14:35	He went a short ways away.
	He fell to the ground and then prayed
	That the hour would pass Him by
	If it was possible at all,
	But to God's will He'd comply.*
14:36	He was saying, "Abba, Father,
	This request to you, I pray.*
	All things are possible for You.
	This cup from Me, take away.
	"However, I am not praying
	According to My own will,
	But what I am really asking
	Is that Yours, You would fulfill."
14:37	He returned and found them sleeping.
	Simon Peter, He did scold,
	"Are you sleeping? Could you not watch
	For a single hour as told?
14:38	"That you don't fall to temptation,
	To watch and pray always seek.
	Indeed the spirit is willing,
	But the flesh is very weak."

14:39	He went away a second time
	And prayed, saying the same word.
14:40	He returned and found once again
	That to sleep they had deferred.

        For their eyes were very heavy,
        And they did not even know
        How they were to respond to Him.
        Their sleep, they could not forgo.*

14:41	The third time He came, He told them,
	"In the time left have you thrived
	In slumber and taking your rest?
	It's done. The hour has arrived.

        "The Son of Man's being betrayed
        Into sinners' hands, and lo!

14:42	He who betrays Me has drawn near.
	Now get up. Let us all go."
14:43	Right then Judas, one of the Twelve,
	Came as He gave this command.
	A large crowd accompanied him
	With both swords and clubs *in hand.

        Now the chief priests, scribes, and elders
        Sent along this multitude.

14:44	The one who was betraying Him
	Gave them a sign *to be viewed.

        He told them, "Whomever I kiss,
        That's the One. Him, you must take
        And lead away under your guard.
        Act when the signal I make."*

14:45	When Judas arrived on the scene,
	Jesus, he instantly faced.
	He said, "Rabbi!" Then he kissed Him.
14:46	Then on Him their hands they placed.

	They grabbed Him, but one standing by
14:47	Drew his sword, *showing no fear.
	He struck the slave of the high priest,
	Severing the slave's right ear.[202]

14:48	Responding, Jesus said to them,
	"Have you come to make a stand
	As against a thief and take Me
	With both swords and clubs *in hand?

14:49	"Every day in the temple courts
	I was with you as I taught,
	Yet did you try to capture Me?
	To attempt this,* you did not.

	"But this is so that the Scriptures
	Might be fulfilled *on this night."
14:50	Then all the disciples left Him
	And ran away *filled with fright.

14:51	A certain youth was trailing Him.
	Now a linen cloth he wore
	To cover up his nakedness.
	That was his clothing, no more.*

	The multitude went to grab him,
14:52	But their grasp, he did elude.*
	Leaving the linen cloth behind,
	He ran away in the nude.

The Poetic Scriptures of Six Writers

14:53   They led Jesus away from there
Into the high priest's sight.
All the chief priests, elders, and scribes
Gathered together that night.

14:54   Peter followed Him from afar
Inside the high priest's courtyard.
While warming himself by the fire,
He sat with those of the guard.

14:55   The chief priests and the whole Council
Sought the witness of many
Against Jesus to have Him die,
Yet were not finding any.

14:56   For against Him many people
Were falsely testifying,
Yet similar testimonies
Nobody was supplying.

14:57   Some even arose against Him,
Testifying with falsehood
Concerning the sanctuary*
Which they had misunderstood.*

14:58   "We heard Him say, 'I will tear down
This sanctuary man made.
In three days, I'll build another.
Without hands, it will be laid.'"

14:59	However, not even in this
	Did their testament agree.
14:60	Then the high priest stood in their midst
	And began his inquiry.
	He said to Jesus, "Do You not
	Answer with any reply?
	What are these charges against You
	That these people testify?"
14:61	He continued to be silent
	And did not give a reply.
	The high priest again questioned Him,
	Hoping He would testify.*
	He said to Him, "Are You the Christ,
	The Son of Him who is blessed?"
	This time Jesus was not silent.*
14:62	"That's who I am." He confessed.
	"You'll see the Son of Man sitting
	On the Powerful One's right,
	Coming on the clouds of heaven.
	The Son of Man, you will site."◆
14:63	Then the high priest tore his garments.
	"He has blasphemed!" was his cry.
	"What further need do we now have
	For others to testify?
14:64	"You all have heard the blasphemy.
	What do you all think?" he said.
	Then all the Council condemned Him
	As One worthy to be dead.

14:65 Then some began to spit on Him,
And they covered up His face
So He could not identify*
Who was inflicting disgrace.*

They were beating Him with their fists.
"Prophecy to us, disclose!"
The guards received Jesus with slaps.
He received numerous blows.*

14:66 Peter was in the yard below.
One maid of the high priest came
14:67 And noticed Peter *standing there
Warming himself *by the flame.

She looked at him and said, "You were
With Jesus the Nazarene."
14:68 But he denied it, "I don't know
Or understand what you mean."[203]

He went outside at the gateway
14:69 And again was detected.
The maid said to the bystanders,
"With them, he is connected."

14:70 Again he was denying it.
After a short duration,
Again the ones standing near him
Rang out an accusation.

"You there, are a Galilean!
You are one of them, therefore."
14:71 "I don't know this Man you speak of."
He said as he cursed and swore.

14:72   Then instantly, a rooster crowed.
            (Now this was the second time.)
            Peter was reminded right then
            That the crowing was the sign.*

            He recalled the words Jesus said,
            "Me three times, you will deny
            Before a rooster crows two times."
            He began to loudly cry.

15:1   Immediately, in the morning,
            After the chief priests made plans
            With the whole Council, elders, and scribes
            To put Jesus in Pilate's hands –

            They carried Jesus whom they bound.
            Him To Pilate, they handed.
15:2   "So, are You the King of the Jews?"
            Pilate asked, *being candid.

            In reply, He said to Pilate,
            "You said *that I am that King."
15:3   The chief priests began charging Him.
            Many charges they did bring.

15:4   Pilate again questioned Jesus,
            "Do you not answer a thing?
            Take note of how many charges
            That these men against you bring?"

15:5	But He answered no more questions
	So that Pilate was aghast.
15:6	Now, at the feast he'd hand to them
	One prisoner for whom they asked.
15:7	There was a man named Barabbas
	Who with rebels had been chained.
	These rebels committed murder
	When in revolt they campaigned.
15:8	The crowd came to Pilate and asked
	If he would do *at this feast
	Just as he did for them before.
15:9	"Who do you desire released?
	"Do you want the King of the Jews?"
	Pilate asked them in reply,
15:10	For he knew the chief priests brought Him
	Due to an envious eye.
15:11	But the chief priests stirred up the crowd
	In order that he instead
	Would release Barabbas to them.
15:12	Again, Pilate to them said:
	"Then what am I to do with Him,
	The King of the Jews, *this One?"
15:13	They yelled again, "Crucify Him."
15:14	He asked, "What wrong has He done?"
	Yet they cried out even louder,
	"Crucify Him! *Crucify!"
15:15	As for this crowd, Pilate had planned
	That them he would satisfy.

　　　　　He released to them Barabbas.
　　　　　Then after he had applied
　　　　　A scourge on Jesus, he then gave
　　　　　Him up to be crucified.

15:16　　Now the soldiers led Him away
　　　　　Inside the palace courtyard
　　　　　Which is called the Praetorium
　　　　　And called together the guard.

15:17　　They called their entire cohort.
　　　　　Jesus in purple they dressed.
　　　　　After weaving a thorny wreath,
　　　　　That wreath, upon Him they pressed.

15:18　　Then they began to salute Him,
　　　　　"Hail! King of the Jews," *they said.
15:19　　Then with a very sturdy reed,[204]
　　　　　They were striking at His head.

　　　　　They were also spitting on Him.
　　　　　Before Him, they were kneeling
　　　　　As if* they were worshipping Him.
　　　　　Mockery they were dealing.[205]

15:20　　They stripped Him of the purple clothes
　　　　　After they all had mocked Him.
　　　　　They put His own garments back on.
　　　　　Then out from there, they walked Him.

15:21　　They led Him to be crucified,
　　　　　But one man passing by there
　　　　　Who was coming from the country,
　　　　　The cross, they forced him to bear.

Simon of Cyrene was the man
Who had been that bystander.
He was the father of two boys,
Rufus and Alexander.

15:22 They brought Him to the location
Of Golgotha, as it's named,
A word that means "Place of the Skull,"
The Aramaic explained.*

15:23 They were trying to give Him wine
Along with myrrh mixed inside,
But He refused to take any.
15:24 Then Jesus, they crucified.

They divided among themselves
All of His clothes, *not just some.
To determine just who took what,
They cast a lot on each one.

15:25 Now it was nine in the morning[206]
When Jesus they crucified.
15:26 His formal charge, "King of the Jews"
Was the inscription supplied.

15:27 Then with Him there were crucified
Two men convicted of theft.
One was crucified on His right
And the other, on His left.[207]

15:29 The ones who were passing by Him,
Contempt they were displaying.◆
They were speaking evil of Him,
Wagging their heads and saying:

	"You who'd raze the sanctuary
15:30	And in just three days somehow
	Would rebuild it (Ha!), save Yourself!
	Come down from the cross *right now."

15:31 In the same way, the chief priests too
Were saying with all the scribes
In the face of one another
With taunting and♦ mocking cries:

"He saved others. As for Himself,
He cannot save anyhow.
15:32 Let Christ, the King of Israel
Come down from the cross right now.

"That way we might see with our eyes
And upon Him place our trust."
Those who were crucified with Him,
Abuses they too did thrust.

15:33 When the hour of noon had arrived,
The sunlight, something did block.*[208]
Darkness engulfed the entire land
'Til the hour of three o'clock.[209]

15:34 At three o'clock, Jesus cried out
"Eloi!" in a clear, loud tone.
"Eloi, lema sabachthani?"
The meaning needs to be known.*

It's meaning is, "My God, My God,
Why Me, have You forsaken?"
15:35 Now, some of the ones standing there
Heard Him *yet seemed mistaken.[210]

	They said, "Look! He calls Elijah."
15:36	A certain one of them raced
	And filled a sponge with sour wine.
	The sponge on a reed, he placed.

He began to give Him a drink.
"Allow this deed," was his plea.
"Let us see if Elijah comes
To take Him down from the tree."

15:37 But Jesus let out a loud cry.
All His breath from Him withdrew.
15:38 The sanctuary veil was torn
From top to bottom in two.

15:39 A centurion stood facing Him
As he saw Him die this way.
"This person was the Son of God.
It's true!" was all he could say.

15:40 There were also some women there.
From a distance was their view.
There were quite a number of them.*
There will just be named a few.*

Here are three:* Mary Magdalene;
Mary who was the mother
Of James the younger and Joses;
And Salome was the other.

15:41 In Galilee these three served Him
And followed Him everywhere.
Many women who came with Him
To Jerusalem were there.

15:42 When evening had already come
On the day of preparation,
The day before the Sabbath rest,
There came a solicitation.*

15:43 Joseph from Arimathea
Was a person of high rating
And one of the council members.
God's kingdom he was awaiting.

He came and entered with boldness
Before Pilate with the prayer
That the dead body of Jesus
Be given into his care.

15:44 But Pilate wondered if Jesus
By then had truly expired.
He summoned the centurion.
"Is He long dead?" he inquired.

15:45 As soon as Pilate learned the truth
From the centurion's word,
He handed over to Joseph
The body *to be interred.

15:46 Now Joseph had bought for Jesus
A fine linen cloth ♦or sheet.
He took Him down and in the cloth
Wrapped Jesus *from head to feet.

He placed Him in a certain tomb
Which had been hewn out of rock.
He rolled a stone against the tomb
So the entrance, it would block.

15:47	Now, where His body had been placed, Two of the women had seen, Mary the mother of Joses, Also Mary Magdalene.

16:1	After the Sabbath had elapsed, Salome and Mary of James Along with Mary Magdalene Bought spices for the remains. This was so that when they arrived They could anoint Him *in the cave.
16:2	It was the first day of the week When they arrived at the grave. Now it was extremely early When they arrived at the tomb, Just after the sun had risen, But a problem came to loom.*
16:3	They were asking one another, "Who will roll the stone away From the entrance point to the tomb On our own behalf *today?"
16:4	As they were talking,* they looked up. They saw the stone rolled away. Now, the stone was extremely large. They entered *without delay.

16:5   They saw a young man sitting down.
           In white clothing, he was dressed.
           Now, to their right he was seated.
           The women became distressed.

16:6   He said to them, "Don't be distressed.
           You seek Jesus the Nazarene,
           The One who had been crucified.
           He was raised *and has left this scene.

           "Behold the place where they put Him.
           Jesus is no longer here,
16:7   But go away and tell the news.
           There's no need for you to fear.*

           "Tell His disciples and Peter,
           'Before you, He goes ahead
           To Galilee where you'll see Him
           Just as to you, He had said.'"

16:8   Exiting, they ran from the tomb
           With fear yet great joy inside.
           They said nothing to anyone
           Because they were terrified.[211]

THE POETIC LETTER TO THE HEBREWS

1:1 Long ago, God spoke many times
And in many different ways
To the fathers in the prophets.
1:2 What about in these last days?

He spoke to us in the one Son
Whom as an heir He assigned
So as to inherit all things.
Through Him the world, God designed.

1:3 The Son radiates God's glory.
He is the exact imprint
Of the very nature of God,
And God, He does represent.◆

He sustains each and every thing
By the power of His voice.
The purification of sins
He has made *by His own choice.

After this purification,
The Son sat down on the right
Of Greatness in the high places,
Raised up to the highest height.♦

1:4 So much better than the angels,
The Son of Greatness became.
Therefore, He has inherited
A far more excellent name.

1:5 For to which one of the angels
Did the Lord God ever say:
"You Yourself are truly My Son.
I've begotten You today."?

Again, to which of the angels
Did this message ever come?
"I'll be to Him as a Father.
He'll be to Me as a Son."

1:6 Again, when He brought to the earth
The Firstborn, ♦He who's supreme,[212]
He said, "All the angels of God
With worship must Him esteem."

1:7 Now, He does say of the angels
In the Psalms He did inspire,[213]
"His messengers as winds, He makes,
His servants as flames of fire."

1:8 But of the Son, He says, "O God,
Your throne forever remains.
The staff You rule Your kingdom with,
Uprightness, it maintains.

The Poetic Letter to the Hebrews

1:9 "You've loved what's right, hated what's wrong.
So, with oil that makes one glad,
God Your God has anointed You
Above Your every comrade."

1:10 And He says, "At the beginning,
Lord, You established the earth.
The heavens are Your handiwork.
The universe, You did birth.♦

1:11 "The heavens and earth will perish,
But forever You will stay;
They'll become old as a garment,
1:12 And You will put them away.*

"You will roll them up as a cloak.
They will be changed like attire.
But You Yourself remain the same.
Your years will never expire."

1:13 Which of the angels has He told,
"At My right hand take Your seat
'Til I make Your enemies as
A footstool under Your feet."?

1:14 Are they not all serving spirits
Sent with the obligation
To serve the ones who are destined
To inherit salvation?

2:1 Therefore, it's essential for us
That more attention, we pay
To all the things which we have heard
So that we don't drift away.

2:2 For the word spoken through angels
Became established ♦and firm.
A just punishment, every sin
And rebellious deed did earn.

Since the aforementioned is true,
2:3 Punishment, how will we elude
If we neglect a salvation
Of such enormous magnitude?

This salvation received its start
When the Lord conveyed *the word.
It was then established for us
By the people who had heard.

2:4 By signs, wonders, and diverse powers
God also co-testified,
And gifts according to His will,
The Holy Spirit did provide.

2:5 For the occupied world to come
Which we are speaking about,
God did not put in subjection
To the angels. *Check Psalms out![214]

2:6	Someone witnessed somewhere saying,
	"Why do You keep man in mind?
	Why do You keep looking after
	The progeny[215] of mankind?

2:7	"You made him just below angels,
	With glory and honor, his wreath.
2:8	All things You subjected to him.
	His feet, You've placed them beneath."

        In subjecting all things to man,
        He's left nothing unsubjected.
        However, we don't see all things
        Under man's rule effected.

2:9	But there is One whom we now see
	Whom just below angels was made,
	Jesus who's been crowned with a wreath
	With glory and honor inlaid.

        He was given this victory wreath
        Since He suffered to the last breath[216]
        That by God's grace in place of all,
        He might experience death.

2:10	Because of God, all things were made,
	And by Him all things exist.
	So it was fitting for Jesus
	That through sufferings *He persist.

        Bringing many sons to glory,
        Through sufferings God perfected
        The leader of their salvation.
        Now they are all connected.*

2:11	For both the One who sanctifies
	And the people sanctified,
	All of them come from the same One.
	As one family, they reside.*
	That is why to call them brothers,
	Jesus possesses no shame,
	Saying these words: "To My brothers,
	I will publicize Your name.
2:12	"In the church's midst, I'll praise You."
2:13	Again, "Trust in Him, I'll place."
	Again, "Look! I and the children
	Whom God gave to Me *by grace."
2:14	Therefore, because in flesh and blood
	The children did participate,
	Likewise, He shared in flesh and blood
	That death's strength, He'd eliminate.
	He died to destroy the devil
	(Who held death's powerful sphere)
2:15	And to save those held in bondage
	Their whole lives by deathly fear.
2:16	For He did not rescue angels.
	He rescued Abraham's seed.
2:17	Therefore, He was obligated
	To become like them indeed -
	Yes, to become like His brothers
	In each and every respect
	In order that He could become
	A high priest *without defect -

	A merciful and faithful priest
	In things which to God relate
	That for the sins of the people,
	He could then propitiate.

2:18 For because while being tempted,
He suffered *yet was not swayed,
Then as for those being tempted,
He now can come to their aid.

3:1 So then, brothers, you who are saints,
Who in heaven's calling share,
Ponder Jesus, the apostle
And high priest whom we declare.

3:2 Jesus was faithful to the One
Who made Him apostle and priest
As Moses was in God's household,
From the greatest to the least.[217]

3:3 For this One's deserved more glory
Than what on Moses was laid
As the builder has more honor
Than the building he has made.

3:4 For a house is built by someone
Whether right here or abroad.[218]
Now everything in existence
Has a builder too. It's God.

3:5	Moses was a faithful servant
	In God's entire household
	For a testimony of things
	Which afterward would be told.
3:6	But Christ, He was a faithful son
	Over God's household, that's us,
	If the boasting about the hope
	We hold firm, also our trust.
3:7	So, as the Holy Spirit says,
	"If today you hear His voice,
3:8	Do not do as your fathers did
	And make hardened hearts your choice.
	"The day they were tried, they rebelled
	In the desert *over needs,[219]
3:9	The place your fathers tested Me.
	Forty years they saw My deeds.
3:10	"That's why with this generation
	I became angry and said,
	'This generation is always
	In their heart being misled.
	"'Never has this generation
	Come to truly know My ways.'
3:11	They won't (as I swore in My wrath)
	Come into My resting place."
3:12	Watch out, brothers, so that no one
	Ever has an evil heart
	Causing faithlessness so that they
	From the living God depart.

3:13	But encourage one another
	Each day while it's called "Today"
	So none of you become hardened
	By sin's guile *in any way.
3:14	For we've become sharers of Christ
	If we hold firm to the end
	Our original confidence
	That to Christ we did extend.*
3:15	Remember what the Spirit says,[220]
	"If today you hear His voice,
	Do not do as your fathers did
	And make hardened hearts your choice."
3:16	For who were those who heard *His voice
	Yet rebelled *against the Lord?
	Was it not all whom Moses led,
	All who out of Egypt poured?
3:17	With whom did He become angry
	For forty years *day after day?
	Was it not the ones who had sinned,
	Whose corpses in the desert lay?
3:18	He swore no entrance to His rest
	To the people who rebelled.[221]
3:19	We see that they could not enter
	Since to faithlessness they held.

4:1 Therefore, let's fear while there remains
A promise to enter His rest
So that to have come short of it,
Not one of you be assessed.

4:2 For we've been told the good news too
Just as even they were told.
However, the word that was heard
No profit to them did hold.

Why it did not benefit them
Was because, *although they heard,
They had never intertwined faith
With their hearing of the word.[222]

4:3 For we are entering into rest
(That is, we who have believed),
The same rest He has spoken of
Which they had never received.*

"They won't (as I swore in My wrath)
Come into My resting place."
Although His works were completed
Since creating earth and space.

4:4 For somewhere of the seventh day
He made this declaration,
"The seventh day God rested from
All His works *of creation."

4:5	Also again in this passage
	Reference to His rest contains,*
	"They won't enter My resting place."
4:6	Therefore, to enter remains.

> Since those to whom the good news came
> Did not enter, though they heard,
> Disobedient to the call,♦
> Having no faith *in the word –

4:7	He again marked a certain day.
	"Today" is how it's been classed.
	In David, He called it "Today"
	After so much time had passed.

> Here's the quote, as already said
> In this letter's prior parts,*
> "If today you all hear His voice,
> Then do not harden your hearts."

4:8	For if Joshua gave them rest
	In their promised habitat,*
	God would not be speaking about
	Another day after that.
4:9	In light of what God has spoken[223]
	In David, *which is unflawed,
	There still remains a Sabbath rest
	For all the people of God.
4:10	For the one who enters God's rest
	Has from his works rested too
	Just as God *after creation
	Rested from what He did do.

4:11 Therefore, let us enter that rest,
Putting into it our all,
So that no one may copy them
And to disobedience fall.

4:12 For this is living and active:
The word spoken by the Lord,[224]
And the word of God is sharper
Than any double-edged sword.

It is so sharp* that it pierces
To the point that it divides
The spirit, the soul, and the joints,
And tissue of bones' insides.

God's word is able to discern
(To make plain the metaphor)*
The thoughts arising from the heart,
Even the motives we store.

4:13 There's no creature hidden from Him.
All are naked and exposed.
His eyes see all. An account by us
To Him must be disclosed.

4:14 So since we have a great high priest
Who through the heavens has passed
(Jesus, God's Son), then let us all
To that confession hold fast.

4:15	For a high priest we do not have
Who has insufficient powers
To sympathize with each of us
In the weaknesses of ours.

No, instead we have a high priest*
Who's been thoroughly tested
In all things just as we have been
Yet by sin unmolested. |
| **4:16** | Therefore, let us with confidence
Come before the gracious throne
To find grace in our time of need
That mercy to us be shown. |
| **5:1** | For each high priest who is chosen
From among men is selected
To act for people in the things
That with God are connected.

This is for the very purpose
That he may present *to God
Gifts and sacrificial offerings
For sins *of those who are flawed. |
| **5:2** | He can relate with compassion
To the ignorant and beguiled
Because by weakness he has been
Surrounded *and defiled. |
| **5:3** | Sacrificial offerings for sins,
He's obligated to make,
Not only for all the people,
But likewise for his own sake. |

5:4 To take this honor on oneself,
There's not one person who does,
But the high priest is called by God
Just as Aaron also was.

5:5 Thus Christ glorified not Himself
So a high priest He'd become.
He who said these words to Him did
(The Psalms this passage is from):*

"You Yourself are truly My Son.
I've begotten You today."
5:6 So also, in another place
To Christ this same One did say:*

"You Yourself, a priest forever!
No end to it will I bring♦
Since it's after the order of
Melchizedek, Salem's king."[225]

5:7 Christ offered in His days on earth
With strong crying and with tears
Both requests and supplications
To the One whom He reveres.

He presented these prayers to Him
Whose power is so immense
To save Him from the grip of death.
He was heard for His reverence.

5:8 Christ came to learn obedience
(Even though He was the Son)
From the things by which He suffered
Until all His work was done.*

5:9   After His work was accomplished,
He is the person who became
Eternal salvation's author
To all who obey in His name.

5:10   It's because Christ became high priest
By God and was designated
According to the order of
Melchizedek, *as was stated.

5:11   About this there's much to tell you,
Yet it is hard to explain
Since in your action of hearing
In sluggishness you remain.

5:12   By now you ought to be teachers,
But your need has reoccurred
For one to teach you the basics,
The beginning of God's word.[226]

You've become in this state of need,
And therefore, this I conclude:*
You are having a need for milk,
Not a need for solid food.

5:13   For everyone who just drinks milk,
No knowledge has he compiled
In the teaching of righteousness
Because he is just a child.

5:14   Solid food is for the mature,
Those who through practice sustained
Distinguish between good and bad,
Their faculties fully trained.

6:1 The first message[227] about the Christ,
For that reason let us drop.
Let's be carried toward the mature.
Rebuilding what's built, let's stop!

Since the foundation has been laid,
Let not these again be poured:
First,* repentance from lifeless works
And faith toward God *as Lord.

6:2 Second,* doctrine about cleansings
And the laying on of hands.
Third,* resurrection of the dead
And final judgment that stands.

6:3 And we'll move on to the mature
If indeed God will allow,
6:4 For it's impossible for some
To repent again anyhow.

Those who have once been enlightened,
And of heaven's gift have tasted,
And have in the Holy Spirit
Actively participated -

6:5 Those who have tasted God's good word
And powers future time *will exude
6:6 Yet fall away, they can't again
To repentance be renewed.

The Poetic Letter to the Hebrews

| | For they would be crucifying
Again for themselves God's Son,
And they would be exposing Him
To shame before everyone. |
|---|---|
| **6:7** | For earth which drinks the frequent rain
So that useful fruit it bears
For those whom the land has been tilled,
The blessings from God, it shares. |
| **6:8** | But by bearing thorns and thistles,
It's nearly cursed, *void of worth.
The end result will surely be
The burning up of that earth. |
| **6:9** | But, dearly loved ones, about you
Of better things we've been swayed,
Things pertaining to salvation,
Although such words we've conveyed. |
| **6:10** | For God is not unjust so as
To forget your love and deed
Which you showed the saints in His name.
You served and still serve their need. |
| **6:11** | But we long for each one of you
The same diligence to show
'Til the end for the certainty
Of the hope *of which you know. |
| **6:12** | This is so that you won't become
Sluggish, but that you'll parrot
Those who through faith and endurance
The promises inherit. |

The Poetic Scriptures of Six Writers

6:13 For when God promised Abraham,
  Since there was no one greater
  To make an oath by, He then swore
  By Himself, *the Creator.

6:14 He said, "I will multiply you;
  I'll bless you as I ordained."
6:15 And thus by being patient,
  The promise, he then obtained.

6:16 People swear by someone greater.
  If they have any dispute,
  The oath is the parameter
  To confirm what's absolute.

6:17 So God guaranteed by an oath
  Since He planned to firmly show
  His plan to the heirs of promise.
  No change could it undergo.

6:18 This way through two unchanging facts
  (For God can't lie *or do wrong)
  We who've fled to grab the hope shown
  Might have a comfort that's strong.

6:19 We have an anchor for our lives,
  A certain and secure brace,
  Hope which enters behind the veil
  Into the innermost place.

6:20 That's where Jesus entered for us,
  As a forerunner assigned,
  Since a high priest, He has become
  After Melchizedek's kind.

The Poetic Letter to the Hebrews

7:1   For Melchizedek, Salem's king,
      A priest of the Most High God –
      Who met Abraham returning
      From smiting the kings abroad.

      Who blessed him *and God the Most High;²²⁸
7:2   To whom Abraham divided
      One-tenth of everything he had
      Which for him God had provided.*

      Whose name means *king of righteousness*,
      And as to his location,*
      King of Salem, or "king of peace"
      Being the right translation.

7:3   Without father, without mother,
      Without genealogy,
      Without the beginning of days,
      No death *record, do we see.

      Melchizedek who had been made
      Similarly to God's Son -
      For Melchizedek, Salem's king*
      As priest remains on and on.

7:4   See how great Melchizedek was.
      The patriarch Abraham
      Gave to him one-tenth of the spoils
      Gained while fulfilling his plan.²²⁹

7:5 Now those who received the priesthood
By Levitical descent
Had a commandment in the Law
To take from folks ten percent.

This means the Levitical priests
From their brothers took ten percent
Although it was from Abraham
That they all had their descent.

7:6 However, this Melchizedek
(Whose descent no one can trace)
From Abraham received one-tenth
Though not part of the same race.

So, he blessed the one who possessed
The promises God extended.
7:7 The greater blesses the lesser
Is a truth that's uncontended.

7:8 So, here we see that men who die
Receive one-tenth *from others,
But there is the testimony
That he lives on, *my brothers.

7:9 One could say, Levi through Abraham
Tithed yet took tithes *by law,
7:10 For he was in his father's loins
When him, Melchizedek saw.

7:11 Therefore, if there was perfection
Through the Levitical priesthood
(For the people had received law
While under this system they stood),

What further need would there exist
For a different priest to arise
According to Melchizedek's
And not Aaron's kind otherwise?

7:12   For when the priesthood becomes changed,
Then out of necessity
A change of law is also made.
Here is how this came to be:[230]

7:13   He of whom are spoken these things
From another tribe has come,
From which no person ever served
At the altar, *no not one.

7:14   For the fact that our Lord arose
From Judah is very plain.
Moses said nothing about priests
That to this tribe would pertain.

7:15   Yet it's more abundantly clear
Since another priest arose
According to the likeness of
Melchizedek *as Psalms shows.

7:16   This priest came not according to
A law of required descent,
But according to the power
Of life with endless extent.

7:17   For He bears this testimony
(This quote in the Psalms, we find):
"You are a priest forevermore
After Melchizedek's kind."

7:18 On the one hand, to set aside
      A prior command, *God elected
      Due to weakness and uselessness,
7:19 For nothing, that law perfected.

      On the other hand, there arose
      An introductory sphere
      To a hope that is much better,
      Through which to God we draw near.

7:20 And to the extent that this sphere
      With an oath was not without
      (For on the one hand, with no oath
      As priests those ones came about.

7:21 (On the other hand, by God's oath
      As a priest, He was assigned,
      For He told Him, "The Lord has sworn
      And will never change His mind.

      ("Yes, *You are a priest forever."),
7:22 So to a greater extent[231]
      Jesus became a guarantee
      For a better covenant.

7:23 On the one hand, the other priests
      Increased greatly in number
      Since from continuing as priests
      Them all, death did encumber.

7:24 However, on the other hand,
      Since He forever remains,
      He holds on to the priesthood
      Which permanently maintains.

7:25	So, those who come to God through Him,
	He can fully save indeed
	Because for them He always lives
	In order to intercede.
7:26	For such a high priest suited us,
	Holy, undefiled, without blame,
	Fully set apart from sinners.
	Higher than the skies, He became.
7:27	He had no daily need (unlike
	The high priests *who by sins were vexed)
	To sacrifice for His sins first,
	Then those of the people next.
	For the sacrifice which He made
	He offered once, for all time,
7:28	For the Law appoints as high priests
	Men who to weakness resign.
	But the saying about the oath
	Which came long after the Law
	Appoints a Son who forever
	Stands perfected, ◆without flaw.

8:1	The main point of the next subject[232]
	Is the kind of high priest we own.
	In heaven, He sat on the right
	Of the divine Majesty's throne.

8:2   He serves²³³ in the holy places
        And in the tent that is true,
        A tent which the Lord erected,
        Not one any man did do.

8:3   For each high priest is appointed
        For the purpose to bring in
        Gifts and also sacrifices
        In relationship to sin.*

        Therefore, it is necessary
        For this One also to hold
        Something which He might bring to God,
        Since He's the high priest foretold.*

8:4   Therefore, if He were still on earth,
        To be a priest, He would not
        Because there are priests who by law
        Offer the gifts they have brought.

8:5   A shadow of heavenly things
        And just its reproduction,
        These priests who were appointed serve
        As seen in God's instruction.

        For Moses had been instructed
        When he was about to erect
        The tent ♦or the tabernacle
        By Him *who's the architect.

        "See to it that you make all things
        By the pattern in each respect
        Which was shown you in the mountain."
        Stated God *the architect.

8:6	A greater distinguished service,
	Jesus has in fact attained
	Inasmuch as He mediates
	Something better God ordained.*
	Yes, a much better covenant,
	Jesus has mediated,
	For upon better promises
	It has been legislated.
8:7	For if the first covenant made
	Was faultless ♦(which it was not),[234]
	An occasion for a second
	Would not ever have been sought.
8:8	For finding fault with them, He says,
	"'Days are coming into view,'
	Says the Lord, 'when I'll accomplish
	A covenant that is new.
	"'With Israel's house and Judah's house
	A new covenant, I'll effect,
8:9	Not like the one with their fathers
	In that day that I did elect.
	"'When by the hand from Egypt's land,
	I took them,' declares the Lord.
	'They stayed not in My covenant.
	Concern for them, I ignored.'
8:10	"The Lord says, 'Here's the covenant
	Which I'll put into effect
	With the household of Israel
	After those days *I elect.

    "'Placing My laws into their minds,
    My laws on their hearts, I will write,
    And I'll become to them as God.
    My people, they'll be in My sight.

8:11 "'And they won't teach any longer,
    Each speaking to another
    (Whether it be a citizen
    Or even their own brother)

    "'Saying, *Experience the Lord!*
    Because from the most lowly
    To the greatest of the people,
    All will already know Me.

8:12 "'For as to their unrighteousness,
    Mercy on them, I will pour.
    As to their sins they've committed,
    I'll remember them no more.'"

8:13 By saying *new,* He then has made
    The first covenant passé.
    What's wearing out and growing old
    Is near vanishing away.

9:1   Therefore, the first covenant had
    Regulations necessary
    For the ministry of the priests
    And the earthly sanctuary.

9:2	For the first part of the tent made
	("The holy places" it's named)
	Held the lampstand and the table.
	The showbread, it too contained.
9:3	Now, behind the second curtain
	("The Holy of Holies" it's named),
	The golden altar of incense,
9:4	This part of the tent contained.

And the ark of the Covenant
Was in this innermost place.
On each of the sides of the ark
Gold overlaid every space.

Within the ark was a gold jar
With manna *unconsumed,
The tablets of the covenant,
And Aaron's rod which bloomed.

9:5	Above the ark were cherubim,
	Creatures reflecting glory,
	Overshadowing the seat made
	To be propitiatory.

Concerning all of these objects,
It is not the time to start
Explaining the significance
Of each and every part.

9:6	When these things had thus been prepared,
	The priests (always repeating)
	Enter the first part of the tent,
	Their services completing.

9:7   However, in contrast to this,
      Just the high priest enters here:
      The innermost[235] part of the tent,
      And that, just one time each year.

      He does not enter without blood
      Which for himself he presents
      And for the sins of the people
      Committed in ignorance.

9:8   The Holy Spirit thus makes clear,
      Access was not yet made plain
      Into the most holy places
      While the first tent does remain.

9:9   This was a parable for now.
      Sacrifices and gifts were brought,
      But to perfect the worshippers
      In their conscience, these could not.

9:10 In relation to food and drink
      And various cleansings too,
      These fleshly rituals were in force
      'Til the time to make things new.

9:11 But when Christ arrived as high priest
      To the good things that have come,
      He entered through the greater tent,
      More complete *than the earthly one.

      This greater tent has been put up
      Without any human hands.
      It is not of this creation.
      In the spiritual realm it stands.*

9:12   Christ did not enter with the blood
Of goats and bull calves applied,
But through His own blood He entered
The holy places inside.

He went one time and for all time
Into the holy places,
Acquiring a redemption
That lasts throughout the ages.

9:13   If heifer's ashes and the blood
Of goats and bulls makes clean,
Cleansing the flesh of the defiled
By a sprinkling routine -

9:14   How much more will the blood of Christ
Cleanse our conscience from dead deeds
For service to the living God
Than the blood of animal breeds.*

For through the eternal Spirit,
He offered Himself to God
Without any blemish at all,
Being perfect and unflawed.◆

9:15   Due to this, He's mediator
Of a covenant, a new one.
His death occurred to pay for sins
Which under the first was done.

This all happened in order that
Those who've been called would receive
An eternal inheritance,
Guaranteed since they believe.*

9:16　　For wherever there is a will,
　　　　It is a necessity
　　　　For the will-maker to be dead
　　　　To possess validity.

9:17　　For a will is in force at death
　　　　Since no power can it derive
　　　　As long as he who made the will
　　　　Continues to be alive.

9:18　　So, even the first covenant
　　　　Was not inaugurated
　　　　Without the use of any blood.
　　　　By blood it was activated.*

9:19　　For after every commandment
　　　　That with the Law did accord
　　　　Had been told to all the people
　　　　As Moses *spoke from the Lord –

　　　　After taking the blood of calves
　　　　And the blood of goats as well
　　　　With water, red wool, and hyssop,
　　　　On the following, blood fell.

　　　　Moses sprinkled the scroll itself
　　　　And all the people and stated,
9:20　　"This is the blood of the covenant
　　　　Which God for you mandated."

9:21　　Likewise, Moses sprinkled with blood
　　　　All vessels which did pertain
　　　　To the service of ministry.
　　　　He sprinkled the tent the same.

9:22	Almost all things are cleansed in blood
According to the Law, *we read,
And without the shedding of blood,
Forgiveness cannot be decreed.
9:23	In light of this, on the one hand,
It was an absolute need
For the copies of heaven's things
To be cleansed by rites decreed.
	On the other hand, there arose
For heavenly things a need
To be cleansed by sacrifices
Better than the ones decreed.
9:24	For Christ did not ever enter
Holy places that were hand-made,
Places which are an antitype
Of the genuine one *God laid.
	But He entered heaven itself
So that now, as to our case,
He would appear on our behalf
Before God's very face.
9:25	He entered not to offer Himself
Often like the high priest *alone
Enters yearly the holy places
With blood that is not his own.
9:26	Or else to suffer many times
Would have been required of Him
Since the creation of the world
In His sacrifice for sin.*

But now at the end of the age,
He has just one time appeared
Through the sacrifice of Himself
In order that sin be cleared.

9:27   And just as it is appointed
That only once people die
And after this there is judgment,
9:28   So to Christ this does apply.

For Christ was offered only once
To bear the sins for the many.[236]
He will be seen a second time
But not for sin, *not any.

His second appearance will be
To bring final salvation
To those who are waiting for Him
With eager expectation.

10:1   For since the Law is a shadow
Of the benefits to come
And is not itself the image
Of those matters, *no not one -

It is not able to perfect
The ones who to God draw near
By the unchanged sacrifices
Constantly offered each year.

The Poetic Letter to the Hebrews

10:2 Or else these offerings would have stopped
Since worshippers would have been
Cleansed one time and no longer have
Consciousness of sins again.

10:3 But in these is the reminder
Of sins every single year.
10:4 That means, the blood of bulls and goats
Cannot make sins disappear.

10:5 So, when He came into the world,
He said, "You desired not
A sacrifice or an offering,
But a body for Me, You wrought.

10:6 "Burnt and sin offerings pleased You not.
10:7 Then I said, 'O God, behold,
I have come to fulfill Your will
As written of Me in the Scroll.'"[237]

10:8 Note that He said in the above.
"Offerings (whether burnt or sin)
And sacrifices, You don't want
And do not take pleasure in."

These sacrifices and offerings,
To the Law they did accord.
10:9 Then next He stated, "I have come
To fulfill Your will, O Lord."[238]

So then,* He took away the first,[239]
Which to the Law did accord,*
To establish the second one,
About the will of the Lord.*

10:10	In that will, *having been fulfilled, We all have been sanctified Through the offering of the body Of Jesus Christ one time applied.
10:11	On the one hand, every priest stands Serving daily as he extends The same sacrifices often Which never can take away sins.
10:12	On the other hand, that One sat On the right of God, ♦Divine, After offering in place of sins One sacrifice for all time.
10:13	As to what remains, He awaits 'Til this event is complete,* When His enemies are placed as A footstool under His feet.
10:14	For by means of just one offering, He *who sits on God's right side Has perfected forevermore All those being sanctified.
10:15	Now also, the Holy Spirit To us *(as we all have read) Testifies long after *the Psalm, For this is what He had said:
10:16	"After those days, this covenant With them, I the Lord will bind: Placing My laws upon their heart, I will write them on their mind.

10:17	"All* their sins and their lawlessness I'll never remember again."
10:18	Where forgiveness of these exist, There's no more offering for sin.

10:19	Therefore, brothers, because we have Boldness within us instilled To enter the holy places By the blood which Jesus spilled -
10:20	(This way He opened up for us As a new and living way Through the sanctuary curtain, Or His flesh, that is to say)
10:21	And since we have over God's house A great high priest, *this now hear:
10:22	In the full assurance of faith With a true heart, let's draw near.
	From a conscience that says we're vile, Our hearts have been sprinkled clean, And our body has been immersed With water that is pristine.
10:23	Let's grip this confession of hope But without hesitation, For He who promised is faithful And has no vacillation.♦

10:24　Let us think how to motivate
　　　　One another, *as we should,
　　　　To love others unselfishly
　　　　And to do deeds that are good.

10:25　Let's not forsake our assembly
　　　　As some have come to adhere.
　　　　Stir one another all the more
　　　　As you see the day drawing near.

10:26　For if once receiving truth's knowledge
　　　　We willfully practice sin,
　　　　A sacrifice concerning wrongs
　　　　No longer remains therein.

10:27　There remains an expectation
　　　　Of judgment that terrifies,
　　　　A raging fire which will consume
　　　　Every foe *who Him defies.

10:28　Since, based on the testimony
　　　　Of witnesses three or two,
　　　　Those rejecting the Law of Moses
　　　　Will die without mercy is true -

10:29　How much more a worse punishment
　　　　Do you think will justly meet
　　　　The person who has trampled on
　　　　The Son of God with his feet.

　　　　Also, the one who deems unclean
　　　　That by which he was sanctified,
　　　　The blood of the new covenant,
　　　　The Spirit of grace, to deride.

The Poetic Letter to the Hebrews

10:30   For we know Him who has stated,
"Vengeance is Mine. I'll repay."
And "The Lord will judge His people"
The Scripture also does say.*

10:31   It is a terrifying judgment,
This falling into the hands
Of the one God who is living.
His judgment forever stands.*

10:32   But remember the former days,
After you were enlightened,
When you endured through a contest
Of sufferings that were heightened.

10:33   When you were openly exposed
To reproach and tribulation,
Or when others went through such things,
You joined in participation.

10:34   For you displayed your sympathy
To the ones who went to jail.
The seizure of your property,
You accepted *without fail.

You accepted it joyfully
Since you know you have in store
Something much better in heaven
That abides forevermore.

10:35   In light of all that has been said,[240]
Your confidence *in the Lord,
Do not ever throw it away.
It has such a great reward.

10:36	For the need of perseverance, Constantly you must fulfill That you might receive the promise After you practice God's will.
10:37	For just a little while longer, The Coming One will arrive And will not delay anymore. So, in perseverance strive.*
10:38	Now, the one who's righteous by faith Belongs to Me and will live, Yet to anyone who withdraws, No delight will My soul give.
10:39	But we're not of those who withdraw Which ends in ruination, But we are of those who have faith For the soul's preservation.

11:1	Faith is the assurance we have In the things for which we hope, The conviction of those matters Not yet in our visual scope.
11:2	For in the aforementioned faith, Were people of long ago Given a good testimony, Recorded for us to know.*

11:3	By faith we realize that the world By the word of God was made So that the things seen have not come From things already displayed.
11:4	By faith Abel offered to God A sacrifice much greater Than the one Cain offered to God As told by our Creator.* When God approved the gifts he gave, "He's righteous" was testified. Through faith, Abel still speaks today Even though he has long died.
11:5	By faith Enoch was transferred up So that death he would not face, And he was not found anywhere Since God took him *to His place. For before this transfer occurred, It had long been testified That he had pleased God in his walk. The Lord was always his guide.*
11:6	Without faith one cannot please *God, For all who come to the Lord[241] Must trust that He really exists And to seekers gives reward.
11:7	By faith Noah when he was warned About things yet to unfold Prepared an ark in deep respect So as to save his household.

>
> He condemned the entire world
> By the faith he did possess
> And according to faith became
> An heir of righteousness.

11:8
> By faith Abraham obeyed when called
> And went to a location
> He'd have as an inheritance,
> Not knowing his destination.

11:9
> He settled in the promised land.
> By faith a stranger became,
> Tent-living with Isaac and Jacob,
> Coheirs of promise, the same.

11:10
> For he was waiting eagerly
> For the city *that's unflawed
> With foundations whose designer
> Also whose builder is God.

11:11
> By faith barren Sarah herself
> Long past the age to conceive,
> Since she deemed Him faithful who promised,
> Conception's power received.

11:12
> From one man, though as good as dead,
> Were born these - ♦people galore,
> Countless like the stars of the sky
> And the sand along the shore.

11:13
> In faith all the faithful ones[242] died,
> The promises not obtained.
> Instead to see them from afar
> And to hail them, they maintained.

The Poetic Letter to the Hebrews

	Strangers and nomads on the earth
	Is how themselves they did view.
11:14	For those who say such things reveal
	That a homeland, they pursue.

11:15 Now if they were really thinking
Of the land from where they came,
They surely would have grabbed the chance
To return back *to the same.

11:16 But as it is, they continued
In eagerness to aspire
For a place that is much better,
A heavenly one, to desire.

In light of their eager desire,[243]
Without shame God has declared
That He be called their God, and so,
A city for them, He prepared.

11:17 When tested, Abraham by faith
Had offered Isaac, his son.
He who received the promises
Was offering his only one.

11:18 "In Isaac your seed will be named."
To Abraham, this was said.
11:19 So, he reasoned that God had power
To even raise up the dead.

So, from a parabolic death,
Abraham received his son.
11:20 Isaac blessed Jacob and Esau
By faith about things to come.

11:21	By faith Jacob blessed Joseph's sons, Each one while he was dying. Then he bowed and worshipped *the Lord While on his staff relying.²⁴⁴
11:22	By faith dying Joseph recalled That *from Egypt's very borders Israel's sons would have exodus And about his bones gave orders.
11:23	By faith Moses' parents hid him At birth for months counting three, For they viewed the child as striking, Not fearing the king's decree.
11:24	By faith Moses (when fully grown) Refused to be called a son Of the daughter of the Pharaoh, But to suffer, he did succumb.
11:25 **11:26**	Suffering with God's people, he chose Than to have sin's passing pleasures, Deeming insults for Christ more wealth Than all of Egypt's treasures. He was looking for the reward.
11:27	By faith he left Egypt's land Without fearing the king's anger As before him, he did stand.²⁴⁵ For Moses endured through it all As a person with eyes stayed On Him who is invisible, Facing the king unafraid.*

The Poetic Letter to the Hebrews

11:28   By faith he kept the Passover
And sprinkled blood *(which was much)
So he who destroys the firstborn
Would their own firstborn not touch.

11:29   By faith they all crossed the Red Sea
As they walked through on dry ground.
When the Egyptians tried to cross,
Every one of them were drowned.

11:30   By faith the walls of Jericho
Fell *with no physical blow
After they had been encircled
For seven days *in a row.

11:31   By faith Rahab, the prostitute
(Unlike those who had not believed)
Did not get destroyed *in the raid
Since in peace the spies, she received.

11:32   What more do I say of such ones?
For me, time will surely fail
If I tell about such people,*
Disclosing in full detail.

Ones like Gideon and Barak,
Samson and Jephthah *(there's more),
David, and also Samuel,
And all the prophets *of yore.

11:33   For through faith these conquered kingdoms.
Promises, they did acquire.
They worked justice, shut lions' mouths,
11:34   And quenched the power of fire.

They escaped the sword's fatal edge.
From weakness they received power.
They were made strong in times of war,
Making foreign armies cower.

11:35 Women received their dead alive.
Some were tortured who expected
No release but saw better lives
When they are resurrected.

11:36 And others received a trial
Where they were both flogged and mocked.
Some were even thrown in prison
And put in chains *that were locked.

11:37 They were stoned, even sawed in two,
Killed by a murderous sword.
They went around in sheep and goat skins,
Oppressed, abused, needs ignored.

11:38 (The world is not worthy of them)
In deserts, they wandered around,
Into mountains and into caves,
Into holes inside the ground.

11:39 Though testified of through their faith,
The promise, no one collected
11:40 Since God foresaw better for us
That with us they'd be perfected.

12:1 So, since we have surrounding us
Such a cloud that is so great,
A cloud of faithful witnesses,
Let's lay aside every weight.

Let us lay aside every sin
Which easily breaks our pace,
And let us run with endurance
What's set before us, the race.

12:2 Focus on Jesus, faith's leader,
Who is its completer too,
Who endured the cross as He kept
The joy set before Him in view.

As for the shame which the cross brings,
No regard, did His thoughts own,
And He has sat down *in heaven
On the right side of God's throne.

12:3 For consider Him who endured
Such hostile opposition
By those sinners against Himself
As He fulfilled His mission.*

That way you will not grow weary.
With surrender, your minds won't flood.
12:4 In your struggle with sin you've yet
To resist to the point of blood.

12:5 Have you completely forgotten
The exhortation *against sin
Which was explained to you as sons?
"Don't take lightly His discipline.

"And don't faint when reproved by Him
12:6 Since discipline the Lord effects
On the one whom He truly loves.
He flogs every son He accepts."

12:7 Keep enduring for discipline.
As sons, God is treating you,
For what son is there whose father
Did not discipline him too?

12:8 But if you're without discipline,
In which every son has shared,
Then you are illegitimate
And not sons *as you've declared.

12:9 If we had our fleshly fathers
To discipline *as we grew,
And we were turned around by it,
Much more this, we all must do:

We must remain in subjection,
Complete submission to give◆
To the Father of our spirits,
And we will then truly live.

12:10 They disciplined as they deemed best
For few days *(if we compare),
But He did it for our own good
So His holiness, we'd share.

12:11	All discipline for the moment
	Seems not joyful but makes us pained,
	Yet peaceful fruit called righteousness
	Yields later to those by it trained.
12:12	Therefore, strengthen your weary hands,
	And your weakened knees, restore.
12:13	Make straight paths for your feet so what's lame
	Be healed and not twisted more.
12:14	Pursue peace with all the people.
	To holy living accord
	Because without holy living,
	Nobody will see the Lord.
12:15	See that no one misses God's grace
	And that there not be any
	Bitter root springing up to cause
	Trouble, defiling many.
12:16	See that there's no fornicator
	Or profane one *among you known,
	Like Esau who for just one meal
	Sold the birthright he did own.
12:17	For you know even afterward,
	When he promptly objected[246]
	And wished to receive the blessing,
	Esau was still rejected.
	For to find any place at all
	For repentance, he did not
	Even though with tremendous tears
	After the blessing he sought.

12:18   You've not come to a location,
        Some place that you all can touch,
        Like blazing fire, darkness, gloom,
        Or a storm that rages much.

12:19   Like a sound of a trumpet blast,
        Or a voice of words *divine
        Which they who heard begged that He'd stop
        Speaking to them *at that time.

12:20   For they could not bear the order
        When to them it had been said,*
        "If a beast just touches the mount,
        It must be stoned until dead."

12:21   So terrifying was the sight
        (The appearance God did make),*
        That even Moses himself said,
        "I am fearful, and I shake."

12:22   But *to a spiritual mountain,
        To Mount Zion you have come,
        And to the living God's city,
        The heavenly Jerusalem.

        And you've come to countless angels
        Gathered in joy, as we're told,[247]
12:23   And to the church of firstborn ones[248]
        Who in heaven are enrolled.

        You've come to God, the judge of all,
        And to these you're connected,*
        To the spirits of righteous ones,
        Those who have been perfected.

The Poetic Letter to the Hebrews

12:24   You've come to Christ,²⁴⁹ mediator
Of a new covenant *applied,
And to the sprinkled blood that speaks
Better than Abel's blood cried.

12:25   See that you don't shun Him who speaks,
For if no escape did they know
When they refused the instruction
Of Him on earth *long ago -

How much more true is it for us
When from Him we turn away,
From Him who's in heaven above,
12:26   Whose voice shook the earth that day.

But now He has promised, saying
"Yet one more time I will shake
Not only the earth but also
The universe *I did make."

12:27   The promised words "Yet one more time"
Declares a removal applied
To shakable things that were made
So what can't be shook will abide.

12:28   Therefore, since we are receiving
A kingdom unshakable,
Let us show gratitude whereby
This is unmistakable:*

We serve God in a pleasing way,
With reverence and awe in view,
12:29   For our God *who is in heaven
Is a consuming fire too.

13:1 Let brotherly love continue.
13:2 Your hospitality, share,
For some have entertained angels
Without ever being aware.

13:3 Keep remembering those in prison
As though with them you are chained.
Keep remembering those mistreated
Since in body you've been pained.

13:4 Keep marriage honored among all,
And its bed, do not defile,
For God will judge fornicators
And the adulterous lifestyle.

13:5 Keep your conduct completely free
From money-adoration,
Being content with what you have
Because *of this quotation:

"I'll never let go or leave you."
This God Himself did convey.
13:6 So then, because God promised this,
We can confidently say:

"The Lord God, He is my helper.
I will never be afraid.
What will a person do to me?"
(From Psalms this quote is conveyed)*

13:7	Remember your leaders, the ones Who to you God's word did state. Note the outcome of their lifestyle. Their faithfulness, imitate.
13:8	Jesus Christ is the same today, Yesterday, and forever.
13:9	Don't be carried off by teachings Many and strange, not ever.
	For it's good to secure the heart By the teachings of God's grace, Not by ritual foods which do not Profit the adherent's case.
13:10	We believers[250] have an altar From which the ones *who presume To serve in the tent don't possess The authority to consume.
13:11	For the blood of the animals As a sacrifice for sin Was by the governing high priest To the holy places brought in.
	But in regards to the bodies Of the animals that were slain, They were carried outside the camp And burned *that nothing remain.
13:12	Therefore, also Jesus *our priest In order to sanctify The people by means of His blood Went outside the gate to die.[251]

13:13	So, let us go outside the camp
	To Jesus, bearing His shame.
13:14	For we seek a future city.
	The one here will not remain.
13:15	Through Him let's offer constantly
	To God a sacrifice of praise,
	That is to say, the fruit of lips
	Which confess His name always.
13:16	Do not neglect to do what's good
	And in fellowship[252] to live.
	For these kinds of sacrifices,
	God is well-pleased that you give.
13:17	Give your leaders obedience
	With submission *paramount,[253]
	For they're watching over your souls
	As they must give an account.
	Practice your part in order that
	With joy their part they might do
	Without any inward groaning,
	For this would not profit you.
13:18	Keep in constant prayer for us,
	For we are convinced *I tell
	That we have a conscience that's clear,
	Wishing in all ways to act well.
13:19	But I especially exhort
	And urge♦ you to do this deed
	That I might be restored to you,
	And that it be done with speed.

The Poetic Letter to the Hebrews

13:20   Now, may the God of peace who raised
   Our Lord Jesus from the dead
   (The sheep's great shepherd who began
   The new²⁵⁴ covenant when He bled)

13:21   Prepare you in every good work
   To do His will as in us
   He works what pleases Him through Christ.²⁵⁵
   Endless glory to Jesus!

13:22   I urge you, brothers, put up with
   This word of exhortation,
   For I wrote this letter to you
   With just brief information.

13:23   You know our brother Timothy
   Has now been released, with whom
   I will see you all *face to face
   As long as he comes here soon.

13:24   Greet all the leaders over you
   And all the saints *in that place.
   Those from Italy greet you too.
13:25   Present with you all is grace!

THE POETIC LETTER OF JAMES

1:1   James, a bond slave, belonging to
The Lord Jesus Christ and God.
Salutations to the twelve tribes
Which have been scattered abroad.

1:2   Regard it all joy, my brothers,
When you face various trials
1:3   Since you realize that endurance,
The testing of your faith compiles.

1:4   And let endurance run its course
Of reaching its perfect goal
So that you lacking in nothing
May become mature[256] and whole.

1:5   If any of you lacks wisdom,
Keep asking from God who to all
Gives generously without scolding,
And on you, wisdom will fall.

1:6	But keep asking in faith. Doubt not,
	For the doubter, one can compare
	To a wave of the sea driven
	Or tossed by the wind here and there.
1:7	To receive a thing from the Lord,
	The doubter must not expect.
1:8	He's one with a divided mind,
	Wobbly in every respect.
1:9	Let the brother with humble means
	Boast that God[257] lifted him high,
1:10	But the rich, that God humbled him,
	For like a wild flower, he'll die.
1:11	For the sun rises with its heat
	Possessing a scorching power,
	And so the sun dries up the grass,
	And from the grass, falls its flower.
	The beauty of the flower's face
	Becomes completely destroyed.
	So, the rich too will fade away
	In the pursuits *they've enjoyed.
1:12	The man is blessed who endures trial
	(Proven as real and unflawed)
	Since he'll receive the crown of life
	Promised to those who love God.
1:13	In temptation let no one say,
	"By God I'm being tempted."
	God tempts no one, and from wrong's lure
	He Himself is exempted.

The Poetic Letter of James

1:14	But each is tempted when he's dragged
	And lured by his own desire.
1:15	Then after that, lust is conceived,
	And offspring, it does acquire.*
	The offspring that's brought forth is sin.
	Then sin grows, *once given breath,
	Until reaching its full-grown state,
	And then sin gives birth to death.
1:16	Stop being deceived, my brothers
	Whom I unselfishly love.
1:17	Each good gift and each perfect gift
	Is actually from above.
	Each gift descends from the Father
	Of the luminaries burning.
	Within Him change does not exist,
	Nor a shadow due to turning.
1:18	Due to His plan, He gave us birth
	By means of the word of truth
	So that of all His creations
	We are a kind of first fruit.
1:19	My brothers whom I dearly love,
	This truth, you already know,
	But let each one be quick to hear.
	In speech and in wrath, be slow.
1:20	For human wrath does not produce
	Righteousness which to God belongs.
1:21	Therefore, lay down all filthiness
	And any remainder of wrongs.

> In the state of humility,
> Receive the word planted within
> Which has the power to rescue
> Your souls²⁵⁸ *from the power of sin.

1:22 But become doers of the word
And not just hearers alone
Who keep on deceiving themselves,
1:23 And here is the reason shown:

> If someone merely hears the word
> And no action does he embrace,
> He's like a man who keeps viewing
> In a mirror his natural face.

1:24 For after he observed himself
And departed *from that spot,
What kind of person he was like,
He immediately forgot.

1:25 But the one who, as to the law
That's perfect, carefully views
That law that brings freedom *from sin
And in that law continues -

> Not as a hearer who forgets
> But as a doer who acts,
> That person will truly be blessed
> In the deed which he enacts.

1:26 If someone thinks he's religious,
And his tongue, he does not restrain,
But he keeps deceiving his heart,
Then that one's religion is vain.

1:27	Two examples of* religion That is pure and without taint Before our God and Father's eyes Is this *action and restraint: To care for orphans and widows In their affliction ♦and pain, And to keep preserving oneself From the world without a stain.

2:1	My brothers, stop holding the faith In Jesus the Christ, our Lord (He who is the glorious One) With a prejudice outpoured.
2:2	If a man comes with a gold ring To your meeting in fine clothes, And a poor man comes dressed in filth, And these greetings, you disclose:*
2:3	You look at the one in fine clothes And say, "Sit here where it's best!" To the poor man you say, "Stand there!" Or "Sit beside my footrest!"
2:4	Are you not then among yourselves Showing discrimination And also becoming judges With evil cogitation?

2:5 Listen, my brothers whom I love.
 What did God save people for?*
 In this world, did He not elect
 To be rich in faith, the poor?

 Did He not choose them to be heirs
 Of the kingdom *that's above
 Which He promised to everyone
 Who upon Him fix their love?

2:6 But the poor you have dishonored.
 Are not the ones who oppress
 And drag you into the courtrooms
 The wealthy people *no less?

2:7 Is it not the wealthy themselves
 Who continually declare
 Blasphemies against that good name,
 The very name which you bear?

2:8 If this royal law in Scripture
 You are really pursuing,
 "Love your enemy as yourself",
 Then very well you're doing.

2:9 But you are committing a sin
 When prejudice is inflicted,
 For by the Law as transgressors,
 You have become convicted.

2:10 For whoever keeps the whole Law
 But trips over one so to fall,
 Then that one has become guilty
 Of violating them all.

2:11	For He who said "Do not commit Adultery *with anyone" Also gave this other command, "Murder must never be done." If you don't commit adultery Yet go and murder someone, A transgressor against the Law You yourself have just become.
2:12	In this manner, keep on speaking, And in this way, always live: As if the law of liberty Its judgment is going to give.
2:13	For judgment is without mercy To the person *who just sins, Not practicing showing mercy. Over judgment, mercy wins.
2:14	My brothers, what's the benefit If someone lacks works *to show Yet keeps on claiming to have faith? Can that faith save him? No!²⁵⁹
2:15	If a brother or a sister (Let us together suppose)* Is lacking daily nourishment And is without any clothes –
2:16	But one of you utters to them, "Go in peace. Keep warm. Be filled." Yet withholds what their body needs. What benefit is instilled?

2:17   Likewise also, in the same way,
       Regardless of what one has said,
       Faith, if it has no works to show,
       According to itself is dead.

2:18   But someone will say *about you
       That you have faith *as you confess,
       But someone will say *about me
       That works I myself possess.

       Your kind of faith that's without works,
       Show to me. ♦Authenticate!
       And the kind of faith that I have,
       By my works I'll demonstrate.

2:19   You believe that there is one God.
       You do well, *but this now hear:
       This, the demons also believe,
       Yet they just tremble in fear.

2:20   But do you, O you foolish man,
       Wish to really come to know
       That faith without works is idle
       Since it has nothing to show?*

2:21   Was it not by works our father
       Abraham was justified
       When he offered Isaac his son
       On the altar *he supplied?[260]

2:22   Note that his faith was working with
       His works *that God expected,
       And by the works which he performed,
       His faith was then perfected.

2:23	The Scripture was fulfilled which says, "In God, Abraham believed, And it was put on his account That righteousness, *he received." And he was called the friend of God.
2:24	So, you see a man *is known To be justified by his works And not by his faith alone.[261]
2:25	Was not Rahab the harlot too Justified by works *in that day When she welcomed the messengers And sent them out another way?
2:26	For just as the body is dead Without the spirit *inside, In the same way faith too is dead Without any works *applied.

3:1	Not many of you, my brothers, Should be teachers *by ambition Since you know a greater judgment We'll receive *in our position.
3:2	We all stumble in many things. If one stumbles not in speech, He can restrain his whole body. Maturity, he has reached.

3:3	If we put bits in horses' mouths To obey as we decide, Slackening or tightening the reigns,* Their whole body too, we guide.
3:4	Look at the ships too. Though so large And driven by winds so great, They're steered by the smallest rudder Where the pilot's whim would dictate.
3:5	The tongue also is a small part, Yet great boastings, it conveys. Take note of how a fire so small Sets a great forest ablaze.
3:6	And the tongue itself is a fire, The world of what is not right. That tongue is placed among our parts. Our bodies, it does ignite.* The tongue defiles the whole body, Setting fire to life's whole course. The tongue also is set on fire, Gehenna being the source.
3:7	By humanity, each species Is being and has been tamed Of wild creatures, birds, and reptiles. Even sea life has been trained.
3:8	But not one person is able To tame the tongue of mankind. It is restless with wickedness. With deadly poison, it's lined.

3:9	By it we bless the Lord and Father, And by it curses we've jawed Against people who have been made After the likeness of God.
3:10	From the mouth comes praises *to God, From the same, curses *to others. That these things in this way occur Should never be, my brothers.
3:11	A spring does not pour out water That's fresh *for your thirst to fill And then pour out from the same hole Water that could make you ill.
3:12	Can olives come from a fig tree, Or figs come from a grapevine? No, my brothers, and neither can Fresh water arise from brine.
3:13	Who's informed and wise among you? Make sure that the works you show In the humbleness of wisdom Out of good behavior flow.
3:14	But if you have harsh jealousy And contention in your heart, Don't lie and cover up the truth, And boasting, do not impart.
3:15	This does not come down from above, This "wisdom" *that you enforce, But is earthly, unspiritual, And demonic in its source.

3:16	Because wherever may exist
	Jealousy and contention,
	There are chaos and evil deeds
	Of every dimension.
3:17	But the wisdom that's from above
	Is first pure *in attribute,
	Then peaceful, kind, considerate,
	Filled with mercy and good fruit.
	It's impartial and wears no mask.
3:18	Fruit which righteousness does bear
	Is sown in peace by the people
	Who practice peace *everywhere.

4:1	The wars and battles among you,
	From what source do they arise?
	From the pleasures which as soldiers
	In your body parts exercise.
4:2	You strongly want yet do not have.
	So what do you do? You kill.
	You envy yet never obtain.
	So you quarrel and fight at will.
	You don't have since you fail to ask.
4:3	You ask and gain no *treasures
	Since you keep on asking wrongly
	To spend it on your pleasures.

4:4	Faithless ones! Befriending the world
	Is fighting God. Don't you know?
	You who plot to be the world's friend
	Set yourself up as God's foe.
4:5	Or do you think that the Scripture
	Is futile in what it affirms?
	"The Spirit made to live in us
	With envy continually yearns."
4:6	God gives greater grace, for He says:
	"God opposes those filled with pride,
	But to the ones who are humble
	He gives grace. ♦It's a gift supplied."
4:7	So, be in subjection to God
	In light of what Scripture does say,[262]
	And stand firm against the Devil,
	And from you, he will run away.
4:8	Come near to God, and He'll come near.
	You sinners, clean hands secure.
	You who have a divided mind,
	Your own hearts, you must make pure.
4:9	Be in the state of misery.
	Mourning and crying, assume.
	Let your laughter be changed to grief
	And your joy be changed to gloom.
4:10	Become humble before the Lord,
	And you, the Lord will exalt.
4:11	As to one another, brothers,
	Stop every verbal assault.

He who speaks against his brother
Or judges him *in his own eyes
Ultimately* speaks against law
And upon it judgment supplies.

And if you keep on judging law
With judgments as you see fit,*
You are not a doer of law
But you are a judge of it.

4:12   There is One lawgiver and judge,
The One who can destroy and save.
You who keeps judging your neighbor,
Who are you *like this to behave?

4:13   Listen now, you people who say,
"Today or tomorrow we'll go
To this city, stay there a year,
Do business, and make profits flow."

4:14   You know not what your life will be
Or what tomorrow engineers,
For you're a vapor which is seen
For a short time, then disappears.

4:15   Instead of that you are to say,
"If it is the Lord's desire,
We will have existence at all
And for this or that aspire."

4:16   As for now you boast in your pride.
All such boasts are evil therein.
4:17   Therefore, he who knows to do good
Yet refrains, to him it is sin.

The Poetic Letter of James

5:1 Listen now, you who are wealthy.
Shed tears and weep loudly too.
Cry over all your miseries
Which are coming upon you.

5:2 The riches you gained have rotted.
Moth-eaten, your clothes have become.
5:3 The gold and silver you've amassed,
By rust they've been overrun.

Their rust testifies against you
And will eat your flesh like fire.
Yes, you have stored up this treasure
For when the last days transpire.

5:4 Look! The wages of laborers
By whom your own fields were mowed,
The wages which you have withheld
Cry out *for what you have owed.

The ears of the Lord of armies,
The harvesters' cries have entered.
5:5 You have reveled upon the earth,
Self-indulgent *and self-centered.

Fattened hearts in a day of slaughter,
For yourselves you foolishly chose.*
5:6 You condemned and killed the upright
Although you, they do not oppose.

5:7	Therefore, brothers, become patient
	Until the Lord comes on that day.
	Note the farmer keeps awaiting
	The earth's precious fruit to display.

        He's patient for it 'til the time
        The early and late rains appear.
5:8   Be patient too. Strengthen your hearts,
        For the Lord's coming has drawn near.

5:9   Against one another, brothers,
        Don't be grumbling anymore
        In order that you not be judged.
        Look! The judge stands at the door.

5:10   Take as an example, brothers,
        Of suffering, and patience too,
        Those who proclaimed in the Lord's name -
        The prophets - *let us review.

5:11   Look! We regard those who endured
        To be in a happy state.
        You've heard of the patience of Job,
        How it, he did demonstrate.*

        And you have seen the outcome worked
        By the Lord Himself which shows
        That He is full of compassion,
        And His mercy overflows.

5:12   Now my brothers, above all else,
        Stop practicing oaths, *I say.
        Don't swear by heaven or by earth.
        Don't swear any other way.

	But when you communicate "yes",

But when you communicate "yes",
Let it mean yes *and that's all,
And your "no" must really mean no
So on you, judgment won't fall.

5:13 Is anyone of you suffering?
Prayers to God, keep phrasing.
Are any in a cheerful mood?
With songs to God, keep praising.[263]

5:14 Is one of you constantly sick?
The church elders let him call for.
In the Lord's name rubbing with oil,
Let their prayers over him pour.

5:15 And the prayer which is offered up
By faith for this weary soul
Will rescue him *from his sickness
And the Lord will raise him whole.

And if he has committed sins,
Forgiveness to him will be sent.
5:16 So, confess to one another
Your sins so as to repent.[264]

Keep praying for one another.
Confess and pray to be healed.
A just one's prayer has great power
When its workings, it does wield.

5:17 Elijah was a human being
With the same nature as ours.
He prayed fervently that there not
Fall on the land any showers.

	And it did not rain on the land
	For three years and six months more.
5:18	Again he prayed. Heaven gave rain,
	And the land, its fruit then bore.

5:19   My brothers, if one among you
       From the truth is led astray
       And someone turns that person back
       To the truth from his sinful way –

5:20   Let him learn that the one who turns
       A sinner from his wayward stride
       Will save his very soul from death
       And a host of sins will hide.

THE POETIC LETTER OF PETER - 1 PETER

1:1 Peter, Jesus Christ's apostle,
To the exiled chosen ones
Of the scattering which took place
To the following regions:

The coastal region of* Pontus,
Galatia *(southward it be),
Cappadocia and Asia,
And Bithynia *by the Black Sea.

1:2 According to God the Father's
Prior decision to know[265]
You all in a personal way,
His choice of you, He did bestow.

The Spirit's sanctifying work
Put His choice into effect
For living in obedience
As His chosen and elect.*

　　　　　And also for the sprinkling
　　　　　Of Christ Jesus's blood.
　　　　　May both grace and peace to you all
　　　　　In multiplicity flood.

1:3　　　Praise to our Lord Jesus Christ's God,
　　　　　Who is our Lord's Father too,
　　　　　For He by His lavish mercy
　　　　　Caused us to be born anew.

　　　　　We're born into a living hope
　　　　　Which in certainty looks ahead♦
　　　　　By means of the resurrection
　　　　　Of Jesus Christ from the dead.

1:4　　　We're born into an inheritance
　　　　　Which can't perish, spoil, or fade,
　　　　　Which in heaven for all of you,
　　　　　Its reservation has been made.

1:5　　　You are continually guarded
　　　　　Through your faith by God's power
　　　　　For a salvation that's ready
　　　　　To be shown in the last hour.[266]

1:6　　　In all this, you greatly rejoice
　　　　　Though now for a time that's brief
　　　　　(And since it is necessary),
　　　　　In many trials you have grief.

1:7　　　This is so the genuineness
　　　　　Of your faith, valued higher
　　　　　Than gold which is perishable
　　　　　Even though tested by fire -

>
> Will result in it being found
> At Jesus Christ's revelation
> As praiseworthy, as glorious,
> And as with high commendation.

1:8
> Even though you did not see Him,
> To love Him has been your choice;
> Although you don't see but believe,
> In Him you greatly rejoice.

> And that with joy unspeakable,
> Filled with glory *that extols

1:9
> Since you're receiving your faith's end,
> The salvation of your souls.

1:10
> Now, concerning this salvation,
> The prophets who had prophesied
> About this grace which was for you,
> Search and inquiry, they applied.

1:11
> They were searching as to what time
> Or nature of time, ♦its sort,
> The Spirit of Christ within them
> Was declaring in their report.

> That is to say, the one given*
> When He predicted *without fail
> The suffering in store for Christ
> And the glorious things to trail.

1:12
> To these prophets it was revealed
> Concerning these things *of grace
> That they were not serving themselves
> But you *in this time and place.

        These things have been announced to you
        Through those who preached the good news
        To you by the Holy Spirit
        Sent from heaven *to the Jews.[267]

        Into these things that have to do
        With salvation *in these days,
        Angels have an intense desire
        To stoop down and fix their gaze.

1:13   Therefore, with your minds girded up
        And sober without cessation,
        Fully hope in the coming grace
        At Jesus Christ's revelation.

1:14   Being obedient children,
        Do not be shaping your ways
        After the desires of your past
        Held in your ignorant days.

1:15   But He who called you is holy.
        So, be holy in all you do,
1:16   For it's written, "Since I'm holy,
        You all become holy too."

1:17   If you address Him as Father
        Who judges fairly always
        According to each person's work,
        Live in fear your earthly days.

1:18   For you know that you were redeemed
        From your conduct which was vain,
        Handed down from your ancestors,
        Not by things which won't remain.

	You weren't bought by silver or gold
1:19	But by the precious blood of Christ,
	Blood as of a lamb unblemished
	And unflawed *when sacrificed.

1:20 Long before the world's creation,
The Christ had been foreknown,
But in these last times for your sake,
To the world the Christ was shown.

1:21 Through Him are believers in God
Who raised from the dead our Lord
And gave Him glory that in God
Your faith and hope would be *stored.

1:22 Since you have purified your souls
In obeying the truth told
For a sincere brotherly love,
Let unselfish love unfold.[268]

Love one another fervently
From the heart, and here is why:
1:23 You've been born anew not from seed
Which decays but which won't die.

You have been born anew from seed
Through ♦the gospel preached before,
The word of God which is living
And remains forevermore.

1:24 Therefore, "All flesh is just like grass,
And all glory it parades
Is just like the bloom of the grass.
The bloom falls, and the grass fades.

1:25 But the word declared by the Lord
Continues forevermore."
And this is the word which was preached
As good news to you before.

2:1 Therefore, because you have laid down
All wickedness and all guile,
Hypocrisies, envious acts,
And all statements that revile –

2:2 As newborn babes, long for the milk
That's without contamination
But is rational that in it
You might grow in your salvation.

2:3 This is under the assumption
That you *whom I have in mind
Have tasted that the Lord Himself
Is oh so very* kind.

2:4 We come to Him, the stone that lives,
Who by men has been rejected.
However, in the sight of God
He is precious and elected.

2:5 And you yourselves as living stones
Are built together solely
As a house that is spiritual
For a priesthood that is holy.

You're to offer sacrifices
That are spiritual, *unflawed.
Such offerings through Jesus Christ
Are acceptable to God.

2:6　Therefore, it's contained in Scripture:
"Look! A stone in Zion, I place,
A chosen, precious cornerstone.
You who trust Him won't have disgrace."

2:7　So, to you who trust, He's precious,
But to those who don't, *it's said:
"The stone the builders rejected
Became the corner, the head."

2:8　And it says to them, "He became
A stone over which to stumble
And a rock that's so offensive
That it causes one to tumble."

For they stumble over the word
(The good news to those who've sinned)◆
Because they're disobedient.
To stumble, they are destined.

2:9　But you are an elected race,
A priesthood with royalty,
A people for a possession,
A nation which is holy.

This is so that you might proclaim
The virtues of Him outright,
Him who called you out of darkness
Into His wonderful light.

2:10	Formerly, you weren't a people, But you're God's people today. You used to not obtain mercy, But now mercy's on display.
2:11	Dear ones, I urge you as exiles And aliens *who on earth stroll To abstain from fleshly desires Which keep warring against your soul.
2:12	Keep your conduct honorable Among Gentiles since they talk Against you as doing evil. Contradict them by your walk.♦ This is so that by your good works Under their observation, They might give God the glory on The day of visitation.

2:13	To all human institutions, Be subject for the Lord's sake, Whether to the king who's reigning Or to officials he might make.
2:14	Submit to kings as those supreme And to officials as if sent By him to punish wrongdoers And to praise those on good bent.

2:15	Because the will of God is this: That by practicing what's good, You make silent the ignorance Of fools *who've not understood.
2:16	Be as free men yet not as those With freedom ♦as a façade, As a veil over wickedness, But act as bond slaves of God.
2:17	Place high value on all people; Love the brotherhood *which ties; Keep on showing reverence to God; With honor the king recognize.
2:18	Household slaves, keep in submission To your masters in all fear, Not only to those good and kind But even to those severe.
2:19	For this is grace, ♦a gift from God:[269] If anyone endures grief, Suffering in an unjust way Due to their godly belief.
2:20	For what kind of glory is there If you keep on enduring When in some way you are sinning And beatings you're incurring? But if you keep on enduring When well-doing you embrace And you are suffering for it, In God's presence that is grace.

2:21	Because for you Christ suffered too, Leaving you a model today To follow along in His steps, You are called to suffer this way.
2:22	Christ never did commit a sin, Nor was guile in His mouth found.
2:23	Although constantly insulted, No insult back, did He sound.
	Although constantly suffering, Not one threat did He express, But He gave Himself up to Him Who judges with righteousness.
2:24	In His body He bore our sins On the tree *where He did forgive So that, after we die to sin, In righteousness we would live.
	By His wound,[270] you all became healed.
2:25	For you were like sheep gone astray, But you have turned to the shepherd, Guardian of your souls, today.
3:1	Likewise, wives, be in submission To your own husbands. Here's why: If any ♦are unbelievers, The word, they always defy -
	They might be won without a word By the conduct of their wives
3:2	After watching the respectful And pure way you live your lives.

3:3	Don't let your outward appearance Be for you as something stressed, Like braided hair, and wearing gold, Or the fine way you are dressed.
3:4	Stress the person veiled in the heart With décor that never dies, A gentle and quiet spirit Which is precious in God's eyes.
3:5	For the former holy women Who in God had their hope rest - By submitting to their husbands, In this way, they also dressed.
3:6	Let me give you one example.[271] Abraham, Sarah obeyed, Respectfully calling him lord. As her children, you've been made. That's assuming that doing good Is your deliberation Without possessing fearfulness Of any intimidation.
3:7	Likewise, husbands, live with your wives With a knowledge *that lacks not, Assigning honor to your wife As you would a fragile pot. Honor your wives as fellow heirs In the unearned gift of life So that your prayers may never be Hindered *by unresolved strife.

The Poetic Scriptures of Six Writers

3:8	Lastly, let all show sympathy. Form your thoughts in like fashion. Show to others brotherly love. Be humble. Have compassion.
3:9	Do not repay evil with wrong. Slander for slander, don't merit, But bless instead since a blessing You all were called to inherit.
3:10	For let the one who really wants To love life and see good days Prevent his tongue from evil words, And no guile, let his lips phrase.
3:11	But let that one turn from evil And begin to practice good. Let that one seek peace *'til it's found And pursue it *as all should.
3:12	For the Lord's eyes see the righteous. His ears hear their petition, But the Lord's face is against those Fulfilling evil ambition.
3:13	And what person will mistreat you If good you've zealously stressed?
3:14	But even if for righteousness You should suffer, you are blessed.

	Don't be afraid of their terror.
	Don't be intimidated,
3:15	But in your hearts let Christ as Lord
	Be wholly dedicated.

	Always be set for a defense,
	Responding* to all who elect
	To ask why you have hope within.
3:16	Speak with meekness and respect.

Always maintain a good conscience
That when they slander your name,
Insulting your good way in Christ,
They then will be put to shame.

3:17 For it is better, if God's will
Should so desire ♦and long,
That one suffer for doing good
Instead of for doing wrong.

3:18 Because Christ too suffered for sins.
Just once *did this, He provide.
As a righteous Man in the place
Of the unrighteous, *Jesus died.

He did this to bring us to God,
That is, His own life to give.*
Although He was killed in the flesh,
His spirit was made to live.

3:19 In that spirit He also came
And a proclamation made
To the spirits in a prison
3:20 Who long ago disobeyed.

Specifically, when God's patience
Was waiting ♦and enduring
In Noah's days when construction
Of the ark was occurring.

In this ark was a small number,
Just eight human lives inside.
All eight lives were brought safely through
By the water *God supplied.

3:21 An antitype called baptism
Now saves you *but in this sense,
Not removing filth from the flesh
But a pledge of good conscience.

Pledging to God in good conscience
Saves you *from condemnation
By Jesus Christ's resurrection
Which proves we have salvation.*

3:22 He's at God's right hand in heaven,
Seated when He entered it.
Angels and all authorities
And powers to Him submit.

4:1 Because Christ suffered in the flesh,
Arm yourselves with that same aim
Since he who suffered in the flesh
Has refrained from sin's *game.[272]

The Poetic Letter of Peter – 1 Peter

4:2 That way you will no longer live
     The time in the flesh that remains
     Indulging in human desires
     But what to God's will pertains.

4:3 For the time that has passed us by
     Was enough to have fulfilled
     The life plan that the heathens have
     Which in you had been instilled.*

     For you lived in licentiousness,
     In drunkenness and in lust,
     In revelries and carousing,
     In idolatries which disgust.

4:4 The heathens are surprised at you
     That with them you do not run
     In the same uncontrolled excess.
     So, they blaspheme *you, each one.

4:5 They will give an account to Him
     Who's ready for the giving
     Of judgment to those who are dead
     And to those who are living.

4:6 For this cause, to the spiritual dead[273]
     The gospel word, we did give:
     Although judged in the flesh by men,
     In their spirit, by God they'd live.

4:7 The end of all things has drawn near.
     So in light of this, *I say,
     Be of sound judgment and sober
     So in earnestness♦ you'll pray.

4:8   Above all things, hold selfless love
        Fervently for one another
        Since, as you demonstrate this love,
        Many sins, that love will cover.

4:9   Be friendly• toward one another,
        Showing hospitality
        Without providing for complaints
        Any opportunity.

4:10   As each one has received a gift,
        In service that gift, then place
        Toward others as good managers
        Of God's many-sided grace.

4:11   If someone speaks, then speak as one
        Speaking as God's words *apply.
        If someone serves, then serve as one
        Empowered by God's supply.

        Do this so that in everything
        God might be glorified then
        Through Christ[274] to whom is the glory
        And power forever. Amen.

4:12   Dearly loved ones, don't be surprised
        By the fire you undergo
        As if a strange thing sprung on you.
        For it comes to test you so.

4:13   But keep rejoicing in so far
        As in Christ's sufferings you share
        So that you might greatly rejoice
        When His glory is laid bare.

4:14	If you're insulted in Christ's name, Consider yourselves as blessed Since the glorious Spirit of God Surely* upon you does rest.
4:15	For let not one of you suffer As one who murders or steals, Or as one who spies on others, Or who in wrongdoing deals.
4:16	If as a Christian one suffers, Let that person bear no shame. Instead, let him glorify God In relation to that name.
4:17	For the season for His judgment Begins with God's house, *I say. If first with us, what end is for those Who God's gospel disobey?
4:18	"If the righteous are saved with strain, Where then will these ones appear: The ungodly and the sinners?" (That's a quote from Proverbs here)[275]
4:19	So then, let all those who suffer While God's will they're pursuing Pledge to the faithful Creator Their own lives in well-doing.

The Poetic Scriptures of Six Writers

5:1	Therefore, as a fellow elder,
	Who to Christ's sufferings attest,
	And as a participant in
	The glory to be undressed –
	I urge the elders among you,
5:2	God's flock in your location,
	Shepherd willingly as God wants,
	Not out of obligation.
	Nor with a corrupt lust for gain,
	But shepherd with an eager walk.
5:3	Don't domineer those in your care,
	But be examples to the flock.
5:4	And when Jesus the Chief Shepherd
	Is revealed, ◆fully displayed,
	You will receive the victory wreath
	Of glory that cannot fade.
5:5	Similarly, you younger men,
	To elders be in subjection.
	Everyone toward one another
	Make this humble election:*
	Clothe yourselves with humility
	Because *Proverbs says someplace,[276]
	"God opposes those who are proud.
	To the humble, He gives grace."

5:6	Therefore, under God's mighty hand
	Be humbled so in due time
	He may, *and not anyone else,
	Your exaltation assign.
5:7	Cast all your worry upon Him
	Since for you He really cares.
5:8	Be sober and be on alert.
	To this, the Devil compares:
	Like a lion, he is roaming
	With a roar *loud and scary,
	Seeking someone to swallow up.
	He is your adversary.
5:9	Stand against him firm in your faith
	Because you already know
	The same sufferings in the world,
	Your brothers[277] now undergo.
5:10	But once you've suffered a short time,
	The God of all grace *sufficed
	Who called you into His glory,
	The eternal glory in Christ –
	He will Himself restore each one.
	He'll fit, set, and strengthen you.
5:11	To Him alone is the power
	Forevermore. It is true.[278]
5:12	A brother full of faithfulness,
	I regard Silvanus to be.
	Through him, I have written to you,
	But I've only written briefly.

I've written to encourage you
And attest with my raised hand[279]
This to be the true grace of God.
Into this grace, you must stand!

5:13   The ones in Babylon greet you
Who are your fellow-elect.
Mark who's my son also wishes
His own greeting to direct.

5:14   Greet one another in this way,
In a holy[280] kiss of love.
To all of you who are in Christ,
You possess peace from above![281]

THE POETIC LETTER OF PETER – 2 PETER

1:1 This letter is* from Simeon
(Who as Peter became known),
A bond slave and apostle of
Jesus who as Christ *was shown.

To those who've been allotted faith
Equal to our faith as priced
In the righteousness of our God,[282]
The Savior, Jesus the Christ.

1:2 My wish is that both grace and peace
Be multiplied to you all
In your personal walk[283] with God
Whom Jesus our Lord we call.[284]

1:3 His divine might has given us
Freely all that has to do
With life and godliness, knowing
Him who has called me and you.

	He called us by His own glory
	And the virtue He's possessed
1:4	Through which He's freely given us
	Promises precious and best.

This is in order that through them
In divine nature you'll share,
Escaping corruption in lust
Which in the world *does ensnare.

1:5 Also for this very reason,
With all diligence applied,
To your faithfulness add virtue.
In virtue insight provide.

1:6 And to insight add self-control,
And to self-control append
Patience ♦or steadfast endurance.
In this, godliness extend.

1:7 In your godliness then supply
A love of the brotherhood,
And in brotherly love supply
A love that's selfless *and good.[285]

1:8 When these are in you and abound,
Useful and fruitful you'll become[286]
In the personal knowledge of
Our Lord Jesus Christ, *the Son.

1:9 For the person who lacks these things
Is short-sighted, even blind,
Since the cleansing of his old sins,
He has not brought to his mind.

1:10	So, brothers, more eagerly make Firm your election and call, For by practicing all these things, You'll never stumble and fall.
1:11	For thus to you the entrance to The kingdom which does abide (The kingdom of our Lord and Savior) Will be lavishly supplied.
1:12	Therefore, I'll always be ready To remind you all I've told Though you know and are firmly set In the truth which you now hold.
1:13	I regard it as only right, As long as I'm in this tent, To stir you up by reminders Since my death is imminent.
1:14	For by our Lord, Jesus the Christ, This truth to me was made clear. So, I know that the removal Of my tent is very near.
1:15	So, I will be very eager That reminders, you receive[287] To have you always remember After this body, I leave.
1:16	For the power and the coming Of Jesus the Christ our Lord, We did not make known by heeding Myths that to slyness accord.

We made it known to you because
Eyewitnesses we became
Of that majesty, ♦that splendor.
That is why this, we proclaim.♦

1:17 Christ received from God the Father
Honor and glory that day
When from the majestic glory
To Christ such a voice did say:

"This is My Son I dearly love,
Whom as My delight, I count."
1:18 We heard that voice from heaven while
With Him on the holy mount.

1:19 And we have the prophetic word
That is more sure, *one we read,
To which you're doing very well
To pay attention ♦and heed.

In a dark place, you follow it
As a lamp that's shining far
'Til the day dawns and in your hearts
Arises the morning star.

1:20 For above all else realize this:
All prophetic oration
Of Scripture never derived from
One's own interpretation.

1:21 For no prior prophecy came
By human will, *which is flawed,
But moved by the Holy Spirit,
Men spoke directly from God.

| 2:1 | But false prophets also arose
Among the people *of old
As teachers will among you rise
Who to pseudo-doctrine hold. |
|---|---|

Heresies that are destructive,
They will secretly bring in,
Denying even the Master
Who redeemed them from their sin.

Thus, they will bring upon themselves
Destruction sudden ♦and swift.
2:2 To their licentious behavior,
Many will eagerly shift.

Due to them, the way to the truth
Will then be desecrated.
2:3 They will exploit you in their greed
By words they fabricated.

Their long deserved condemnation
Is not standing idly by,
And their eternal destruction,
No sleep, does it occupy.

2:4 For since God did not spare angels
After they had missed the mark
But gave them up, being reserved
For judgment somewhere that's dark -

This place is known as Tartarus
Where ropes of darkness await
All the angels who have rebelled.
'Twill be their eternal state.*

2:5 Since He spared not the ancient world
But preserved Noah (the eighth
To enter in the ark of God),*
A herald of righteous *faith -

Since He spared not the ancient world
After pouring on mankind,
Characterized as ungodly,
A flood *globally designed –

2:6 And since Sodom and Gomorrah,
The cities *of wicked fame,
He condemned to devastation
Until ashes they became

(This functions as an example,
This swift judgment which destroyed,♦
To future ungodly people
That judgment they won't avoid) -*

2:7 And since He rescued righteous Lot
Who was being worn right down
By the licentious behavior
Of lawless men *in that town

2:8 (For righteous Lot while living there,
In what he both heard and saw,
Was torturing his righteous soul
By their acts against God's law) -

2:9	So the Lord knows to save from trial Those who live the godly way And to keep under punishment The unjust 'til judgment day.
2:10	Specially those who live behind The flesh in its sinful ways Which leads to moral corruption. Glories, they also dispraise.
	They are both daring and self-willed. They do not tremble ♦or fear When speaking blasphemies against The glories *in heaven's sphere.
2:11	Whereas angelic messengers (Though greater in strength and might), As for a blasphemous judgment, Against them do not indict.
2:12	But as far as these *false teachers, Like beasts which have no reason Naturally born to be captured And slaughtered *in due season
	(In this condition they blaspheme, And of knowledge, they are void) - As beasts are destined for slaughter, They will also be destroyed.
2:13	They will receive unrighteousness As their pay for deeds not right. They consider it as pleasure To revel in broad daylight.

They are just spots and blemishes
Reveling in all deceit,
And they do this during the time
That with you at feasts, they eat.

2:14 They have eyes filled with adultery
And sinning eyes that don't rest.
They keep luring unstable souls.
Hearts trained in greed, they've possessed.

They are children under a curse!
2:15 Leaving behind the right way,
They followed the path of Balaam
And so have been led astray.

Balaam, the son of Bosor loved
The wage of unrighteous pay.
2:16 But he received a sharp rebuke
For his own transgressing way.

A donkey who's naturally dumb
(Speaking in a human voice)
Prevented the prophet Balaam
From making a crazy choice.

2:17 These false teachers are dried-up springs
And clouds driven by a gale.
For them, a place has been reserved
Where deep darkness does prevail.

2:18 For when spouting puffed up folly,
They lure fleshly lusts along
Of those who have hardly escaped
From the ones living in wrong.

	They lure them to licentious acts,
2:19	Promising them liberty,
	While they themselves exist as slaves
	To corruption *which can't free.

        For whatever conquers someone,
        To that thing he's been enslaved.
2:20   So the state of these false teachers
        Are judged by how they've behaved.[288]

        Let's assume they've escaped the world's
        Defilements *(which them enticed)
        By a real knowledge of our Lord
        And Savior Jesus the Christ.

        Let's say they're entangled again,
        Continually overcome.
        For them, the last state has turned out
        To be worse than the first one.

2:21   It would have been better for them
        Not to have personally known
        The way leading to righteousness
        Than that righteous life to disown.*

        Once personally knowing it
        Then turning from the commands,
        The holy commands given them,
2:22   This proverb's fulfillment stands:

        "A dog returns to the vomit
        Which from its own mouth did flood,
        And once it's washed, a swine returns
        To wallowing in the mud."

3:1   This is now your second letter
          Which, my dear ones, I designed.
          In both, I've tried to waken up
          With reminders, your pure mind.

3:2   Specifically, to remind you
          Of the words *already told
          Which had been spoken long before
          By holy prophets *of old.

          And also to remind you of
          The commandment to you brought
          By your apostles who relayed
          What the Lord and Savior taught.

3:3   First of all, understand this truth:
          In the last days *there'll be talk.
          Mockers will come with their mocking
          While by their own lusts they walk.

3:4   "Where's the promise of His coming?
          For since the fathers have died
          All things remain as it has been
          From creation's start!" they'll chide.

3:5   For they let this fact escape them:
          By the word God had declared,
          The heavens arose long ago,
          And the earth too was prepared.

	Out of water, the earth arose.
	Between water, it was placed,²⁸⁹
3:6	By which the world existing then
	By flood water was laid waste.

3:7 But both the heavens and the earth
(The current one *we admire)
By the very same word *of God
Have been reserved for fire.

Yes, both the heavens and the earth
For judgment day have been stored,
Also the complete destruction
Which on the godless are poured.

3:8 But, my dear ones, don't overlook
The fact that in the Lord's way
One day is as a thousand years
And a thousand years, one day.

3:9 So, in regards to His promise,
Though slowness this some would call,
The Lord, He is not being slow
But is patient toward you all.

For He is not determining
For certain ones to perish
But for all people to make room
That repentance, *they cherish.

3:10 The day of the Lord will arrive
As a thief coming around.
In that day, the heavens themselves
Will pass with a roaring sound.

But elements will dissipate,
Burning in the atmosphere.
Also, earth and the works within
Will then be found ♦and made clear.

3:11   What kind of people must you be
Since all will thus dissipate?
To holiness and godliness,
Your conduct must correlate.

3:12   For you're then anticipating,
As well as hastening on,
The coming of the day of God
Due to which *all will be gone.

By a burning which is by fire,
The heavens will dissipate,
And elements will be dissolved
By a heat intensely great.

3:13   But according to His promise,
We wait with fervor applied[290]
For new heavens and a new earth
Where righteousness does abide.

3:14   Therefore, dear ones, be diligent
While for these you wait with aim
So that you may be found by Him
In peace without spot or blame.

3:15   And consider our Lord's patience
As His continued work to save,
As our dear brother Paul wrote you
By the wisdom him God gave.[291]

3:16	God gave it in all his letters,
	As every letter reflects,*
	When speaking in them of these things.
	Some things he wrote are complex.
	The untaught and unstable twist
	His words *in their deduction
	As they do the other Scriptures
	But to their own destruction.
3:17	Therefore, dear ones, because you know
	About these things beforehand,
	Keep on guard so as not to fall
	From the firmness where you stand.
	Don't be led astray by errors
	Which the lawless have proclaimed,
3:18	But continue growing in grace
	And in knowledge that you've gained.
	That is, knowing Jesus the Christ,
	Our Lord, in a personal way.
	To Him be the glory both now
	And 'til the eternal day.

THE POETIC LETTER OF JUDE

1:1   Jude, a bond slave of Jesus Christ,
         Also a brother of James.
         To the called, loved in Father God
         And kept in Jesus Christ's name.[292]

1:2   My wish for you is that mercy
         To you all be multiplied,
         Also that peace and love to you
         Be abundantly supplied.

1:3   While working with all diligence
         To you, my dear ones, to write
         About our common salvation,
         Necessity gripped me tight.

         I held the need to write to you,
         Urging you all to contend
         For the faith which was once for all
         Handed to the saints *to fend.

1:4   For certain men, ungodly ones
Have snuck in through the back door.²⁹³
Already this judgment of theirs
Has been written of before.

These men change our God's grace into
A sin license to elect.
Our sole Master, Our Lord Jesus Christ,
They continually reject.

1:5   I determine to remind you,
Though you've known all beforehand,
That the Lord first saved a people
Once for all from Egypt's land.

Then secondly, them He destroyed,
The ones who did not believe.
1:6   And I remind you of angels
Who to their rule did not cleave.

But they left their own dwelling place.
Their judgment, He has reserved
In eternal chains under gloom
On that great day *as deserved.

1:7   Just as Sodom and Gomorrah,
And the surrounding cities,
Are displayed as an example
In a similar way to these.²⁹⁴

They indulged in sexual grossness.
Others' flesh was their desire.
They're a model of those suffering
Justice by eternal fire.

1:8	However, in the same way too,
	The flesh, those dreamers²⁹⁵ defile.
	And they reject authority.
	Glories, they also revile.
1:9	But when Michael, the archangel
	Argued with ◆him who opposes,
	Dialoguing with the Devil
	About the body of Moses -
	He dared not even to pronounce
	A judgment which would accord
	With blasphemy but instead said,
	"May you be rebuked by the Lord!"
1:10	But these blaspheme what they don't know,
	And as beasts with reason void,
	Whatever they naturally know,
	In those things they are destroyed.
1:11	Woe to them since they proceeded
	To follow after Cain's way,
	And were plunged into the error
	That arose from Balaam's pay.
	Woe to them because they perished
	In Korah's hostility.
1:12	They're hidden reefs in your love feasts,
	Yet with visibility.²⁹⁶
	For they eat together with you,
	And themselves, they boldly tend.
	They are clouds that have no water,
	Blown away by any wind.

	They're fruitless autumn trees, twice dead,
	Uprooted, *bearing no more.
1:13	They are violent waves of the sea
	Foaming their shame *on the shore.

       They are stars which wander about,
       No symmetry in their ways.♦
       For them, a place has been reserved
       Where deep darkness always stays.

1:14   Enoch, the seventh from Adam
       Prophesied of these as well.
       "Behold, the Lord came with His saints,
       Innumerable." he did tell.

1:15   "He came to place judgment on all
       And to rebuke all life, ♦each one,
       Concerning all their godless works
       Which were impiously done.

       "He came to rebuke every life
       For all the harsh insults hurled
       Which were spoken against Him by
       Godless sinners *in this world."

1:16   These are discontented grumblers.
       Their own lusts, they try to obtain.
       Their mouth declares arrogant words,
       Marveling at faces for gain.

1:17   Dearly loved ones, recall the words
       Which the apostles foretold,
       Those sent by our Lord Jesus Christ.
       What they were saying, *behold.

The Poetic Letter of Jude

1:18   They were telling you constantly,
"In the last time will be taunts
By those who continually go
After their ungodly wants."

1:19   These are those people among you
Who division always press.
They are driven by their nature.[297]
The Spirit, they don't possess.

1:20   Dear ones, building up yourselves in
The most holy faith *we observe,
Praying in the Holy Spirit,
1:21   In God's love yourselves preserve.

And in God's love yourselves preserve
As that mercy you wait for
Given by our Lord Jesus Christ
Unto life forevermore.

1:22   Have mercy on those who waver,
1:23   But others, out of the fire
You must rescue by snatching them.
Of this, you must never tire.[298]

And still others, have pity on,
But in fear it must be piled,
Despising the undergarments
Which by their flesh are defiled.

1:24   To Him who can prevent your fall
And who can cause you to stand
In the presence of His glory
In a joy that is so grand –

1:25   To the only God our Savior
Through our Lord Jesus the King[299]
What follows I ascribe to Him,*
With which to Him I now sing.*

To Him is glory, greatness, might,
And rule *again and again
Before all time, in the present,
And forevermore. Amen.

ENDNOTES

1   Derived from Genesis 17:19.
2   Jacob became known as the deceiver after tricking his father into blessing him instead of Esau (Genesis 27:12).
3   Ram is only mentioned in genealogies.
4   Derived from Numbers 2:3. Nahshon became the chief of the tribe of Judah.
5   Rahab was the harlot from Jericho who trusted in God and joined the Israelite culture. See Joshua 6:25.
6   This is derived from the first chapter of Ruth. Moab was well over 100 miles from Bethlehem as the crow flies. The journey required circumventing the Dead Sea, which could easily double the mileage.
7   Derived from 2 Samuel 11:3. This is the shameful story of David's adultery with Bathsheba and murder of Uriah.
8   The kingdom became divided. The northern kingdom included ten tribes of Israel, and the southern kingdom included the tribes of Judah and Benjamin. Only the southern kingdom of Judah was concerned with the succession of kings being from the line of David.
9   Derived from 1 Kings 15:6,7.
10   Derived from 1 Kings 15:14.
11   Derived from 1 Kings 22:43.
12   The Greek writings transcribed the Hebrew for Joram and Jehoram exactly the same. See 2 Kings 8:16.
13   Uzziah was the great-great-grandson of Jehoram. The same exact term (rendered as *became father of or fathered*) is used here in the Greek text as is done throughout this genealogical record. The term is used loosely to refer to a direct descendent, whether actually or legally.
14   Derived from 2 Kings 15:5.
15   Derived from 2 Kings 15:35.
16   Derived from 2 Kings 16:3,4.
17   Derived from 2 Kings 18:5.
18   Derived from 2 Kings 21:1.

19 Derived from 2 Kings 21:22.
20 The last three lines are derived from 2 Kings 22:8,11.
21 This phraseology puzzles scholars. Jechoniah was the grandson of Josiah, not his son, and he had only one brother (1 Chronicles 3:15,16). He was also exiled into Babylon by Nebuchadnezzar (Jeremiah 27:20). Some suggest that there was an error in copying. However, there is no evidence of a scribal error. Others state that Jehoiakim was also called Jechoniah. No evidence exists for this explanation either. Besides, Jehoiakim was never deported to Babylon, but his two sons were. See 2 Kings 24. The best explanation is that the term *fathered* or, as some translations put it, *begot*, is used loosely to refer to any descendant (see verse 8 notes concerning this word). The term *brother* is also used loosely to refer to relatives.
22 More literally, *and his brothers*. Since Jechoniah had only one brother, the term must refer to relatives including cousins.
23 Derived from Jeremiah 52:13.
24 1 Chronicles 3:19 lists Zerubbabel as Pedaiah's son. Pedaiah was Shealtiel's brother. Every other place Zerubbabel is called the son of Shealtiel. Either Pedaiah died and Shealtiel married the widow making Zerubbabel his stepson, or Shealtiel adopted Zerubbabel.
25 Derived from Ezra 4:3 and Haggai 1:1,8.
26 Throughout the genealogical record, Matthew has without fail followed the pattern of a certain person fathering someone else. He breaks that pattern here. Instead of saying Joseph fathered Jesus by Mary, a pattern that would match verses 5 and 6, he leaves the father unnamed by saying that Jesus was fathered by Mary. This sets up the next narrative giving the nature of the conception.
27 More literally, *the angel of the Lord*. The angel was called *an angel of the Lord* in verse 20, although the KJV contains the word *the* instead of *an*. The Greek text lacks the article *the* in verse 20 but inserts it here four verses later even though it is the same angel. This was a Greek way of saying, *the previously mentioned angel of the Lord*. The angel of the Lord was a key figure in the Old Testament but never is mentioned in the New Testament. Many scholars believe that Jesus was the angel of the Lord in the Old Testament.
28 This line really comes from verse three which states that all of Jerusalem became troubled by their question.
29 More literally, *His mother Mary*.
30 *A minor one* is poetic elaboration on the particular prophet Matthew is quoting, Hosea 11:1. Hosea is one of the twelve minor prophets.
31 Matthew does not state that Archelaus was Herod's heir. He states that Herod was his father.
32 Matthew does not quote a specific prophet but summarizes what the prophets (plural) communicated about the Messiah. To call a person

a Nazarene was to degrade them, much like the term nigger does in American culture. At least four prophets spoke of this degradation: Isaiah (53), Daniel (9:26), Zechariah (13:7), and David (Psalm 118:22).

33 Isaiah 40:3 is quoted. Isaiah was referring to Yahweh, and Matthew applies this divine name to Jesus.

34 Derived from Isaiah 11:2.

35 The first sentence spoken from heaven is from Psalm 2:7, referring to the final king of Israel. The last sentence is from Isaiah 42:1, referring to the suffering servant. Here the Father was declaring Jesus as both the Messiah and His servant who would have to suffer. Never in Jewish history had the Messiah and God's suffering servant been identified as the same person. The Father makes that identification in this declaration.

36 Because many translations have rendered this, *if You are the Son of God*, some have erroneously concluded that Satan was trying to make Jesus doubt His Sonship. However, the language of the Greek text assumes the statement to be fact. Therefore, I have translated it, *since You are the Son of God*. Satan was tempting Jesus to be another kind of Messiah, different than the suffering servant the Father declared Him to be at His baptism.

37 This is poetic elaboration on why Jesus left Nazareth, derived from Luke 4:28-30. Matthew only records that Jesus left. Luke records His rejection by those in the synagogue as the cause for leaving Nazareth.

38 More accurately, *He healed every disease and illness in the people*. The word *every* is reflected in the words, *and did not refuse*.

39 The crowds are not described as being present until the end of chapter 7. The picture seems to be that Jesus positioned Himself on the mountaintop so everyone could hear as He taught His disciples.

40 Derived from the end of chapter 7 where it states that the crowds were amazed at His teaching.

41 This should be pronounced as one syllable. The word *blessed* means happy.

42 More literally, *will not pass away*.

43 More literally, *the kingdom of heaven*.

44 The object of what this person lives and teaches is not explicitly stated by Matthew but is implied from the context as being the entire Law.

45 More literally, *the kingdom of heaven*.

46 Gehenna was a dump southwest of Jerusalem which was constantly burning. It was a place for burning garbage and the dead bodies of criminals. In Jewish thought, it came to be used as a metaphor for eternal judgment.

47 Matthew quotes Jesus as shifting from addressing them all as a group to addressing an individual. In modern English the word *you* can be singular or plural. But the Greek language distinguishes between you

singular and you plural. You can see the change between singular and plural in the KJV since Old English used ye and you for the plural and thou, thy, and thee for the singular (see verses 23-26, 29,30, 36, 39-42). This back and forth shift continues throughout the next two chapters. When switching to you singular, one might imagine Jesus going up to a specific disciple and looking that disciple in the eye while teaching. He might then move to a different disciple, addressing him. He might then look up, scanning the group, as He switches to you plural. I have not always distinguished between singular and plural in the rhyming translation since Jesus's words for the individual was still to be applied by everyone.

48   Most translations call the action of the husband *divorce*. The word has the basic meaning *to release from*. In this context, it is a release from the marriage relationship. However, it is not a passive release of letting go, but a forceful act.

49   The language used by Matthew forbids a translation that resembles, *causing her to commit adultery*. Matthew puts the action of committing adultery in the passive voice. In other words, the action of committing adultery is not the woman's action (which would require the active voice), but is put upon the woman by someone else. She is not forced to commit adultery, but adultery is forced upon her although she has not committed it. Jesus was stating that, in general, Jewish society wrongly assumed that every divorced woman had committed adultery.

50   A slightly different word for committing adultery is used here which only differs by a few letters. It is a deponent verb, which means that it only has an active meaning (the subject does the action) even though it has a passive form.

51   The proposed prayer was not intended to be a prayer in itself but a guide to prayer. See Luke 11:4 note.

52   Some translations contain the ending, *for Yours is the kingdom and the power and the glory forever. Amen.* However, all Greek copies prior to the fifth century lack this. Many later manuscripts have varying adaptations of the above ending. The ending was most likely taken from 1 Chronicles 29:11 and added to make it into a prayer to recite.

53   One certainly could interpret Jesus's words as saying that we are promised God's forgiveness when we forgive others. The tense used by Matthew could picture instances of forgiving others, or it could be viewed as a snapshot of a person's life. In light of Mark 11:25, we have to opt for the latter. See Mark 11:25 notes.

54   The action verbs are in the Greek present tense and therefore communicate not a one-time action but an ongoing action of asking, seeking, and knocking. It is a picture of persistence.

55 The question asked expects a negative answer as the Greek text makes clear. *Such a father is unknown* is poetic elaboration on that negative answer.
56 This question expects a negative answer as in the previous verse. This line elaborates on that answer. Notice in the examples that the father seems to be trying to fool his son with a gift that somewhat resembles what is being requested. A stone might resemble a loaf, and a snake might resemble a fish.
57 Literally, *for this is the Law and the Prophets.*
58 The first two sentences in this stanza translate rhetorical questions expecting a negative answer.
59 A Roman official, better known as a centurion.
60 Jesus literally said, *Let the dead bury the dead.* He is speaking about those who are spiritually dead. There is no good excuse for putting off following Jesus.
61 The Greek copies vary as to the name of this region. Besides Gadarenes, some have Gerasenes and others have Gergesenes. Mark and Luke record the same incident but call the region, Gerasenes (see Mark 5:1; Luke 8:26). However, even the Greek copies of Mark and Luke have the same variety of names. Some scholars suggest that the different regions overlapped this town.
62 Matthew does not give the name of the town. Some might mistakenly think Jesus's own town here to be Nazareth. However, He changed His base of operations to Capernaum.
63 More literally, *He got up and went home.*
64 The word *awe* elaborates on the word *fear*. This was not the kind of fear that terrified them but struck them with awe since they praised God.
65 Derived from Luke 5:29.
66 More literally, *the blind men came to Him.*
67 In the original text, verse 1 reads *Simon who is called Peter.* That information is put here.
68 Derived from Matthew 16:18.
69 *Otherwise* is more literally, *but if it is not worthy.*
70 See Matthew 5:22 note.
71 *On high* is more literally, *who is in heaven.* This applies here and in the next verse.
72 Translations simply say that Jesus went into their cities (i.e., the cities of the twelve disciples). This does not mean that Jesus went to preach in their hometowns. There was a separation of Jesus from His twelve disciples as they went into cities to do as instructed in chapter 10. Whatever city they entered was their city to which they were to minister. After they finished their tasks, Jesus then would enter that town and preach and teach.
73 More accurately, *the poor are being evangelized.*

74 Jesus is referring to the prophecy of Malachi 4:5 which states that Elijah the prophet would come to Israel before the great and terrible day of the Lord comes.
75 Poetic elaboration. Jesus is quoting Hosea 6:6.
76 Although Matthew did not explicitly state that Isaiah spoke the words God instilled, it is obviously implied. The literal translation would be *what was spoken through Isaiah the prophet.*
77 *The world* is more literally *nations* or *Gentiles.* The same applies to verse 21.
78 The liberation from the demon is not stated by Matthew but is implied by the Pharisees' reaction in verse 24.
79 Literally, *the Holy Spirit.*
80 This sentence is poetic elaboration, summarizing the next verse.
81 Implied.
82 Only a handful of Greek manuscripts do not contain this verse, two of them being the earliest copies of Matthew. However, the internal evidence weighs against its omission, since the next verse would not make sense without it.
83 The last two lines of this stanza are poetic elaboration on the seeds multiplying into fruit of various amounts.
84 More literally, *but it has not been given them.*
85 The Greek text does not specifically make knowledge the object of what people have or don't have. This is implied by the previous verse of knowing or not knowing the mysteries of heaven's kingdom.
86 Poetic elaboration. Immature tares look exactly like wheat. Not until close to harvest time does the appearance of the tares differ from the wheat. Tares are poisonous.
87 The Greek text uses a different word for seed that is sometimes translated as *grain.* I have included both translations here.
88 Many scholars have identified this as the black mustard plant which grows to a height of ten to fifteen feet.
89 The Greek text calls the standard of measure a saton, which is roughly equal to 1/3 of a bushel. The text states that the woman put leaven in three of these measures of flour, or roughly a bushel.
90 The quote is from Psalm 78:2.
91 Derived from the scriptural introduction to Psalm 78:1 which reads *A Maskil of Asaph.*
92 *In groups* is derived from Mark 6:39.
93 Although this was new territory for Jesus in His travels, these men recognized Him from their encounter with Him in their travels.
94 More accurately, *Israel's house.*
95 Implied.
96 Derived from the next verse.
97 More literally, *flesh and blood did not reveal but My Father in heaven.*

98 Poetic elaboration. The meaning of Jesus's words have been debated by scholars over the centuries. From this passage comes the erroneous picture that Peter is now at the pearly gates of heaven either admitting or denying entrance. The term *kingdom of heaven* is only used by Matthew. Up to this point, it has been mentioned 18 times and refers not to heaven but to salvation. It is synonymous with the term *kingdom of God* and *kingdom of Christ*. At the moment of faith a person is transferred from the kingdom of darkness into this kingdom (Colossians 1:13). Therefore, the keys refer to the stewardship of sharing the gospel of the kingdom, which is salvation in Christ. Whoever accepts it by faith will be freed from the power of darkness or sin represented by Hades' gates. Whoever rejects it will remain bound by the power of darkness. However, this is not the work of a man but of God as seen in the idea that whatever is done on earth will already have been done in heaven. Jesus is now seated in heaven as the King and has been building His church through the gospel message as believers spread the gospel. Therefore, this stewardship, although given to Peter first as seen in Acts 2 in the salvation of the 3000, is given to all who genuinely confess Jesus as the Christ, the Son of the living God (see Matthew 28:18-20).

99 Poetic elaboration. I believe that Matthew is making a play on the words, *Peter* and *stumbling stone*. Prior to the confession of Jesus as the Christ, the Son of the Living God, Peter was known to those around him as Simon son of John. Because of his confession, Jesus then called him Peter, which means rock. Here the Rock becomes a stumbling stone.

100 Most translations read *Satan* where I have *adversary*. The Greek word often translated as *Satan* literally means *adversary* as all Greek lexicons define. Jesus was not talking to Satan but to Peter, which the text plainly states. Therefore, it is best to refer to the meaning of the word as a description of Peter.

101 This line elaborates on a particle in the Greek text that sets Jesus's statement in the next verse as a contrast. One could translate it, *on the one hand Elijah is coming and will restore all things, but on the other hand I tell you that Elijah has already come*. Jesus obviously is contrasting what He is saying with what the scribes had been saying about Elijah. Therefore, what the text implies, I have plainly stated in this line.

102 See Matthew 13:31 notes.

103 Verse 21 is not found in the earliest Greek copies of Matthew. It was probably added by later scribes to harmonize with Mark's gospel (see Mark 9:29).

104 A didrachma is a double drachma or two drachmas.

105 Matthew does not explain the purpose of collecting the double drachma. I have provided the additional information that it was a tax imposed on Jewish males for the temple.
106 The Greek text calls this coin a stater which was equivalent to two didrachmas, enough to satisfy the tax for two males.
107 More literally, *give it to them*.
108 The earliest Greek copies omit verse 11. It was most likely added in order to harmonize with Luke's gospel (see Luke 19:10).
109 Matthew introduces verse 19 with this statement. I have placed it at the end of the address.
110 These slaves were government officials who were given stewardship over parts of the kingdom. Part of their responsibility was to generate revenue and turn it in.
111 Literally, *one hundred denarii* which was equivalent to one hundred days of wages for the common laborer.
112 Derived from verse 29. The king was given all the details by the other slaves.
113 Literally, *Therefore*.
114 It is difficult to determine what Jesus means by *word*. To what word is He referring: His word on marriage and divorce, or the word that the disciples just said, namely, that it is best for a person not to ever get married? In light of the following comments by Jesus, I understand that he is referring to the disciples' conclusion. While marriage is God's intent for mankind in general, it is not His intent for everyone specifically. To some, it has been granted never to marry and only these have the ability to hold to this life. We must understand marriage as a sexual relation. So Jesus is speaking about those who have the ability to abstain from sexual relations. They are not to be criticized for abstaining but allowed to hold to this kind of life. Everyone else (those who don't have the ability to abstain from sexual relations for the rest of their lives), must see marriage as God's intent for them but in the sense that Jesus taught. Male and female must become one flesh for life.
115 Implied.
116 What I have rendered as *to reach your goal*, many translations render as *perfect* or *mature*. The man does not desire to be perfect in the sense of sinless, nor does he desire to be mature. He desires to grab hold of eternal life. That is his goal. The Greek word has the most basic meaning of completion, which is meant in this context. For Jesus is answering the man's question of what he still lacks in gaining eternal life.
117 Derived from Luke 18:23.
118 Literally, *the kingdom of God*.
119 Literally, *Behold*.

120 The phrase *I swear it* is derived from verse 28 where Jesus said, *the truth to you I now tell.*
121 More literally, *and did likewise.*
122 Poetic elaboration. Their chant came from Psalm 118:25,26.
123 Psalms as the location of the quoted Scripture is not mentioned by Matthew. Jesus is referring to Psalm 8:2.
124 Matthew does not call it a curse. The disciples called it this in Mark 11:21.
125 More literally, *immediately.*
126 The Greek copies of Matthew vary as to the order of the responses by the two sons in the parable as well as the answer given to Jesus. It is difficult to determine the original. Most versions have the reverse order than what I have. The NASB has the same order that I have. In the end, the order does not change the story.
127 More literally, *like angels of heaven.* The similarity is in relationship to marriage only. As angels have no marital relations, neither will humans in the resurrection life.
128 The earliest and best manuscripts do not contain verse 14.
129 The words *and climb* are poetic elaboration derived from Jesus's command in verse 16 to flee into the mountains.
130 The subject of what is near is unexpressed. Some translations say *He is near* and others say *it is near.* Jesus began answering three questions posed by His disciples in verse 3. The three questions are asked in this order: (1) When will the complete destruction of the temple buildings occur? (2) What is the sign of Your coming? (3) What is the sign of the end of the age? Jesus answered the third question first in verses 5-14. The gospel being preached to all the nations was that sign. Jesus then answered their first question second – the time of the complete destruction of the temple where not one stone would be left on another. This answer extends through verse 35. He warned the disciples to look for the abomination of desolation, the rising of the false christs and teachers, and the false claims of His coming, assuring them that His coming would be visible and known to all the earth's tribes. The lesson of the fig tree applies to the signs relating to the complete destruction of the temple, which Jesus stated would occur before that generation passes away. This complete destruction occurred in 70 A.D., forty years later. The second question about the sign of His coming was answered last of all in the remaining verses of this chapter.
131 More literally, *keep being ready.*
132 Derived from verse 15.
133 Derived from verse 15.
134 Derived from verse 25.
135 Poetic elaboration on the word *covenant.* As the first covenant was enacted with blood (Exodus 24:8), so also the new covenant. Although

Jesus had not died yet, He speaks in the present tense picturing His blood putting the new covenant into effect.

136 The fact that it was the right ear that was chopped off is derived from the gospel accounts of Luke and John.

137 Matthew does not say that Pilate was sent from Rome. This information is derived from historical records. Pilate was sent to rule as governor of Judea in A.D. 26. He made his place of residence in Caesarea.

138 The presence of the religious leaders is derived from the next verse.

139 Derived from the next two verses. Pilate did not want to condemn Jesus to death, and yet he did not want to go against the crowd's wish out of fear of being seen by Rome as an ineffective governor. Therefore, he sought to entice them to free Jesus by placing a terrible alternative before them, the release of Barabbas.

140 A cohort consisted of approximately 600 soldiers.

141 Literally, *from the sixth hour until the ninth hour.*

142 Matthew does not state that these particular bystanders misunderstood Jesus's words. It is plausible that they understood it but twisted Jesus's words, turning *Eli* into *Elijah,* in order to mock Him. These had to be Jewish bystanders for the Roman guards would be ignorant of such things.

143 Implied. Jesus's life was not taken from Him, but He chose to let His human spirit depart from His body. See John 10:18.

144 Derived from John 19:38.

145 This was a governmental seal that threatened the death penalty upon anyone breaking the seal. It would be impossible to move the stone without breaking the seal.

146 Matthew assumes the reader knows that it was a crime for a Roman soldier to sleep while on duty. No innocent soldier would admit to this crime and certainly would not tell others about it. Therefore, the Jewish leaders had to bribe them generously and convince them that they would never be punished for this crime.

147 Matthew does not specifically state who was present in this group. The reader may conclude that only the eleven apostles were there. However, given Jesus's instructions to the women to tell His brothers to go to this mountain, it is best to conclude that the group encompassed all the followers of Jesus. This is probably the appearance to over 500 people to which the apostle Paul refers in 1 Corinthians 15:6.

148 A common misinterpretation of the opening verse of Mark is that the beginning of the gospel is when John the Baptist appeared and began preaching. However, the Greek text simply reads, *The beginning of the gospel of Jesus Christ, the Son of God*. There is no verb to make it a complete sentence. This was the way Greek writers entitled a document. Therefore, this is the title of Mark's entire writing. The

149   beginning of the gospel spans from the preaching of John to the resurrection of Christ.
150   Poetic elaboration. The words spoken are from Psalm 2:7 and Isaiah 42:1. See Matthew 3:17 notes.
150   Poetic elaboration. Jesus assumes that the man knows the ceremonial cleansing laws given in Leviticus 14.
151   Derived from verse 8.
152   Derived from Luke 5:32.
153   The Greek text does not clearly identify who came to Jesus and asked this question. One might assume that it was both John's disciples and the Pharisees since they were just mentioned. Matthew 9:14 singles out John's disciples as asking this question. Luke 5:30-32 records the scribes and the Pharisees asking the question.
154   The idea of despair is derived from Matthew 9:15.
155   Derived from Matthew 9:17.
156   Derived from Matthew 12:9 which indicates that his happened right after Jesus made the statement of being Lord of the Sabbath.
157   Literally, *unclean spirits*.
158   Derived from Matthew 16:16.
159   Mark's account leaves out the specific identity of His "real mother and brothers." Matthew records Jesus as referring to His disciples.
160   The last two lines of this stanza are poetic elaboration on the seeds multiplying into fruit of various amounts.
161   Mark does not state God to be the forgiver, only implies it.
162   More literally, *tribulation and persecution*.
163   English translations present these two questions as rhetorical. In the Greek text, the answer is given for each question.
164   Derived from Luke 8:18. Mark only states that what this one has will be taken away. Luke states that even what this one thinks he has will be taken away.
165   More literally, *the unclean spirits*.
166   The woman was already healed when she touched Jesus's garment. Why then do most translations read Jesus telling the woman to go in peace and be healed? The tense Jesus used was one that emphasizes ongoing action. Jesus was assuring her that the healing was permanent.
167   Mark does not call him Jairus here, but simply designates him as the synagogue leader.
168   *Hoopla* is poetic elaboration on the weeping and wailing. It was a common Jewish practice to have professional mourners weep and wail.
169   This line and the previous line are poetic elaboration, revisiting the first question posed.
170   Although this was new territory for Jesus, He was recognized by those who had previously encountered Him. Matthew 14:35 records that the men of that place were the ones who recognized Jesus.

171   This phrase has puzzled scholars. A word-for-word translation of this line would be, *by fist they wash the hands*. Many suggest that it refers to a thorough washing.

172   A Hebrew term that referred to something set aside as a gift to God. The person still owned "the gift" until sometime in the distant future when it was to be given.

173   Verse 16 is not found in the two earliest Greek manuscripts of the 4th century but is found in two 5th century manuscripts.

174   Derived from the next verse.

175   Jesus was in this area when He cast out Legion into the herd of pigs (see Mark 5:20). He returns again to the region, but this time in the middle of it. The Greek text indicates He went "up" into the middle of Decapolis. The Sea of Galilee was below sea level. The middle of Decapolis was above sea level. Thus, He went up or made His ascent into this area.

176   Virtually all translations read, <u>no</u> *sign will be given*. However, the word translated as *no* is really *if*. Mark did not complete the statement by Jesus but left the reader hanging – *if a sign will be given to this generation-*. From the other gospels, we learn that the only sign that will be given is the sign of Jonah (Matthew 16:4; Luke 11:29). Why then did Mark not record the rest? Perhaps, Jesus gave the "if statement" first, then interrupted Himself by giving an illustration of discerning the sky as Matthew records before giving the "then statement."

177   Mark does not give the disciples' answer to this question as Matthew does.

178   See Matthew 16:23 notes.

179   More literally, "according to their own only." This is a Greek idiom meaning that it was just them only.

180   Derived from Matthew 17:19.

181   Most Greek copies read, *prayer and fasting*. Only the two earliest copies omit the word *fasting*. There is one earlier copy that appears to have the word *fasting*, but it is impossible to verify. With fasting being a common discipline in the early church, there would be no reason to omit the word fasting if it were original. On the contrary, if the original did not contain the word fasting, there would be a strong reason to add it. Jesus cast the demon out, not by fasting, but only by praying. Jesus was in constant communication with the Father and never did anything on His own (see John 5:19).

182   Verse 44 and 46 are the same words found in verse 48. But verses 44 and 46 are not found in the earliest Greek copies. Evidently, copyists felt that the words from Isaiah should have been quoted three times, after each condition of being maimed, lame, and one-eyed, instead of just once.

183   Although Jesus does not state this, He uses the language of Isaiah 66:24.

184 The fact that all will be salted by fire is a difficult statement. Some translations take the liberty to replace the metaphor of being salted with being tested. In the next verses, Jesus states that salt is good and that believers are to keep the salt within themselves. This is a reminder of a previous teaching that believers are the salt of the earth (see Matthew 5:13). Here Jesus is urging believers to be salty by living in harmony with one another. I took the liberty to make that clear by re-emphasizing that salt is good and believers must be salty.

185 The two earliest Greek copies omit this line. Although it is clear from Matthew 19:5 that Jesus said this, Mark abbreviated his account.

186 Literally, *Therefore*.

187 This love was not a feeling. Otherwise, a different Greek word would have been used. The Greek word used here is agape which refers to an unselfish love regardless of how one feels. Translations that emphasize feelings have missed the point of the passage. He looked at the rich man first. Then in reaction to what He saw, he decided to love him. This is not to say that He did not love him before. The word love is in a tense that emphasizes pointed action. Jesus looked at the rich man and decided to love him in a specific way, namely by communicating his true need.

188 Literally, *the kingdom of God*.

189 The last two lines of this stanza are derived from verse 30.

190 More literally, *mother or father*. Likewise in the next verse.

191 More literally, *brothers or sister*. Likewise in the next verse.

192 The phrase *I swear it* is derived from verse 29, *I tell you the truth*.

193 Literally, *one on Your right and one on Your left*.

194 Derived from John 18:11.

195 More literally, *the coming kingdom*.

196 The tenses Mark used in quoting Jesus are very important. The Greek present tense is used in the action of the believer forgiving, which means that it is not referring to instances of forgiveness but a lifestyle of forgiveness. The Greek aorist tense is used in the action of God's forgiveness, which means that it is referring to instances of forgiveness. So the idea is that the person who has the lifestyle of forgiveness will receive God's forgiveness for every sin. Verse 26 is omitted by the earliest Greek copies which was derived from Matthew 6:15. The derived verse just states the opposite: *if you do not have the lifestyle of forgiveness, then neither will your heavenly Father forgive your sins*. However, Matthew's quote uses two completely different sets of tenses then Mark's quote. See Matthew 6:14 notes.

197 More literally, *he must take the wife*. This is an obvious reference to marriage.

198 More literally, *angels in heaven*. The comparison to angels is only in the area of marriage. One must not press the likeness to angels any further than that.

199 A quadrans was worth 1/128 of a day's wage for a common laborer. The two coins were each called a lepton which was a coin with very little value.
200 Derived from Matthew 24:14.
201 The subject of what is near is unexpressed. Translations vary between *he* and *it*. The primary subject is the destruction of the temple. It is the only question that Mark recorded that the disciples asked (see verse 4), although Matthew records a three-pronged question. Therefore, verses 28-31 apply to the sign of the temple's destruction. See also Matthew 24:33 notes.
202 Mark does not identify which ear was cut off. This information comes from the gospels of Luke and John.
203 Some translations read that a rooster crowed right after Peter's first denial. It is difficult to determine by the Greek copies if Mark wrote this or if it was added by copyists. The two earliest copies omit it.
204 Although Mark does not describe the reed as very sturdy, the Greeks knew this reed to be sturdy. Modern readers may mistakenly think this reed to be flimsy.
205 Derived from the next verse.
206 More literally, *the third hour*. Mark used the Jewish method for the time.
207 Verse 28 is omitted by the earliest and best Greek copies.
208 Some have tried to explain the darkness as an eclipse that naturally occurred. However, as in all the gospels, all these events are presented as arising because of the death of Jesus.
209 Mark gives the times as the sixth hour and the ninth hour. Since He used the Jewish method of time, this corresponds to noon and three o'clock.
210 See Matthew 27:47 notes.
211 The gospel of Mark officially ends here. Greek scholars agree that any additional words seen in translations were not from Mark. They were added by someone else because it was believed that either Mark was unable to finish the gospel or that the original ending was lost. Most scholars hold to the latter. However, a third possibility is more plausible to me. Since the gospel of Mark was inspired by God, then the abrupt ending is inspired as well. Mark entitled the book, *The beginning of the gospel of Jesus Christ, the Son of God* (see 1:1 notes). The women failing to report the good news of His resurrection out of fear was not the ending of the gospel. That was part of *The beginning of the gospel of Jesus Christ*. How the gospel progresses is up to us who claim to be Christ's disciples. Will we overcome our fear and report the good news that Jesus has risen?
212 The word *firstborn* has only two meanings: (1) the first one born in a family; (2) one who rules. The second definition developed out of the

213 first. The firstborn son in a family eventually became the head or ruler of the family when the parents died. This term became applied to one who possessed supreme authority. The second definition applies here.
213 Poetic elaboration. This is a quote from Psalm 104:4.
214 The following verses are from Psalm 8:4-6.
215 More literally, *the son of man*. This is not a reference to Jesus as the son of man. It is a term that refers to the human race which descended from Adam. God put all things under the rule of mankind (Genesis 1:28). But the son, or progeny, failed to effectively rule everything.
216 More literally, *because of the suffering of death*.
217 Literally, *whole*. Moses was faithful in the entire household of God.
218 Literally, *every*. The statement is true for every house.
219 This is a reference to Exodus 17:1-7 where the sons of Israel quarreled with Moses over their lack of water.
220 Literally, *in what was said* or *in the saying*. The Hebrew writer is referring back to verse 7 and so has the Holy Spirit in mind as the speaker.
221 The writer put this in the form of a question along with the answer: *to whom did He swear that they not enter His rest, but those who rebelled?*
222 The Greek text is very difficult and has given rise to different understandings. The KJV states that the word preached was not mixed with faith *in those who heard*. However, all the sons of Israel heard. Some versions change the translation of the Greek word that has been translated all along as *hearing* to *listening* (e.g., ESV). This is a solution, but the point of the context is that everyone heard. Some go with a variant reading in an early manuscript that presents the word *heard* as not mixing faith in with the hearers (e.g. NAS). But this shifts the blame on the word instead of the hearers. This is contrary to the context that warns the readers against repeating the faithlessness of the sons of Israel. My solution is to understand the participle, translated as *those who heard* (KJV) or *those listening* (ESV), as not referring to the hearers but to their hearing.
223 Literally, *therefore*. The Hebrew writer is drawing a logical conclusion.
224 Literally, *the word of God*.
225 The Hebrew writer does not identify Melchizedek as Salem's king. That information comes from Genesis 14:18.
226 Literally, *the sayings of God*.
227 What is the first message about the Christ? The Hebrew writer has a Jewish audience, and so it refers to the Old Testament teaching about Christ. The subjects mentioned have to do with the Old Covenant which was just a shadow of what was to come (Hebrews 10:1). Repentance from lifeless works and faith in God as Lord was only a partial revelation (Isaiah 45:20-22). The full revelation was in Jesus Christ (Hebrews

1:1). We must trust Christ as Lord. The doctrine of cleansings (literally, baptisms) and the laying on of hands had to do with the sacrifices and the cleansing rites the priests had to go through after laying their hands on the goat (see Leviticus 16:4,5,21,24,26). Jesus is our priest and sacrifice. The resurrection of the dead and eternal judgment was a meager understanding in the Old Testament. Christ's work of grace for believers, which began at the cross and will be finished at Christ's second coming, is the full understanding (1 Thessalonians 5:23,24; 1 Corinthians 15:50-57).

228 Derived from Genesis 14:20.
229 Poetic elaboration taken from Genesis 14:14-16. Abraham's plan was to rescue Lot from his captors.
230 Literally, *for*. It is the common word used to introduce an explanation.
231 The Hebrew writer picks up where he interrupted himself in verse 20.
232 Scholars are divided over whether the main point has to do with the previous discussion or the following discussion. Those that choose the former have to make the main point the many points covering the many verses to follow. It is my opinion that the main point is just one – the kind of high priest we own. Then what follows gives details of that main point.
233 More literally, *a servant*.
234 The Greek text presents a kind of conditional sentence that assumes something contrary to fact. The words in parenthesis elaborate on this condition.
235 Literally, *the second*.
236 The term the Hebrew writer uses is *the many* not simply *many*. This is the same terminology found in Isaiah 53:11. Daniel uses the term to refer to the genuine people of God (Daniel 9:27; 11:33,39; 12:3). See also Romans 5:15,19.
237 Literally, *a roll of the scroll*. This refers to a collection of scrolls making up the Old Testament. The roll refers to an individual scroll, and the scroll refers to the entire Old Testament.
238 The Greek text reads, *O God*.
239 The Hebrew writer does not explain what *the first* and *the second* are. One could simply say that *the first* refers to the Old Covenant and *the second* to the New Covenant. However, in this context, *the first* refers to the first part of the quote he explains in verse 8 – God not being pleased with sacrifices and offerings which were under the Law. *The second* refers to the second part of the quote which he explains in verse 9 – Christ coming to do God's will. Sacrifices under the Law had to be done away with in order to establish what God wanted. Christ offering His own body as a one-time sacrifice did away with the Law of sacrifices and established God's desire.
240 Literally, *therefore*.

241 The Hebrew writer uses the word *God* here.
242 The Hebrew writer simply writes *all died*. Certainly he is not referring to all the descendants of Abraham, for most of them were not faithful. He must be referring to the faithful ones.
243 Literally, *Therefore*.
244 The Hebrew writer takes this information not from the Hebrew Bible but from the Greek translation which adds the action of leaning on his staff (Genesis 47:31).
245 Poetic elaboration is used to make clear that this refers to the second time Moses left Egypt. The first time he left in fear (Exodus 2:14,15). The second time he left in faith standing before Pharaoh without fear (Exodus 5:1).
246 Derived from Genesis 27:36.
247 *As we're told* is poetic elaboration derived from Luke 15:10 of the angelic assembly rejoicing over those sinners who repent and become saved from their sins.
248 Some translations do not put the word *firstborn* in the plural, even though the Greek text pluralizes the word. The firstborn inherit all that their father owns. Believers are called firstborn ones because all believers inherit all that their heavenly Father owns. Unlike in an earthly family where only one can be the firstborn, in the heavenly family, every child of God is His firstborn.
249 Literally, *Jesus*.
250 The word *believers* is poetic elaboration.
251 More literally, *to suffer*.
252 Many translations read *share* instead of *fellowship*. The Greek word is used 19 times in the New Testament, but only once in this letter. The word literally means *what is common*. It takes on the flavor of sharing material things in Romans 15:26; 2 Corinthians 8:4; 9:13 since the context demands it. Here, the context does not demand it and should be seen as it is most commonly used, a spiritual sharing, fellowship.
253 One might wonder the difference between obedience and submission. The Greek word for obedience carries the idea of being persuaded. So a person obeys out of persuasion. However, submission is an act done whether persuaded or not. Many decisions made by leaders are not a matter of right or wrong but of opinion. A person must submit to their spiritual leaders whether they agree with their opinion or not. Submission also carries the idea of a willing arrangement under authority. Therefore, all negative attitudes are eliminated in the act of submission.
254 The Greek text reads, *eternal covenant*. This eternal covenant is the new covenant. See Hebrews 9:13-15.
255 More literally, *Jesus Christ*.

256 Most translations read *perfect* instead of *mature*. The Greek word can carry either idea. Here, the goal of trials is to grow the Christian, not to transport them to immediate perfection. See Philippians 3:12,15 where this word is used in both senses.

257 The word *God* is not in the Greek text in verses 9 and 10. The text commands the poor to boast in his exaltation and the rich in his humiliation. I have interpreted the exaltation and humiliation to be the action of God in bringing them to salvation. God raised the poor to his spiritually high position in Christ and humbled the rich in his submission to Christ.

258 James uses the term *soul* in the same way Matthew 26:38 uses it, to refer to the mind, will, and emotions. Therefore, the salvation in this context is not from sin's penalty, but from sin's power.

259 The Greek text contains the word *no*. It is a rhetorical question expecting a negative answer.

260 The words *he supplied* are derived from Genesis 22:9. Abraham built the altar to sacrifice Isaac.

261 Some may think this to be a contradiction of Romans 3:28, where the apostle Paul states that a person is justified by faith apart from the works of law. However, Paul and James have two different issues in mind. Paul is addressing the false understanding that righteousness before God is attained by following religious rules. James is addressing the false understanding that righteousness before God is attained by a mere assent to facts about God. Paul uses the term *works* in a bad sense (as a means of righteousness), where James uses it in a good sense (as a result of righteousness). Paul uses the term *justify* to mean declared righteous by God, where James uses it to mean to be shown righteous to people.

262 More literally, *therefore*.

263 The words *to God* and *to the Lord* are not stated but implied.

264 The idea of repentance is contained in the word confession, which means to speak the same. We are to speak the same about our sin as God does, which requires us to repent.

265 The word is translated by most versions as *foreknowledge*. This word is often interpreted as meaning the knowing of facts beforehand. However, the word must be seen in a relational sense of God knowing us. When we come into a faith relationship with God, we become known by Him (see Galatians 4:9). Therefore, God's foreknowledge is a prior decision to have a relationship with us. See also Romans 8:29.

266 More literally, *the last time*.

267 Peter is referring to Pentecost when the Holy Spirit was sent to the Jews (see Acts 2).

268 Two different Greek words for love are used by Peter. The first translated as *brotherly love* requires affection. The second translated as *unselfish*

love is an unselfish act for another's good regardless of one's feeling. Both are important in the church.

269 It is hard to imagine how suffering unjustly as a believer would be called grace. We think of grace as the gift of salvation. But the teaching of the New Testament is that suffering for the faith is intimately connected (John 16:33; Acts 14:22; Romans 8:17; Philippians 1:29). Grace is defined as an undeserved gift. Suffering unjustly in Christ's name is certainly undeserved.

270 Almost all translations read *wounds*. However, in the Greek text, it is singular. Jesus was so beaten and battered that to Peter it all appeared as one big wound. Isaiah 52:14 prophesies that His appearance would be marred more than any human being.

271 More literally, *as*.

272 Scholars are divided over the meaning of this passage. Some think Peter is speaking of a believer suffering to the point of dying since the idea of a sinless state may be understood. However, Peter is referring to a person who suffers for doing right. At that point, they are not sinning.

273 Peter does not specify what he means by the dead. I have interpreted it as the spiritual dead. Others think that Peter refers to those believers who had died because of persecution. To me it makes better sense that the gospel is preached to unbelievers so that their spirit may live even though it may mean persecution by men.

274 More literally, *Jesus Christ*.

275 Poetic elaboration. Peter is quoting the Greek version of Proverbs 11:31.

276 Poetic elaboration. Peter is quoting the Greek version of Proverbs 3:34.

277 More literally, *your brotherhood*.

278 More literally, *Amen*, which means *truly*.

279 The Greek word Peter uses was used for a person testifying in a court of law as a witness.

280 Peter does not describe the kiss as holy. However, it certainly is to be understood as such.

281 There is no verb in the Greek text connected with peace. It simply reads, *peace to you all who are in Christ*. This is not a wish, but an exclamation of fact. See notes on 2 Corinthians 13:14 and Galatians 1:3.

282 The deity of Jesus Christ is very plain in the Greek text.

283 The Greek word which I have translated as *personal walk* is translated as *knowledge* by most translations. This word refers to a personal knowledge gained by experience as opposed to a knowledge as a collection of facts. Therefore, this knowledge is relational in this context.

284 The deity of Jesus Christ is again declared in this verse by Peter, although most translations make it seem like *God* refers to the Father and not Jesus Christ. The Greek text is not as clear as the previous verse. However, in light of the plainness of the previous verse, one need not deny the same understanding of this verse.

285 This translates the Greek word *agape* which is a selfless love that acts regardless of one's feelings towards another.
286 More literally, *neither useless nor fruitless.*
287 Implied.
288 The last two lines of this stanza are drawn from the conclusion that the last state has become worse than the first.
289 Many translations read *out of water and through water.* The preposition translated as *through* can refer to an interval of time or space. Perhaps Peter pictures the earth between water, above it and beneath it (Genesis 1:6-8).
290 The Greek word reflects not a simple waiting but one that waits with eagerness or with expectancy.
291 Peter simply writes *the wisdom given him* which implies that God gave it to him.
292 More literally, *in Jesus Christ.*
293 More literally, *snuck in unnoticed.*
294 It is not clear what *these* refer to. It is my opinion that it refers to the previous two examples just discussed: unbelieving Israel and the fallen angels.
295 Jude is referring to the ones in verse 4 who snuck in among his readers.
296 Poetic elaboration on the idea of what they boldly do as explained in the next stanza.
297 The Greek word used is the adjective form of *soul.* One could say, soulish. This word is only used in contrast to something spiritual and so is often translated as its opposite, natural or unspiritual. See 1 Corinthians 2:14; 15:46; James 3:15.
298 The Greek tense Jude uses in the action of rescuing is one that is ongoing. Believers should find themselves continually working to rescue people from the fire of judgment. It is not clear if Jude is referring to rescuing unbelievers from eternal judgment or rescuing sinning believers who are experiencing God's discipline.
299 More literally, Jesus Christ. Jude ends this letter with a doxology.

www.ingramcontent.com/pod-product-compliance
Lightning Source LLC
Chambersburg PA
CBHW032358100526
44587CB00010BA/202